FAMILIES APART

Families Apart

. . . .

Migrant Mothers and the Conflicts of Labor and Love

Geraldine Pratt

University of Minnesota Press
Minneapolis
London

An earlier version of chapter 3 was written in collaboration with the Philippine Women Centre of British Columbia and appeared as "Circulating Sadness: Witnessing Filipina Mothers' Stories of Family Separation," *Gender, Place and Culture* 16, no. 1 (2009): 3–22. An earlier version of chapter 5 was written with the Philippines–Canada Task Force on Human Rights and appeared as "International Accompaniment and Witnessing State Violence in the Philippines," *Antipode* 40, no. 5 (November 2008): 751–79.

Published by the University of Minnesota Press
111 Third Avenue South, Suite 290
Minneapolis, MN 55401-2520
http://www.upress.umn.edu

Library of Congress Cataloging-in-Publication Data

Pratt, Geraldine.
Families apart : migrant mothers and the conflicts of labor and love / Geraldine Pratt.
Includes bibliographical references and index.
ISBN 978-0-8166-6998-1 (hc : alk. paper) — ISBN 978-0-8166-6999-8 (pb : alk. paper)
1. Foreign workers, Philippine—Canada. 2. Women foreign workers—Canada.
3. Women household employees—Canada. 4. Filipinos—Canada. 5. Working mothers—Canada. 6. Immigrant families—Canada. 7. Mother and child—Philippines.
8. Philippines—Emigration and immigration—Social aspects. 9. Canada—Emigration and immigration—Social aspects. I. Philippine Women Centre of British Columbia II. Title.
HD6305.F55P73 2012
331.4089'9921071—dc23
2011044419

Printed in the United States of America on acid-free paper

The University of Minnesota is an equal-opportunity educator and employer.

20 19 18 17 16 15 14 13 12   10 9 8 7 6 5 4 3 2 1

Dedicated to the fierce and generous women of the
Philippine Women Centre of British Columbia, who struggle
for social justice in Canada and the Philippines. Their restless, creative,
and grounded theorization and action inspires
new visions of solidarity, new approaches
to transnationalism, and commitment
to engaged public life.
This book is yours.

Contents

Acknowledgments

THIS BOOK IS BASED ON A SERIES OF COLLABORATIONS: with members of the Philippine Women Centre (PWC) of BC, the Filipino Canadian Youth Alliance, the Philippines-Canada Task Force on Human Rights, and Vancouver theater artists (in particular Alex Ferguson and Caleb Johnston). It grew out of, was nourished by, and lives within these collaborations; there is very little to say beyond this. The book would not exist without the hard work of these organizations and individuals, and the generosity of domestic workers and their families who agreed to revisit what were often painful experiences for the purpose of community education and social transformation.

The collective nature of this book goes beyond this. The academy, when it is working well, is an extraordinary place of friendship and exchange. Many friends and colleagues have reacted to preliminary oral presentations and written chapters with the generosity of their time and engaged criticism, and by sharing ideas and sources that they might have kept for their own. Special thanks to Cindi Katz for reading the manuscript not once but twice! I thank members of the PWC for their careful reading and commentary of the manuscript as a whole. Thanks so very much to Trevor Barnes, Derek Gregory, Chris Harker, Jennifer Hyndman, Victoria Rosner, Melissa Wright, and Sarah Zell for their close reading of good chunks of this book in preliminary stages, and to Ted Alcuitis, Ning Alcuitis-Imperial, Oliver Belcher, Jennifer Chun, Jessica Dempsey, Merryn Edwards, Dave Featherstone, Judy Han, Rick Heynan, Dan Hiebert, Caleb Johnston, Merje Kuus, Kirsten McAllister, Pablo Menzies, Tyler Pierce, Gillian Rose, Jackie Stacey, Juanita Sundberg, and Tracy Zhang for their reactions and contributions to individual chapters.

Several small academic conferences and workshops provided extraordinary opportunities for learning, and their influence is evident in a number of the chapters. Thanks in particular to Sneja Gunew for her invitation to present a barely hatched version of "Listening to Mothers' Stories" at the Decolonizing Affect conference in Vancouver in June 2006; to Nora Chiang for her invitation to present a preliminary fragment of "Waiting" at the Symposium of the IGU Commission on Gender and Geography at the National Taiwan University in November 2007; and to Sallie Marston and Jan Monk for their invitation to develop "Listening to Mothers' Stories" as the Jan Monk Distinguished Lecture in 2008. Thanks to Jennifer Chun for organizing a session on the introductory chapter as part of the Global and Transnational Ethnography workshop series at UBC, and to the participants who gave so generously of their time and suggestions.

The ideas swirling around at the following workshops were formative: the Transnational Feminist Praxis workshop organized by Richa Nagar and Amanda Swarr at the University of Minnesota in 2006; the Mobility and Insecurity Working Meeting at the Centre for International and Security Studies, York University, Canada, organized by Luin Goldring in May 2008; the Mapping North American Youth Cultures Workshop at the Center for Interdisciplinary Studies of Youth and Space at San Diego State University organized by Stuart Aitken, Tom Herman, and Fernando Bosco in August 2008; and the Antipode Summer Institute held at the University of Manchester in May 2009. Reactions at community-based conferences have been essential and extremely productive: in particular, conferences held by the National Alliance of Philippine Women in Canada in May and November 2006 and November 2008; and community research symposiums held by Metropolis BC in 2006 and the Affiliation of Multicultural Societies and Service Agencies of BC in 2010.

Much of the research has been conducted by community researchers. I fight my urge to thank individuals by following the PWC's request that I simply thank the collective, in line with the spirit of their work and their sense of community. Thank you for your hard work and the opportunity to get so close to your extraordinary commitment to collective struggle. I thank as well Caleb Johnston and Mike Thomason for transcription beyond that done by the PWC. Thanks to Maria Trache of Edudata Canada for facilitating data access and her analysis of BC Ministry of Education data, the BC Ministry of Education for access to this data, François Bertrand for coordinating and analyzing the Canadian census data, and Eric Leinberger for his excellent cartographic skills. Thanks to Caleb Johnston, Sean Parlan, Lyle Stafford, and the PWC for sharing their photographs, and to Keiron for his permission to use his image. Huge thanks to Sarah Zell and Cherene Holland for their meticulous copyediting. I thank Jason Weidemann and the team at the University of Minnesota Press for their enthusiasm for and work on this project.

The generous support of the Social Science and Humanities Research Council of Canada and Metropolis BC has been very much appreciated. Staging a play involves an immense amount of fundraising and other types of support, and I thank the British Columbia Arts Council, the Canada Council for the Arts, the Playwright Theatre Centre, the PuSh International Performing Arts Festival, and the Vancouver Foundation. Time and space at the Munk Centre at the University of Toronto in 2008 were essential to allow me to understand why these individual chapters needed to hang out together as a book.

As ever, thanks to Tohmm, Elspeth, and Denise—for walking and talking.

Abbreviations

BCCHRP	British Columbia Committee of Human Rights in the Philippines
CAFGU	Civilian Armed Forces Geographical Unit
CCP	Communist Party of the Philippines
CIC	Citizenship and Immigration Canada
EI	Employment Insurance
ESL	English as a Second Language
FCYA/Ugnayan BC	Filipino Canadian Youth Alliance/Ugnayan Ng Kabataang Pilipino Sa Canada
GABRIELA	General Assembly Binding Women for Reforms, Integrity, Equality, Leadership, and Action
HAU1	Hebbel am Ufer Theatre 1
IMF	International Monetary Fund
KARAPATAN	Alliance for the Advancement of People's Rights
LCP	Live-In Caregiver Program
LEP	Labor Export Policy
NAPWC	National Alliance of Philippine Women in Canada
NGO	Nongovernmental organization
NPA	New People's Army
OCW	Overseas Contract Worker
OFI	Overseas Filipino Investor
OFW	Overseas Filipino Worker

PuSH	International Performing Arts Festival
PWC of BC	Philippine Women Centre of British Columbia
RESPECT	European network of migrant domestic workers' self-organization, trade unions, NGOs, and supporters that campaign for the rights of all Migrant Domestic Workers in private households, both women and men, regardless of immigration status
SCAA	Special CAFGU Active Auxiliary
SIKLAB of BC	Sulong Itaguyod ang Karapatan ng Manggagawang Pilipino sa Labas ng Bansa [Advance the Rights and Welfare of Overseas Filipino Workers]
Ugnayan BC/FCYA	Ugnayan Ng Kabataang Pilipino Sa Canada/ Filipino Canadian Youth Alliance

Collaborating with the Philippine Women Centre: Cultivating a Debate

O N A BEAUTIFUL SUMMER EVENING IN 2005, I approached a small stucco house in a working-class neighborhood in Vancouver. The Philippine Women Centre of BC had arranged an interview with a domestic worker who had recently reunited with her three children, and my research collaborators from the center, Cecilia and Glecy, would be there. In response to my knock, a visibly irritated, physically imposing older white man opened the front door. So obvious to organizers at the center, they had assumed that I would know that the domestic worker and her family would live in the basement of the house. The rental unit was accessed at the side of the house and through the laundry room. When I was led into the living space, Cecilia and Glecy were already there, and the seven of us crowded into the small low-ceilinged room. If I was unsettled by the generosity of the domestic worker's decision to serve us a meal—spaghetti and meatballs—my discomfort about arriving empty-handed only increased as she told her story.

The story began in a conventional enough way, as stories of migrant domestic workers go: long periods of separation from her family while she worked first in Hong Kong and then in Vancouver, an unfaithful husband, followed by marital breakdown. She spoke mostly in Tagalog, and I drifted in and out of the conversation. The emotional currents were also uncomfortable and difficult to read. The mother repeatedly stated that although she had wished for the reunification with her children for years, it had been hard, and her children seemed ungrateful for all that she had done to achieve it. As she repeated this lament, her eldest daughter, in her late twenties, rolled her eyes. At one point, a tinny rendition of the Canadian anthem erupted from my purse; my son's ring-tone selection was embarrassing musical proof of my foreignness.

Soon the energy and purpose of the meeting changed, and we set to work in a differently concentrated way. The domestic worker revealed that they were a family in crisis. The police and an ambulance had been called several days before when the younger daughter had assaulted her mother; a gash on the domestic worker's face still bore testimony to this event. The circumstances leading up to this are both complicated and terribly simple: a serious mental illness hidden from immigration officials to enable her child's immigration to Canada, an inability to pay for medication to control her daughter's illness, and anxiety about approaching health officials to get the necessary drug prescription for fear of the repercussions of disclosure. Charges had been filed, the daughter had spent a night in jail, and now her mother was desperate to undo the legal process that she had set in motion when she charged her daughter with assault. More mundane, but equally important, she felt overwhelmed by the paperwork necessary to enroll her son in school. Our research interview was rendered irrelevant, but the opportunity that it created was not. We spent the rest of the evening sorting through the documentation necessary to enroll her son in school and planning a course of action for her daughter. Soon after the interview, the domestic worker took her daughter to the emergency room, where she was admitted to a mental health facility in order to stabilize her condition. This is activist research, a process that has evolved in my long-term collaboration with the Philippine Women Centre of BC.

The emotional intensity of this experience stuck and created attachments to the family we interviewed that night. We have done further interviews and have followed the progress of this family's life together in Vancouver. This book presents stories about this family and other Filipino families in similar circumstances in ways that we hope might allow them to challenge the reader about this issue, which more broadly can be conceived as a massive reorganization and disorganization of intimacy and family life within the worldwide expansion of temporary labor migration. We hope the reader will understand the pain and trauma of family separation. Where such receptivity might lead is an open question that is pursued throughout the book.

The mobile authorship within this text moves between "I" and an unstable "we." The "I" is the voice of a never quite comfortable white academic, and I use it when it is appropriate to convey the particularity of that experience. The pages written here would be blank without my collaboration with the Philippine Women Centre (PWC). The concern about family reunification is also their concern, having observed these troubled reunifications within the Filipino community in Vancouver and recognized the need for more systematic research. Without our collaboration, I might not have been able to do the interviews at all or would have done them in a radically different way, and the interpretation and analysis of them undoubtedly would be different and likely thinner.

We first came together in 1995 over an interminable feminist concern—the devaluing of care work—to collaborate on a project researching the experiences of Filipino overseas domestic workers in Canada. Because the Live-In Caregiver Program, the program that enables the migration of domestic workers to Canada, is one of the largest and longest-running temporary worker programs in Canada, it is an important case of a worldwide trend toward temporary migration as a governmental strategy for managing profitability and debt through flexible flows of labor. Neither this government program nor the issues of devalued care work have gone away since we began our research—quite the contrary, and we have deepened our assessment and criticism of them through a series of studies that traces experiences of family separation and the fate of Filipino domestic workers and their families in Canada over the long term. Like domestic work, our research collaboration never seems to be done, and as the issues multiply, so have our collaborators. Some studies have drawn on the help of the Filipino-Canadian Youth Alliance (FCYA), others on the Philippines-Canada Task Force on Human Rights, and still others on the work of professional theater artists.[1] We experiment here with ways of telling about migrant experiences to further proliferate our associations to work together toward a different (and better) future.

Families Apart involves telling and collecting and journeying out in an effort to assemble and mobilize an intercultural audience of Filipinos and non-Filipinos by experimenting with different ways of storytelling. It takes shape as an open-ended series of encounters, episodic rather than linear in form, moving between a singular academic voice and the "we" of various research collaborations, between Vancouver and the Philippines, and between genres of "evidence-based" social-scientific research, testimony, theatrical performance, and (nonfictional) narrative and personal writing. We hope to unsettle a widespread complacency that we have detected around some forms of transnational labor and create new attachments to those who suffer different forms of state violence, both in Canada and the Philippines.

Judging Temporary Labor Migration

In recent years, the Philippine Women Centre of BC has invited me to join some of its press conferences, where the center presents analysis and criticism of the Live-In Caregiver Program (LCP). The events I have attended have followed a similar format: four women seated at a table at the front of the room, with a microphone passed back and forth from a community organizer, who asserts the need to scrap the program, to one or two domestic workers who testify to their experience as migrant workers, and then to me to speak as an academic about our collaborative research. At the last press conference, a reporter from one of the major daily newspapers sat at the back of the room and pressed hard on the PWC's position that the program must be scrapped. "Why do women keep coming from the Philippines if it is so bad?" "Are you really saying that you want to close off this possibility for Filipino women to immigrate to Canada?" "Do you see no way of reforming the program to make it better?" During the press conference, I sensed the questions to be combative and hostile, but when she stayed behind to discuss the matter further, this journalist seemed genuinely perplexed by our answers to her questions. She simply could not understand why the PWC would want to shut down this opportunity for immigration.

Members of the Filipino Canadian community raise identical questions at community forums, and there is no consensus about the LCP among Filipino community organizers. Since 2008, Filipino activists in Vancouver have disagreed about the PWC's insistence that the program be scrapped, and this has been one factor that has led to a splintering among activists on migrant issues. Women who share the same passions for migrant rights and who collaborated closely together on our first research project in 1995 now represent different organizations: the PWC and Migrante International–BC, split in part because of their differing positions on the possibility of reforming the LCP. Without sidestepping the intense pain, anger, and loss associated with this separation, we can find hope in this vigorous disagreement over analysis and action by understanding it as an important moment of agonistic politics that marks the potential and promise of radical democracy. This is theorizing—not as if, but because it matters.

There is reason, however, to be alert to the ways that a strange hybrid of the principled stances of the PWC and Migrante International can be co-opted. In a press conference in December 2009, Conservative Canadian immigration minister Jason Kenney turned the catchy phrasing of the PWC on its head when he stated: "So we don't want to end the program, as some would have us do. But we need to mend the program, to improve it, to fix it."[2] This statement could be taken as an instance of simultaneously listening to, ignoring, and co-opting activist energies around migrant issues in Canada.

The Canadian immigration minister's commitment to this foreign worker program is in line with state and supragovernmental institutional thinking around the globe. In an influential 2005 report, the Global Commission on International Migration concluded that, worldwide, the old paradigm of permanent immigrant settlement is giving way to temporary or circular migration. Almost half of these temporary workers are women, often migrating alone to provide for their families. As Leah Schmalzbauer puts it: "In the global south, mother work increasingly mandates migration."[3] The Global Commission recognized three well-established criticisms of temporary migration: (1) it often creates a second-class category of worker, (2) separation has negative consequences for family life, and (3) there is a risk that migrant workers will overstay their work visas and slip into a precarious undocumented status. But, on balance, the commission concluded that, managed properly, the benefits of temporary migration outweigh the costs. It recommended that governments learn from a country such as the Philippines, which, as the world's largest exporter of labor, has "a wealth of experience" providing large numbers of temporary migrants to the global labor markets. "In simple terms, the [receiving countries] are running short of working-age people, while the [sending countries] have such people to spare." Sharing their citizens in this way, countries such as the Philippines enjoy "enormous benefits" from migrants' remittances, along with diasporic investments, which are considered to be much more "dependable and stable" than traditional forms of external funding or development aid.[4] The commission identified women (as compared to men) as exemplary in this regard, remitting especially high proportions of their incomes and putting their remittances to most effective use. Temporary migration is, in the words of the commission, a "win-win" situation for both the receiving and sending states.

This expression of enthusiasm for a profound spatial reorganization of relations of intimacy and familial, work, and political life is an easy target of criticism, reducing as it does human lives to units of labor, living resources, vectors of capital flows, or isolated body parts (for example, the report speaks of "brain circulation" replacing "brain drain" with the hopes of avoiding "brain waste"). It seems to celebrate individual migrants' so-called choices from the distanced appraisal of capital flows and state revenues, and to take histories of uneven development as an unfortunate but unquestioned starting point.

But the case for temporary migration goes beyond the calculations of government and state agencies, and it is defended from the perspective of migrants as well by analysts positioned across the political spectrum. Immigration Minister Jason Kenney expresses his "pride" in the Live-In Caregiver Program from the perspective of migrants on the grounds that it "helps Canada fulfill its caretaker needs and it provides new opportunities for those who come through the program."[5] But equally, Martin Ruhs and Philip Martin have recast the situation as "win-win-win," recognizing the capacity of migrants to earn higher wages through migration.[6] Daniel Bell and Nicola Piper are among those who argue that *critics* of temporary migration often betray a narrow and Eurocentric perspective. They reason that temporary workers' choice to trade off certain rights for access to jobs and a higher standard of living for themselves and their families should be theirs to make, and an insistence that full citizenship rights be extended to migrant workers will likely result "in a one-way ticket back home," as well as limited opportunities for future migrants.[7] Temporary visas for domestic work, they note, provide one of the few avenues that many women have to migrate with state-authorized work permits. "Why is it," they ask, "that liberal democratic theorists typically fail to identify the conflict between their ideals and the actual needs and interests of migrant workers?"[8] They think the answer has something to do with the way that liberal democratic thinkers frame questions of justice within the nation-state, pushing the interests of actual migrants from view as they trumpet liberal principles of equality within the territorial borders of their nation-state.

This question of scale recurs as a quandary. Judgments about justice are often comparative. Canadian temporary-worker programs are considered good compared to those of many other countries, and wages are superior to those in the Philippines. But to what should assessments of the rightness or wrongness, fairness or unfairness, of a temporary-worker program be compared: to conditions of work and life within a particular nation-state, to temporary-worker programs in other countries, to some universal standard of human rights, or to conditions of life at home? There is no agreement. We are, Nancy Fraser claims, in a time of "abnormal justice" and the literal "topography of debate is itself an object of dispute." "[C]urrent debates about justice have a freewheeling character. . . . Not only substantive questions, but also the grammar of justice itself, are up for grabs."[9]

Aside from uncertainty about the scale and scope of comparison, Fraser argues that deliberations about justice are often misframed geographically and that existing territorial arrangements exclude those who should be heard. She argues that we need provisionally to question and reconfigure the spaces of politics and governance through public dialogue in which all those subjected to a particular governance structure have moral standing and can participate equally. Our research collaboration can be understood as an effort not to speak for but to bring domestic workers and their children more fully into public debates about the justice of a temporary-worker program to which the Canadian state is firmly committed. As much as prescribing an answer, we are assembling an archive of migrant testimony that speaks to their lived experience of family separation on the assumption that domestic workers and their families have moral standing and should participate equally in debates about this temporary migration program.[10]

Creating a public archive of testimony and an avenue for dialogue is, however, not enough. The effects of temporary-work programs are not immediately evident in experience, and they become apparent, we argue, only over the long term. They not only creep through the lives of migrant workers but also into the lives of their children. And the effects of geography are more extensive and pernicious than Fraser suggests. Expanding the scale or scope of public debate will not in itself make visible much that geography hides, nor will it dismantle the boundaries that delineate what can and cannot be heard. We need to do more to unsettle complacency, to reenvision responsibility and establish the grounds for a more comprehensive discussion of the justice of temporary-work programs.

Opening Sightlines

Our first research workshop in 1995 began with a song, "Kung Alam Mo Lang Violy." Sung in Tagalog by the twenty or so Filipino domestic workers and community researchers gathered at the PWC, it was kindly translated into English for me. Feel free to sing along.[11]

Koro:	Chorus:
Kung alam mo lang Violy	If you only knew, Violy
(repeat once)	(repeat once)
Kung alam mo lang Violy	If you only knew, Violy,
ang totoo	the truth

Kung alam mo lang Violy	If you only knew, Violy
(repeat once)	(repeat once)
Matagal ka na nilang niloloko.	You've been fooled for a long time.
May midyum tirm development	There is a medium-term development plan
Uutangin ang imbesmeynt	Borrowing money for investment
Panot na ang enbayrunmant	And exploiting our resources
Tuwang tuwa ang gobernment.	The government is rejoicing.
Pinay ay di komoditi	A Filipina is not a commodity
Por export sa ibang kantri	For export to other countries
Wala namang sekyoriti	Without security
Lagi na lang gunugulpi.	And always abused.
Pangingilkil lang ang alam	Corruption is all they know
Gobermit walang pakialam	The government doesn't care
Pinay pambayad ng utang	Filipinas are used for debt payment
Sa IMF at World Bank.	To the IMF and World Bank.
Hoy alam ko na Eddie	I already know, Eddie
(sing twice)	(sing twice)
Hoy alam ko na Eddie ang totoo	I already know, Eddie, the truth
Hoy alam ko na Eddie	I already know, Eddie
(sing twice)	(sing twice)
Matagal mo na kaming niloloko.	That you have been fooling us for a long time.

During the long day that followed this song, domestic workers always began their stories in the Philippines with their frustrations about government corruption and nepotism in the workplace. But I remember listening more closely as they described their lives as Canadian domestic workers. Over the years of writing on this issue, I have rarely begun narrating their stories before they arrived on Canadian soil. Although for their migration they could not have been more explicit about the immediacy and significance of their lives in the Philippines, the domestic workers came to life for me somewhere *during* their flight across the Pacific Ocean.[12]

Economic processes reach deeply into the intimacies of Filipino migrant families as they are squeezed into and through the time-spaces of global capitalism. The scattering of individual family members across the globe as temporary workers is now an important component of such processes. Debates about temporary labor migration are truncated or incomplete, however, because much of this process *and its consequences* are unevenly visible, a result of the material, concrete timing and spacing of labor migration.

Families Apart addresses three spatiotemporalities that structure what can and cannot be readily sensed about temporary migration. First, the consequences of what may appear to be temporary or short-term migration become apparent only in the long term. This book destabilizes assumptions about the temporariness of temporary migration. For many migrants, it is not short term, in itself or in its implications for family members. Second, family separation occurs across great distances, and so it is fairly invisible to those positioned in the global North. The lives of husbands and children left behind in the Philippines have a shadowy existence when domestic lives are viewed from the perspective of Canada. We try to bring this separation into view. And though it might seem that family separation would be all too apparent to migrants themselves, a driving impulse behind this research has been to make experiences of separation visible to migrant families, to open communication about (sometimes traumatic) experiences that look and feel very different on either side of the Pacific Ocean, for those living and working in Canada and those at home in the Philippines, experiences that few family members wish to dwell on or discuss.

Third, my selective listening to what domestic workers had to say at our first workshop is indicative of a pervasive tendency to sense the world in selective ways, within national or specific cultural frames. Framing is, as Judith Butler notes, a "politically-saturated operation of power,"[13] and what we see and do not see, hear and do not hear—and consent to as citizens of a nation—is framed by our positionality within long histories of colonial ventures, uneven economic development, national formation, relations of gender, class, and race, and so on. The issue is, as Butler notes, not just epistemological (that is, a matter of what we can know) but ontological (a matter of what we believe to exist). Framing affects the conditions under which individuals and groups are recognizable as fully human and as subjects capable of making claims to justice. We speculate that Canadians consent to the violence of importing women to care for their families not only because it is in their immediate interests to do so but also because of their inability to see noncitizens as fully deserving of the intimacies they take for granted as integral to family life. This book houses experiments—textual and performative—in circulating our research on and with Filipino migrant families to disrupt Canadians' passive consent to and complacency about labor export and import and the separation of Filipino migrant families across extensive distances for long periods of time. In chapters 3 and 4 in particular, I describe how we crafted and circulated our research to create intercultural discursive spaces in which claims to justice can be posed, heard, and discussed, and in which domestic workers and those who are likely to hire them can address and respond to each other in sustainable ways.

The disruption of passive consent and new relations of responsibility can have profound effects, putting Canadians (as well as Filipinos) into the world differently.[14] What happens, Butler asks, "when a frame [that governs differentially valued life] breaks with itself?"[15] She argues that taken-for-granted reality is thrown into question, along with relations of authority that structure hierarchies of human worth. As the world's largest labor diaspora, much has been claimed for the ways that Filipino citizens inhabit the world. San Juan, for instance, asks: "Can the Filipino diaspora expose . . . the limits of genetic and/or procedural notions of citizenship?" and "In what way can the Filipino diaspora serve as a paradigm for analyzing and critically unsettling the corporate globalization of labor?"[16] But as Nina Glick Schiller notes, it is equally important to disrupt the assumed sedentariness of the nations to which Filipinos migrate.[17] Maintaining a sharp distinction between migrants and presumed sedentary national subjects is a hallmark of a nationalism that feeds exclusionary immigration policy. It sustains assumptions that immigrants pose threats to an imagined social cohesion, which further justifies the proliferation of circulating or temporary migrant worker programs. It hides the fact that we all, in different ways and to varying extents, participate—knowingly and unknowingly—in transnational social and political-economic fields. Migrants and so-called natives often share values, norms, and experiences because they are jointly embedded in these networks and fields. But equally, seemingly sedentary Canadian nationals may become less familiar to themselves if they learn to see the ways in which their national subject position is implicated in processes that are invisible to them, both within their own country and beyond it. In this, we follow a long-standing argument in feminist, postcolonial, and now "new cosmopolitan" studies for the need of those in hegemonic cultural formations to become estranged from their selves as a prerequisite to entering into relations with others.[18] We focus on situated, grounded, and material conditions of connection, relations, and implication rather than a generalized sensibility of cosmopolitanism. Chapters 3 and 4 experiment with ways of positioning comfortable, middle-class Canadians in a complicated, destabilizing relationship with the testimony of domestic workers and their children, in chapter 4 through a testimonial play that we created from our research transcripts in collaboration with Vancouver-based theater artists.

Working with Ian Baucom's notion of melancholic attachment,[19] in chapter 4, the argument is made that attaching to Filipino migrants' experiences of loss opens non-Filipinos to an expansive cosmopolitan interestedness in the Philippines (as distinct from a generalized cosmopolitan sentiment), including an interest in the material conditions that drive migration.[20] Chapter 5 discusses how we can begin to listen (necessarily in a specific and partial way) to what domestic workers and the Philippine Women Centre have always said about their migration experiences: that they are located both in the Philippines and in Canada. More generally, this chapter pursues a way of thinking about the form that cosmopolitan interestedness might take, and how a material, politically engaged interestedness looks and how it works differently than humanitarianism or an ethic of "caring at a distance." Within a specific, nongeneralizable narrative of one group of Canadians' journeying to witness Philippine state violations of human rights, there emerges a wide-ranging argument about the possibilities of collaborating in relations of solidarity across the global South and North. This narrative is also performative in the sense that it forces the reader to take a close interest in the Philippines as one group of Canadian human rights activists experience it. Chapter 5 is not about labor migration; it is one instance of where attachment to the issue of Filipino labor migration might take you. It is practicing rather than professing cosmopolitan interestedness.

The Continuum of Violence and Its Erasure

In June 2006, the BC Committee of Human Rights in the Philippines organized a conference on human rights violations in the Philippines in solidarity with the international campaign "Stop the Killings in the Philippines." After a panel, in which the extent and extremity of human rights violations in the Philippines were enumerated, a white Canadian woman from an ally organization asked the question: "If things are so bad in the Philippines, should progressive Canadians still support scrapping the Live-In Caregiver Program?" A panelist from the Philippines quickly confirmed her organization's support of the PWC's position to scrap the LCP. But the question was telling: of how quickly Canadians imagine Canada in general, and a temporary work migration program in particular, as a refuge from a menacing Third World.

As a narrative of Canadian human rights activists not only witnessing but being acted upon by state violence in the Philippines, chapter 5 risks solidifying rather than displacing preconceptions of national difference and distance by confirming deep-rooted preconceptions of the Philippines as a site of chaos and Canada as a site of law and order. The hope is that the sequence of chapters in this book works against such a tendency: the discussion of state violence in the Philippines follows our analysis of the violence inherent to a temporary domestic worker program in Canada. We take seriously the notion that this temporary labor program subjects those enrolled in it to a form of social death, and that time working as a noncitizen creates enduring social exclusion for domestic workers and their families after they settle in Canada. We read across the erasure of violence in two national contexts, attempting to expose the vulnerability to violence in both places.

Of course, extrajudicial killings in the Philippines and the violence of temporary migration programs take place in entirely different registers: one form of state violence operates—literally—beyond the law, the other within the law, with popular consent. It is the criteria of law that typically separate the "good" states from the "bad." Further, many would see the violence associated with temporary work programs as nonpolitical, as the "fallout" of economic processes. As Susan Buck-Morss notes, "The violence caused by economic activity is not perceived as political violence. So long as the law is obeyed, it is not a state concern. Indeed, relations of economic exploitation are seen as quasi-natural."[21] This may be one reason temporary migration programs are often represented and justified by governments as a managerial response to economic imperatives, market or employer demand, or individual choices to migrate. But all modern societies, including liberal democratic ones, possess what Buck-Morss, following

Walter Benjamin, calls "a wild zone" of sovereign power that is supra- or prelegal. The legal exercise of this sometimes-violent power, especially on insiders who are expected to be protected from it, can reveal "something rotten" in the law.[22] When a temporary migration program leads to the systematic marginalization of (future) citizens and their children, the argument of chapter 2, this reveals "something rotten" within the legal migration system and the exercise of a kind of state violence, less spectacular and decisive than extrajudicial killing to be sure, but one that destabilizes assumptions about geographies of order and goodness, and opens a space to question the (Canadian) state's monopoly on assessments of and claims to justice. It might jolt (some of) us out of our passive consent.

Testimony and Affect

At the launch of the three-year participatory research project of the National Alliance of Philippine Women in Canada in 2006, I spoke on the plenary panel, presenting some of the research that forms the basis for this book, ending with long quotes from youths speaking of their experiences of separation from their mothers. They spoke of not recognizing their mothers when they visited the Philippines, of being fearful of speaking to them on the phone, about their mothers leaving while they slept and their bewilderment upon awakening. I interpreted the literal repetition of the same words and frozen images across interviews, conducted over the span of years, as symptoms of trauma. Cecilia Diocson, chairperson of the National Alliance, followed as the last speaker on the panel. At the podium, she became tearful as she started to speak about the situation of Filipinos. She finished by saying that she had prepared a text but had decided to speak from her heart after hearing the testimony of the youths. The session was then opened for questions and discussion.

There was a long silence before anyone ventured to speak. Finally a woman asked what the Canadian government was going to do to recognize the skills of Filipino nurses. The chair of the Filipino Nurses' Support Group got up from the audience to answer. She too was fighting tears and said she was having a hard time after hearing my presentation. It became clear that many in the audience were moved to tears by the testimonials from the Filipino youths. A longtime activist with the BC Committee for Human Rights in the Philippines finally stood up and said that tears are necessary but that the Filipino community needs to convert these tears into anger. He spoke of the need to connect the LCP experience to a broader analysis of imperialism. I left the event feeling uneasy about my place within it: who am I to move a Filipino audience to tears by ventriloquizing the youths' memories of trauma?

When I presented this same research some months later to government and service workers concerned with migration, most of the audience appeared unmoved by the youths' testimony. A colleague who had organized the event observed: "Yeah, they're a pretty hard-hearted bunch."

A central argument of this book is that Filipino migrant domestic workers are caught in the vice of competing neoliberal policies of governments in sending and receiving countries, and rather than paying rich returns their enterprising ambitions as migrants often end in social and economic exclusion—for themselves *and* their children. But the critical force of this analysis is shadowed by a gnawing concern that it could play its own role in the marginalization of migrants. By rendering the marginalization of Filipino foreign workers in Canada as a problem that must be acted upon (that is, as an "actionable problem"), we run the risk of representing Filipinos as a marginal population, one that could be seen to threaten the stability of life in Canada. Such a concern is not entirely fantastical. Consider that Filipinos in the United States, since the heightened security of national borders established after 2001, compared to other residents who originate from outside the United States, have experienced one of the highest rates of "noncriminal removals," and roughly half of these cases involved Filipinos who were permanent U.S. residents. A concern of the Critical Filipina and Filipino Studies Collective is that the Filipino population in the United States has become an object of racial profiling.[23]

By collecting and circulating testimonials that place domestic workers within their families, and especially in relation to their children, our aim is to reclaim their humanity beyond their economic value as workers and the racialized category of Filipina. An individual Filipina caregiver enrolls her entire family when she migrates; her labor as an individual migrant worker involves the cooperation and help of mothers and husbands and children and grandmothers and sisters and aunts and uncles spread between Canada and the Philippines. Chapters 1 and 2 reveal some of the affect and emotions that circulate (or fail to circulate) among migrant families as they strive to maintain intimacy across great distances. But equally, I consider the ways that testimony to these experiences does or does not travel, or can be made to travel. Chapters 3 and 4 experiment with putting the testimony of domestic workers and their children into circulation, to produce and circulate affective intensities through our research practices. Our intent is to galvanize emotional and political responses within the Filipino Canadian community and beyond, to individual lives rather than a generalized, racialized population.

In this, elements of our project fall within a wide interdisciplinary interest in emotions and affect, the latter broadly referring to a capacity to both affect and be affected. Migrant domestic work is, on the one hand, a quintessential form of affective labor. Affection and emotional care are bought and sold, the worker often transmogrified into "one of the family."[24] A migrant domestic worker extracted from her own family for its collective survival is a telling instance of the extent to which capitalist processes have penetrated the intimate spaces of "our" lives. But what Patricia Clough calls the "affective turn" in contemporary scholarship also gestures toward something excessive to this capture of affect in emotions, the body, the classifiable, and as a commodity.[25] Theorists have been drawn to affect because it refers to intensities that are simultaneously enrolled in *and* fractionally escape from or are excessive to technologies of power, classification, and normalization. Nigel Thrift refers to this as the "push" of life, and Ben Anderson finds in affect a "resource for hope."[26] Chapters 3 and 4 fit squarely within this affective turn; in the former, I trouble over how to circulate emotional testimony; in the latter, I consider as a resource for politics the intangible affective intensities that flow within a theatrical space, between actors and audience and between audience members.

There are all kinds of convincing reasons to be skeptical about many of the claims made about affect, as well as about the political significance of circulating narratives of personal loss and sacrifice with the intent of provoking an affective and political response. Circulating racialized women's emotional stories risks scripting them in a familiar state of victimhood. It risks consolidating their racialization. Sianne Ngai notes that what some might perceive as exaggerated emotional expressiveness—for instance, Filipinos tearing up in response to the youths' testimony—"seems to function as a marker of racial or ethnic otherness in general"; "to be 'animated' in American culture is to be *racialized* in some way."[27] And although I contrast Filipina emotionality to unfeeling (implicitly white) bureaucrats in the scenario at the beginning of this section of the introduction, heartfelt response to the testimony of the youths from these government workers would not extricate us from a complicated politics of race, class, and national difference. This is because sentimentality and a capacity to empathize with the sorrows and pain of others have long been taken as self-validating hallmarks of the (implicitly white) liberal, cosmopolitan bourgeois subject.[28] Further, the emotionality of much contemporary public debate is a source of concern rather than comfort. Lauren Berlant has written extensively about the growing prevalence of moral-emotional rhetoric in the U.S. public sphere and the ways in which morality and feeling often stand in for more nuanced critical political debate.[29] This most definitely includes public debate about immigrants and refugees.[30] Clive Barnett detects a privileging of affect over cognition in recent theoretical accounts of affect— what he calls "ontologizing affect"—and argues that this obscures and leaves unresolved democratic commitments to the principle of participation by all affected interests.[31] The tendency within this literature to construe affect as a means of manipulating political subjects offers, he argues, shaky ground, both for an affirmative politics of affect and commitments to democratic politics.

But feelings or affect are not at odds with, and need not replace, nuanced thought or critical democratic politics. Although critical of the way that affect and politics are currently theorized, Barnett, for one, offers many examples of what he terms "reconfigurations of affect-with-reason" (as opposed to perspectives that privilege either rationality or affect).[32] We think through our senses, and the conceptual break between rationality and affect is a spurious and ideological one, long a target of feminist criticism because of the ways it has been used to exclude and dominate those deemed "too emotional" for rational critical debate. Our focus is on how through affect and emotion we can open up or close down (rather than replace) deliberative public debate. Emotions are resources around which communities can organize, to make claims in a public domain. Experiences of trauma and loss need not shrivel from political engagement; rather, they can provide deep—enduringly painful—reservoirs for political mobilizing. Affect and feeling also condition receptivity to listening and acknowledging and responding. Much of this book worries at *how* to circulate testimonials from domestic workers and their children to shape such possibilities, to create intimacies that maintain important distances between those who testify to their experiences and those who witness these testimonials. *Families Apart* does not just report on the content of migrants' lives from a position of distanced appraisal; we aim to keep our own affective relations to this issue moving, toward the listener or reader, with the intent of reconfiguring their relationship to both the issue of temporary migrant work and to their own sense of self and place in the world. Experiencing complicated, contradictory emotions can be a means toward, but not a replacement for, critical thought; it can provoke but not replace more extended discussions about social justice. "If testimony and documentation are to have a politics and not just an ethics," Rothberg writes, "they must be oriented toward the creation of publics, toward circulation and not just exposure."[33] Tears need not flow in isolation. They can be a means of "collecting" a collectivity and a step toward a broader analysis of imperialism.

The Labor of Collaboration

During an informal reflection on our collaboration over the years, in 2006 Cecilia Diocson revealed some reasons our research on family separation and reunification had gone so slowly: "The interviews—before, [the youths] did not want to do [them]. But now that they have a feeling of ownership, they're very assertive in going out and interviewing, and using [the interviews] in the programs at the Centre." A year and a half later the interviews still were not done. Sitting in the back room at the Kalayaan Centre (then home of the PWC), me looking despondently at some short focus-group transcripts in Tagalog, from memory Cecilia said something like this: "Gerry, this is also a part of what we are studying, the stalled development of our youth." Our research process, I realized, no longer bent to the protocols and priorities of the university but instead invited me to incline myself toward a fuller, more embodied experience of what we sought to understand.

Two years later, I looked again at those transcripts and reread them for their plentitude instead of lack. With distance, I could hear the chatter of male youth—the back and forth of one-liners and jokes and half-revelations—where I had expected and wanted the earnest testimony more likely offered by an adult.

In July 2010, I observed another exercise in prising wants from needs. I was at a workshop attended by six Filipina migrant domestic workers, sponsored by a nonprofit organization in Vancouver and facilitated by an evangelical Catholic mission, to which I have been invited after presenting our research to a coalition of immigrant service agencies. One exercise asks each migrant to report on five "wants" that she plans to strip away as she strives toward a simpler but full life. Their lists included the following:

sending remittances every second month instead of every month; calling their children in the Philippines less often; using a landline rather than cell phone; buying a one- instead of two-zone bus pass; using Faresaver bus tickets instead of a monthly bus pass; borrowing movies from the library rather than renting videos. I imagine my long-term research collaborators' skepticism about the activities taking place in this room—and I miss them, even as I marvel at the resourcefulness and tenacity of these migrant women. And I take pleasure in the intimacy of strangers' arms folded around my shoulders and waist as we pose for the photograph that ends the session.

After fifteen years of working together, a lone, white, middle-class university researcher observing a migrant workshop is an unfamiliar experience (even if she is introduced as an advocate, as was the case at this "values workshop" for migrants). Our association has been sustained by our belief that joining forces pushes scholarship and activism into places that neither can go alone. Collaborating with theater artists has taken us one step further along a trajectory of creating new performative spaces of engagement. On the one hand, Filipino families were no doubt more willing to share their stories with us because they could speak fluently in Tagalog or another language of the Philippines, frequently with those who have lived through similar experiences. They shared their experiences with the expectation that their testimonials would be put to use to try to transform the conditions that they had suffered and would like to see changed. On the other hand, working with a university researcher allowed the PWC access to government data and funding sources that might not otherwise have been available, and our collaborative research may have been taken more seriously within the Filipino community (and beyond) because of its association with a university researcher. It is clear even from these few examples that we brought very different resources within enduring hierarchies of power relations. A structural imbalance creates the conditions for our relationship; it is also what we have striven to expose and work against. Through our productively compromised collaboration, we have tried to create a process of knowledge creation that answers to different communities of interest operating within varying protocols of accountability. The questions that guide our research always have emerged in the first instance from within the Filipino activist community, although we also think and write about them in the context of wider scholarly debates. And as Cecilia notes above, taking ownership of the process has been essential to the participation of community members and their use of our research in organizing work. Our collaborative process has enabled us to address another kind of violence: the epistemic violence that is often understood to be endemic within Western scholarship on "Third World women," when such women are taken as objects to know rather than subjects capable of knowing and theorizing the conditions of their world, and representations of them circulate as valuable commodities within scholarly circuits of knowledge production and career advancement.[34] We have searched for ways of working together to speak to a plurality of audiences. Sometimes we present our research together at press conferences and community forums and conferences, but more often we present it separately: the academic speaking in academic contexts, community researchers through press releases, media interviews, lobbying governments, and community forums. In what follows, I try to convey some of the liveliness of this process and the ways that our research already has been circulating in the world, even as this book puts it into the world in a new and different way.

There is a sense in which the trajectory of the book—from Vancouver to the Philippines; from one form of state violence to another; from containment to venturing across borders into new spaces—is pure artifice. The simplest explanation is to say: this is what we have been in the middle of for the past six years. A concern to theorize and write about ways of circulating testimonials came from the shock of the emotional reactions to initial oral presentations of our research material. This heightened a sense of responsibility toward those who narrated their pain and loss for us, and worries about the political stakes involved in circulating these testimonials within and beyond the Filipino community. The chapter on our testimonial play exists because of our collective need to reflect upon the possibilities of that practice for mobilizing a wider public debate. That is, our concern is as much about future practice of the PWC as it is about advancing scholarly debate on the potentials of theatrical performance. The chapter on witnessing in the Philippines emerged because some of us were involved with this alongside our research project on family separation and reunification, reflecting the bifurcated nature of Filipino activism in Canada and the United States: simultaneously focused on systemic racism in North America and popular democratic struggle in the Philippines. To bring you into our worlds in this messier way is to invite you into our lived research practice.

Our way of doing research models two epistemological points. First, our long association has been a series of encounters across our many differences (both within the PWC, among various organizations at the Kalayaan Centre, and between myself and organization members); it offers proof of the possibility of bringing together and sustaining a relationship with those who do not share an identity, but rather a commitment to work together toward loosely framed, continuously evolving, common ends.[35] We began as feminists who shared a concern about how care work in Canada is grossly and persistently undervalued and the gendered, racist, and colonial assumptions that maintain this situation. But second, what makes such encounters ethically and politically promising, in Sara Ahmed's view, is the possibility they offer to get "closer to others in order to occupy or inhabit the distance between us."[36] Inhabiting this distance, she argues, opens each person in such encounters to other unheard or unfinished histories and geographies, to other encounters, or, in Ahmed's phrasing, "other others": "It is through attending to the multiplicity of pasts that are never simply *behind* us, through the traces they leave in the encounters we have in the present, that we can open up the promise of the 'not yet.'"[37] To Ahmed's focus on temporality, we add: to the multiplicity of spaces that are never simply distant from those that we inhabit.

Ahmed views a collectivity as a process of "collecting together" through such encounters, collecting without presuming a common ground or identity. Through this notion, she aims to navigate through and around critiques of the underlying Eurocentrism of feminist universalisms—for example, universal notions of gender equity—and the splintering of feminist organizing through cultural relativism.[38] Collectivities emerge in practice rather than principle precisely through the hard work of learning in concrete, specific terms how we are positioned differently through and within processes of global capitalism, in this case the expansion of temporary work programs. This book emerges from a process of "collecting together," a collaboration between a university researcher and the PWC. Since then, we have brought the Filipino-Canadian Youth Alliance into our research process, followed by the BC Committee of Human Rights in the Philippines, then several Vancouver-based theater artists. There is some overlap among the first three groups, but each moment of collecting brought more and different people into the encounter. The excursion to the Philippines in the concluding chapter can be understood within such a process of collecting together. Encountering Filipina temporary domestic workers and their families—really doing the hard, sustained work of encountering them—is to be opened to other geographies and histories. It puts the world together

differently, erasing some lines on our taken-for-granted maps and bringing other borders into view.

We begin with a temporary work program in Canada and open ourselves to the other others in our investigation. Through this collaboration,
we hope to facilitate a more expansive dialogue about the justice of temporary work migration in Canada, the Philippines and beyond, and to unsettle assumptions about relations of exclusion and belonging within and
beyond borders.

CHAPTER 1

Enterprising Women, Failing Children: Living within the Contradictions of Neo(Liberalism)

The site of separation, the line marking the limits of (domestic) liberty . . . marks the site of our murkiest conceptualization, and our most dramatic apprehension.

—R. B. J. Walker, "Conclusion: Sovereignties, Exceptions, Worlds"

WHEN THE PCW AND I BEGAN TO INTERVIEW LISA about her time working as a live-in domestic worker for Canadian families, her answers were brief. Despite working for numerous, in some cases abusive, employers and revealing fragments from her third employment situation, which had the makings for a dramatic story, she truncated her account by stating: "I actually stayed with them for a while and finished my contract with them. I just wanted to finish my contract so that I could finish my twenty-four-month requirement under the LCP, leave them and finally get my family." Asked how long she stayed with this abusive employer, she said it was more than a year, but she repeated, "I just wanted to finish my contract so that I can get out of the LCP. My main purpose was to get my family. So I had to sacrifice and stayed with them [the employers]." Asked for more details about her employment, Lisa drew the interview back to her life after the LCP: "Even if it's two o'clock in the morning, I would [walk the dog]. I did this just so that I can finish the contract." Probed for details about overtime wages, she indicated that there were none but insisted, "I didn't mind. As long as I can finish the contract. I just wanted to finish my twenty-four months with them so I can get my family." Lisa's husband offered that these employers often failed to pay on time. Again, when asked about overtime wages, she said: "No. My sole focus is my family and how to get them here." And so the conversation moved—finally— to Lisa's application to sponsor her family's immigration to Canada.

Lisa is one of roughly 21,000 individuals authorized to work in Canada through a temporary work-visa program, the Live-In Caregiver Program (LCP), most of whom are women and the vast majority Filipina.[1] Although almost all have family responsibilities in the Philippines and many, like Lisa, have left children there, they are admitted on temporary visas as individual workers.[2] These workers are part of a much wider reliance on temporary migrant workers in Canada. Nandita Sharma dates the massive expansion in temporary work migration to Canada to the introduction of the Non-Immigrant Employment Authorization Plan in 1973 and estimates that between 1973 and 2004 more than three-quarters of workers recruited to Canada came through temporary work rather than permanent settlement programs. Because of restricted geographical and labor market mobility, all migrant workers are, in her view, legally positioned as unfree labor, and she judges the existence of two different regulatory structures for national and foreign subjects to be a form of apartheid. Sharma notes that "violence is materialized not only in how national states are able to prevent certain people's actual mobility into national space but in constructing certain people as falling outside the ideological—but not territorial—boundaries of this space."[3] Étienne Balibar also labels as apartheid a similar increase of migrant workers within the European Union. Neither insiders nor outsiders, they labor on one side of a border under different legal conditions from national subjects and reproduce their lives (and those of their families) on the other.[4]

If the LCP is part of a general trend, it is an extreme case. Like most temporary migrant programs, it denies domestic workers fundamental mobility rights as well as rights to live with immediate family members. Beyond this, the requirement to live in their employers' homes creates the conditions of serfdom under the terms of the United Nations Supplementary Conventions on the Abolition of Slavery, the Slave Trade, and Institutions and Practices Similar to Slavery.[5] Although states party to the conventions, including Canada (which ratified it on January 10, 1963), have agreed to abolish these practices, the number of work permits issued annually under the LCP, in line with temporary-worker programs more generally, has risen dramatically in the new millennium, from 2,684 in 2000 to 9,816 in 2009.[6]

Apartheid and slavery: such words may seem overblown and histrionic when applied to liberal-democratic societies in which state authority is grounded in an ethic of individual freedom. Yet, as Barry Hindess notes, liberty and domination are joined in liberal thought and practice "like two sides of a single coin: the value of one may appear on the face, but the figure of the other is firmly stamped on the reverse."[7] On one face, liberal government aims to foster the well-being of the population as a whole and to strengthen the resources of those subject to government. As distinct from domination or discipline, an ethics of freedom (choice, responsibility) is the means of governing a population. Government in advanced or neoliberal societies operates "at a distance," shaping individuals' conduct through calculation, depending on the capabilities of individuals to act upon themselves as ostensibly free, rational, and responsible subjects through a "calculative relation to life."[8] Different forms of power and rule—liberal government, sovereign power, discipline, domination—nonetheless coexist and interlock in liberal societies. And they are not practiced equally on different groups of people. Speculating about the growth of state racism, Foucault argued that the modern state justifies differential relations of power and domination by introducing a biological break between the population and inferior races. Without doing so, he argued that the modern state "can scarcely function."[9] While the population is subject to government, inferiorized races can be subjected to the violence of sovereign power.[10] In Foucault's view, state racism developed as the only means to justify "the murderous function of the State"; inferiorized races can be sacrificed to regenerate or make more vital the population. By killing, Foucault explained, "I obviously do not mean simply murder as such, but also every form of indirect murder: the fact of exposing someone to death, increasing the risk of death for some people, or, quite simply, political death, expulsion, rejection, and so on."[11] The importation of women from the global South under conditions of indentured servitude to care for Canadian children, seniors, and the disabled can be read as an instance of sovereign power, whereby Filipino women are sacrificed for the vitality of the Canadian population. Canadian families prosper by tapping into a global supply of well-trained workers who labor and live under conditions that are unacceptable to national citizens.[12]

If this scenario of state power seems plausible in outline, it is clearly lacking in nuance and detail. Lisa tells of her willingness to sacrifice herself for a period of time in order to sponsor her family's migration to Canada. She is directing our attention away from the violence of the LCP to the benefit of family migration. Even if Canadian governments insist that the LCP is not an immigration program, the opportunity that it affords to migrate permanently after it has been completed is unusual.[13] Currently over 90 percent of foreign nationals who enter Canada as live-in caregivers apply for permanent residence, and 98 percent of these applicants are successful.[14] Since the mid-1990s, when family reunification following the LCP began in large numbers,[15] the program has been significant for Filipino communities in Canada. Through the 1990s, roughly one-third of Filipinos immigrating to Canada landed through the LCP, and the proportion increased to 40 percent in 2009.[16] In Vancouver, the significance of the LCP for the Filipino community is even starker: in 1998, 48 percent of Filipino arrivals in Vancouver came through the LCP, either directly or as sponsored family members.[17] Binarized breaks between the Canadian population and an inferiorized racial other, and between liberal forms of government and sovereign power, thus simplify the complexities of geography, power, politics, and social exclusion. And they do so in ways that prevent us from fully appreciating the catastrophe that is the LCP.

Two theoretical adjustments are required. First, a focus on the vulnerability of Filipino domestic workers to the arbitrary exercise of the sovereign power of the Canadian state not only repeats a familiar tendency to begin and end stories in the metropoles of the global North; it obscures the geographical complexity of the power relations in which domestic workers coming to Canada are immersed.[18] It is not only that their citizenship rights are fragmented and scattered across different nation-states—some political rights here, some economic rights there—in ways that often weaken their claims to rights and entitlements in all places.[19] More than this, their subjugation to sovereign power in Canada is parasitic on their enrollment in a neoliberal project of government in the Philippines expressed through its labor export policy (LEP). There is no doubt a "savage asymmetry" between these two national neoliberal projects of government.[20] As San Juan notes, "Brutalized migrant labor throughout the world thrives on the intensified inequality of nation-states, particularly the intense impoverishment of 'third world' societies of Africa, Latin America, and Asia."[21] The neoliberal projects of government in the Philippines and Canada are bred in the asymmetries of uneven development. But of interest here is the fact that, for the Filipino domestic workers maneuvering and caught between the LEP and LCP, these national neoliberal projects are nothing short of contradictory. Governance in advanced (or neo) liberal societies, Nikolas Rose argues, involves the translation between the objectives of authorities wishing to govern and the personal projects of individuals who are the subjects of government: "If translation processes operate without disruption ... the autonomy [of the subject] can be allied with, aligned with, such objectives as economic success, national popula-tion policy . . . and the like."[22] In the case of Filipinas coming to Canada as domestic workers, there are some profound disruptions in the translation process as they move between the crisscrossing neoliberal projects of the Philippine and Canadian states.

Second, skeptical as we might be about official stories of inclusion, the systematic marginalization of Filipinos in Canada can raise troubling ques-tions about state violence precisely because it rubs against these official stories and liberal principles of equality. Legg argues that theorists such as Agamben offer too simplistic a reading of sovereignty in part because they overemphasize the arbitrary decision-making capacity of the sovereign and fail to problematize the articulation of sovereign and other types of power relations, including liberal principles and practices of governance.[23] Dis-entangling the awkward articulation of liberal principles and migrant worker programs also sharpens our analysis of a second set of contradictions in which domestic workers in Canada are caught: between two meanings of citizenship. One meaning of citizenship is tied up with the boundary or threshold question of who is rightly included or excluded from member-ship within a particular liberal democratic community. This is distinct from the meaning of citizenship within a given community, as a bundle of entitlements and responsibilities. The two notions of citizenship operate within different regulatory and normative frameworks: one exclusionary or particularistic, the other universalizing. Even if the sovereign right to exclude guest workers at the territorial borders of the nation is largely un-questioned or accepted as liberalism's (illiberal) enabling condition, visible and explicit exclusion of those living within the national territory generally is not: the "inner logic of democracy and a commitment to liberal princi-ples require the full inclusion of the entire settled population."[24] As Linda Bosniak puts it, liberal citizenship is hard on the outside and soft on the inside.[25]

These two meanings of citizenship are typically seen as complemen-tary rather than contradictory because of the spatial imaginary that keeps them sequestered, one from the other: membership questions are under-stood to take place at the border of the nation, norms of universality are located within that bounded territory. In Bosniak's words: this is a "neat solution to a messy problem."[26] But the separate-spheres model does not hold up in practice, and "the national border dividing citizens from out-siders extends deep inside the community territory."[27] The folding of the border into the inside—Bosniak grasps for an apt description through various spatialized terms, such as imbrication, introjection, and introgression—is apparent "most directly and graphically in the person of the alien."[28] For such resident noncitizens, "the border effectively follows them inside."[29] Guest-worker programs such as the LCP would seem to violate liberal principles of universality because, even though temporary foreign workers have been admitted into the community, they do not enjoy equal rights. They are required to abandon their rights to live with their immediate families. They typically labor at below-market rates of pay within the national context in which they work. Registrants in the LCP are required to work in a particular occupation, for a single employer, and to live in their employers' home. Further, migrant workers' perpetual vulnerability to deportation makes them unlikely to exercise whatever formal rights they may hold. In Michael Walzer's words, long-term guest workers are effectively ruled "by a band of citizen-tyrants."[30]

Because guest workers so obviously violate the norm of universality, when liberal political theorists ask whether "normative maps of democracy have room" for resident noncitizens, any space they find is cramped and compromised.[31] As Mayer puts it: "In tolerating such programs our hands do get a little dirty." Mayer finds some normative space for guest-worker programs when "the moral costs of the dirt are less than the price foreign labor pays for the purist policy" of being denied entry on strict grounds of liberal justice.[32] Mayer's "liberal egalitarian theory of exploitation" determines that guest-worker programs are justifiable only when guest workers migrate from a position of sufficiency (that is, they are not coerced to migrate by desperation) and, knowing and deducting the costs of guest work (low quality of work, separation from family, and so on) would still choose to make the journey. Alternatively, other liberal thinkers find normative wiggle room in the principle of time: they reason that the liberal norm of universality is not offended if the noncitizen resident has the opportunity to naturalize within a reasonable period of time.[33] By this principle, the LCP is just: after twenty-four months in the guest-worker program, registrants are eligible to apply for permanent resident status and sponsor their families.[34] Within this liberal compromise, the Canadian government is blending programs that operate within entirely different social relations.[35] After women complete the requirements of the LCP, they reencounter the Canadian state—no longer as isolated workers employed in slavelike conditions, but as immigrants embedded in their own family relations. They seem to be moving across the biological break from those whose lives can be sacrificed into politically qualified life (or into the body of the population). On these grounds, Carens remains open to the possibility that the LCP is, as some claim, "a model of well-managed temporary immigration."[36]

But do domestic workers have full knowledge of costs and benefits or of what is a reasonable period of time, and does naturalization so easily smooth the experience of being suspended between the two meanings of citizenship, neither fully outsider nor insider? On these questions, liberal theorists are of little help, and hence their liberal principles are rendered inoperative. Michael Walzer, an early and influential critic of guest-worker programs, speculated that naturalization would correct the effects of alien status: "They would soon be like domestic [local] workers, unwilling to take on hard and degrading work or accept low rates of pay."[37] But is that really the case? On the matter of what comprises a fair amount of time, Carens ventures that "denying people the right to have their families with them for more than three months would be harsh and for more than a year would be unconscionable." But he recognizes that no normative principle can dictate the limits of justifiable forced separation regulated by guest-worker programs. In the end, he determines that just standards must be based on "common understanding of ways in which people settle into the societies in which they live."[38]

We situated our study of the ways that domestic workers and their families settle into Canadian society within this lacuna in liberal normative assessment. We argue that the liberal compromise around an illiberal program does not work but, rather, has led to the unwitting production of social and economic exclusion across a significant portion of the Filipino Canadian community, including the children for whom domestic workers like Lisa have sacrificed.[39] It is not only that women coming through the LCP are themselves deskilled through the process; in eerie and rapid repetition, their children relive many of their mothers' experiences. Domestic workers and their families are caught at the thresholds of a number of contradictory (neo)liberal compromises. Something has to give under the pressure of these contradictions; we argue that it is the families immigrating through the LCP that are buckling under their weight.

The blind spots that exist within the gaps of these contradictions make it difficult, however, to build this empirical argument. In particular, because the Canadian government sees temporary worker programs and

immigration as distinct,[40] official statistics are fragmented, and those collected for the LCP are not easily integrated with governmental analyses of
the productivity and well-being of the Filipino community as a whole.
This disjuncture between statistical analyses is telling because what the
state enumerates gives a sense of its priorities: "To problematize . . . requires to be counted. . . . What is counted . . . is what is problematized. To
count a problem is to define it and make it amenable to government. To
govern a problem requires that it be counted."[41] So as we struggle to count
the long-lasting effects of indentured servitude so as to formulate it as a
political problem that Canadian policy-makers might address, we must
also inquire about the limits of such a strategy. We will ask, following
Edkins and Pin-Fat, what are the possibilities of "refusing the grammar of
sovereign power's language game?" by constructing political narratives in
other terms.[42]

Entrepreneurial Migrants

Filipinos coming through the LCP are a small but growing faction of a vast
Filipino labor diaspora: in 2007, Canada followed Italy in having the highest annual increase in new hires of Overseas Filipino Workers (OFWs);
by 2008, it ranked ninth worldwide as the destination for newly and rehired land-based OFWs, and in 2009 it was second only to Taiwan for new
hires of caregivers, no doubt reflecting the recent expansion of the LCP.[43]
Currently more than 8 million Philippine nationals are working abroad in
more than 190 countries, the majority (approximately 85 percent) on temporary labor contracts.[44]

As Kelly delicately puts it, the Philippines' long and brutal history of colo-
nialization "has left it peculiarly susceptible to arguments that prioritized the
global scale."[45] By the 1960s, economic liberalization and export-oriented
development were prerequisites for receiving structural-adjustment loans
from the IMF and the World Bank. Struggling with payment requirements
and rising unemployment, President Ferdinand Marcos, in 1974, established a labor export policy and created state agencies to assist in the deploy-
ment of Filipino workers overseas. Succeeding presidents have further
institutionalized the policy,[46] to the extent that the very meaning of citizenship in the Philippines has been transformed. In *Migrants for Export*,
Rodriguez identifies a new form of "migrant citizenship," a key component
of which is the "right" to overseas employment. Women have fully accessed

this "right," and by 2006 more than half of those leaving the Philippines to work overseas were women.[47] In 2009, women comprised 52.8 percent of newly hired land-based OFWs (as opposed to seafarers), mostly working in a range of care professions: 40 percent as household service workers, 7 percent as nurses,[48] 5 percent as caregivers, 5 percent as "charwomen," and another 2.4 percent as housekeepers.[49] That this policy has generated extremely large sums of foreign capital for the Philippines, there is no doubt: remittances of overseas contract workers to the Philippines doubled from 2000 to 2006, from U.S. $6.05 billion to $12.76 billion, and over 7 percent of households in the Philippines now depend on international remittances as their main (not just supplemental) source of income.[50] Filipinos in Canada accounted for 1.9 billion (roughly 11 percent) of total remittances in 2009, trailing only the United States in the amount of money remitted by overseas Filipinos.[51] The appeal to the receiving countries is also clear: Parreñas identifies Filipina migrant workers as the "servants of globalization." They are slotted into insecure, low-paying jobs by "capitalist scripts" that operate through persistent gendered and racialized inequalities.[52]

But why and how do Filipinas slot themselves into these scripts? The answer goes beyond economic considerations and takes shape within a complex constellation of economic, political, social, cultural, and affective forces. Women coming to Canada through the LCP are highly educated: in 2009, 63 percent applying for permanent resident status had at least one university degree, and a further 33 percent had some university education, a nonuniversity diploma, or a trade certificate.[53] These high levels of educational attainment are symptomatic of the Philippine government's commitment to the production of skilled labor as a key national resource and source of "comparative advantage" within the global economy. Neferti Tadiar likens Filipina overseas contract workers to cosmic gamblers, who "have made what we might recognize as the global economy a vague, unencompassing kind of cosmic order" in which they try their luck.[54] They weigh their options about finding employment adequate for their needs or commensurate with their educational training within this cosmos, against the widening disparity between rich and poor (the Philippines has one of the highest levels of income inequality globally)[55] and persistent political corruption. A culture or ethos of migration has developed such that "a sense of life lived at a larger scale than the village, town or nation is seldom absent from the everyday experience of a large proportion of the population."[56]

The Philippine state and labor brokers intensify and institutionalize this experience by drawing on a potent mix of neoliberalism and discourses of empowerment; Catholic, nationalistic, and gendered ideals of suffering and sacrifice; and cultural notions of cooperation and indebtedness. *In Marketing Dreams, Manufacturing Heroes,* Guevarra examines what she calls the governmentalization of the Philippine state through its management of labor migration, and outlines a proliferation of governmental techniques deployed to create overseas migrants as responsible, entrepreneurial subjects.[57] In 1988, President Corazon Aquino cast overseas Filipino workers as "the new economic" or "modern day heroes," as have subsequent presidents. As Guevarra writes: "The [then] current administration of Gloria Macapagal Arroyo repeatedly touts the Philippines as the 'Home of the Great Filipino Worker' and calls upon overseas Filipino workers to recognize their role as the new 'investors,' the 'new aristocrats,' and the 'ambassadors of goodwill' who have a crucial responsibility to build the country's economy and promote a positive image of the Philippines."[58] Shifts in the language used to describe overseas workers bear the traces of an increasingly neoliberal outlook, moving from Overseas Contract Worker (OCW) to Overseas Filipino Worker (OFW) in 1995, to President Arroyo's use of Overseas Filipino Investor (OFI) in 2001. The *Handbook for Filipinos Overseas,* printed by the Commission on Filipinos Overseas in 1999, could not be more explicit about the expected entrepreneurial and nationalistic outlook: "By the 21st century, the Filipino is envisioned to be: mobile, flexible, entrepreneurial, nationalistic and tolerant."[59] The Philippine government has instituted pre-employment and pre-departure seminars for OFWs, during which norms of responsible conduct are taught, including information on how to submit remittances, handle familial responsibilities, buy insurance, make education plans, and invest earnings in business ventures rather than squandering overseas earnings on consumer goods. It has formulated modules on labor migration to be taught in elementary and secondary schools. On a weekly Saturday television show, President Arroyo was known to extol the virtues of overseas employment.[60] In all of this, since the Migrant Workers and Overseas Filipinos Act of 1995, the state now presents itself as a manager, merely facilitating the aspirations of its citizens acting in their own and their family's interests: "State officials claim that they are not 'promoting' overseas employment but simply 'managing' labour migration and facilitating the desires and choices of their citizens to seek 'greener pastures' elsewhere."[61]

Entrepreneurial Domestic Workers

Techniques of government are one thing; understanding how they are lived by those subjected to them is another. We turn to consider how a mixture of constraint, choice, responsibility, and sacrifice reverberated through interviews with mothers who have migrated to Canada through the LCP.[62] They told stories of planning and calculation seasoned by good fortune or luck. They certainly saved and invested in education and other ventures. Rosita's story of leaving General Santos City (three-time award winner for the "Most Competitive City" in the Philippines), for instance, reveals the weight of her many responsibilities:

> What happened in that [private] school is I was stuck to my duties and responsibilities because the institution, the principal and our supervisors trusted me so much that they gave me lots of responsibilities, not only teaching in the classroom but being an activities coordinator. And what is not fair is that those teachers who are not handling other activities have the time to pursue their studies, like taking a master's degree. Because they have the time and I don't have the time. . . . I couldn't have the chance because I was stuck with those other responsibilities. Another reason I left that school is that I didn't feel that I was happy the whole time I worked there. That's why I said, instead of finding luck in the Philippines, going to other schools, I would try to find my luck in Canada where my sister came before me. And just be strong and leave everything. Leave my kids in the care of my family.[63]

With a Bachelor of Science degree in Education, she earned only 500 pesos a month when she began teaching at this school in 1983; seventeen years later she was earning only 9,000 pesos a month (around U.S. $180)[64] and was now supporting three children on her own.[65] "Sometimes I ended up with nothing in my pocket because they are deducting everything [including her children's private school fees]." "I was really concerned about the future of my kids. . . . There's no way I can really give them a better education if I just stay in the Philippines. . . . So I agreed with my sister that we try our luck here in Canada."

Liberty also left the Philippines when her three children were older, age 13, 12, and 9. She had completed two years of a Bachelor of Arts degree, and described her family background in Manila as middle class, evident in the fact that she was a stay-at-home mother until leaving the Philippines to do overseas contract work. Her husband worked in the Middle East as a contract worker for over a decade before Liberty herself left, but his remittances home had become sporadic, and on one occasion she had to ask neighbors for food. She had been planning for many years to work abroad, but it was not until her eldest son was about to enter high school that her plans became concrete: "In my mind, I wanted him to start in a private school. I paid for his entrance test. After three weeks, the school board said that the results would be posted. . . . And I was so happy and excited: he was number 8, in the top 10. And I said, 'Oh, my son, come, come, your number, look at your name there.' But on the other side of the board, it's the tuition fee." She was unable to pay the fees and her son could not attend. But within months "God listened to my . . . to what I said" and her aunt, who had been working as a domestic servant in Hong Kong, notified her of employment in Hong Kong: "It was always my dream, you know, [to provide] the best education that I could give to my children at my own expense." Liberty's husband (whom she subsequently divorced when he started a relationship with the other Filipino household servant while they were working for the same employer in Hong Kong) did not want her to work abroad, but "I told him that 'I have dreams, big dreams for my children.'"

Leaving her children in the care of her parents in Manila, she stayed in Hong Kong for seven years, working for the same wealthy family. When this family moved to Vancouver, they selected only one of their three helpers in Hong Kong to come with them: "It was me because I had been with them the longest and I had taken care of the kids. I was very lucky that they brought me here from Hong Kong. . . . When they asked me to go with them, I said yes at once. . . . I thought Canada was a new environment and would give a new experience. Also, I would have a new [higher] wage rate. . . . So I was really excited." After living in Vancouver for three years, her employers were discouraged by the economic prospects there and returned to Hong Kong. They wanted Liberty to return with them, but "this time I told them that I am thankful [to them] for bringing me here to Canada, but I am also looking for opportunities for my kids."

Maria traced a similar route into overseas contract work, but in her case she and her husband made the decision together. When her eldest son was in his third year of high school (and her youngest child was just 6 years old), "I decided with my husband to find a better opportunity. We wanted money to be able to send our children to school. I had work in the Philippines. I was working for twenty years. We were making good money and my husband was teaching at [a private school] and at a public high school. But our salaries were not sufficient. So we talked and agreed that I would leave the Philippines to work and earn some money to be able to help the family and send the kids to college."

Maria left in 1990, first for two years in Singapore and then she came directly to Canada. Her remittances were dedicated to her children's education and to accruing assets that they could use for the purposes of immigration. Her husband reported: "I saw to it that the money coming in I don't touch because it is for education. Because my salary was enough for us to survive. So that amount she sent us must be for the education of the kids. I don't touch it for my personal use." They were also able to buy a piece of land planted with coconuts and a two-hectare mango grove, which they cultivated in an enterprising way: "I told them in the Philippines that they should use the land and not leave it empty. So my second child is busy working and taking care of the land at the same time."

Maria sent all but $40 of her earnings home each month, until she began to save to sponsor her family: "I didn't go to parties or have a good time because I wanted to get my husband and son. My friends were complaining that I wasn't going out with them. But I told them that I was planning to sponsor my husband and my son, and I am saving all my money that I get [as a domestic worker]. Finally, with God's help, I was able to get them. . . . I spent all of my whole life for my family."

Maria's frugality in Vancouver may have been extreme, but the themes of hard work, sacrifice, and careful planning were constant.[66] Lisa sent home $500 from her monthly net income of $770: "As much as I could afford I would send to them. I have no savings as I sent everything to the kids." Jeanette sent half of her $750 net monthly income home to her two young children and husband: "So very little was left for my expenses here. Luckily my aunt [also living in Vancouver] gave me some of her used clothing, especially jackets for winter, so I did not have to buy my clothing anymore."

The costs of supporting families in the Philippines, living in Vancouver, and saving to sponsor their family to join them are high relative to domestic workers' salaries,[67] and women often work at more than one job. Jeanette applied first for her own permanent resident status and then later for her family because of the expenses both in Canada and in the Philippines:

Before they arrived I had three jobs. When I got my landed visa,
I was a live-in caregiver, but I told my employer that I wanted to
live out. It was all right with her. Then I had another job, a
part-time cleaning job, then after the cleaning I had another
under-the-table job again. I needed to earn more because of the
expenses I had to pay for sponsoring my family. Just before they
arrived, I had two full-time jobs. The other one was with the friend
of my other employer. I had to work long hours. I usually started at
eight [A.M.] and finished at eleven in the evening. . . . I even had to
borrow money from my second employer to pay for their [air]fare.
I had to pay that every 15th of the month. That was aside from the
money I borrowed from my aunt. [Interviewer: You had debts all
over, huh?] Yes, and then I had to pay for the apartment. . . . After
they arrived, I gave up the other job. I had only one full-time job
[as domestic worker] and two part-time cleaning jobs.

When Jeanette's husband and children arrived, her husband took on the
burden of multiple jobs: "I told her to quit her other job so she could
review [for the Nursing Board exam]. I had to have several jobs too: one
full-time and two part-time jobs. Sometimes I would come home at 2 A.M.,
then get up early again to go to another job." Majoring in marketing for a
commerce degree, her husband worked in the Philippines as a salesman
for International Harvester. In Vancouver, he has worked at 7-Eleven (which
he quit because of what he interpreted to be discrimination), a gasoline
station (where he was held up twice), and as a maintenance worker. After
taking a four-month course at a community college, he now works part-
time as a health aid worker.

Jeanette's advice to Filipinos in a similar situation is "not [to be] choosy
about their work. Take whatever work is available. Maybe they can find a
better one later on. They need to gain Canadian experience first. Pray. Do
not forget to ask for God's help. And try to be understanding of each other's
situation." But her success regaining her professional qualifications is unusual (although not unique); she is, for instance, the one nurse among
seven we interviewed who had regained her professional standing. (She
currently works at a residential care facility for seniors.) Only one teacher
among four had requalified as a teacher in Canada. (With a Bachelor of
Science degree, she taught in elementary school in the Philippines for four
years. Retraining in Canada in early childhood education, she now works

at a day-care center.) Most of the women continued to work as house-keepers (7), as home-support workers (7), providing elder care (2), or working as nurses' aides (2). (Two other women were working as office cleaners, two as minimum-wage retail clerks, one as a waitress, and another was employed in computer training.)

Deskilling has frequently been noted as one of the outcomes of the LCP experience,[68] because women lose their skills during the years that they work as caregivers. The point must also be made that there is a circular relationship between deskilling and family separation. In the years immediately after completing the LCP, many women have few resources for retraining because they are sending large sums of money home and saving to bring their families to Canada. That is, they are simultaneously enrolled in citizenship projects in the Philippines and Canada. They are living migrant Philippine citizenship: working overseas and remitting responsibly to their family members as they simultaneously work toward their permanent resident status in Canada and bringing their families to Canada. Because of their obligations to save money and support their families, the most common retraining strategy is to take a short six-month part-time or full-time course that allows entry into the most precarious jobs in the field of health care. The LCP, followed by family immigration, is thus a regulatory structure that effectively seals women's fate as a well-educated cadre of lowly paid, vulnerable employees, working long hours, often in an increasingly privatized health-care industry. Women who must save to sponsor their families have few resources to develop their own "human capital" in Canada, and they are typically already deskilled by the time their families arrive, often working multiple, insecure jobs. Under such circumstances, even enterprising women find it difficult to realize their ambitions.

Family is, as Nikolas Rose notes, a key site of government through freedom, and the "responsibilized" aspirations of individuals are often realized through their families.[69] This is decidedly so among immigrants, who anticipate that the costs of migration will be repaid in succeeding generations.[70] Hopes for children's educational success and bright futures were central to many women's narratives. When Susan's daughter's sponsorship was first denied: "I called up immigration here. I told them: Why should I come here if not for my daughter? I came here alone hoping that one day I could bring her here and join me so that we can be together. It would be meaningless for me to be here if I could not get my daughter to join me." Susan wants her daughter to get a university education: "That is my goal.

I hope she listens to me." From Lisa: "I just told them [her children] that I sacrificed for them. I left them for the good of our family for so many years. So that I could earn money for their education. It is useless if they cannot finish their education because this is all that I can give them. This is the primary reason why I am here in Canada and left them."

"But now that they are here," Lisa continued, "they don't want to finish high school and they just want to look for jobs. This seems to be the common practice among Filipino kids here. Then it's better that they go back to the Philippines and study there because my purpose in bringing them here is for them to get higher education and eventually take care of themselves." It is this practice among Filipino children in Vancouver—so disruptive of their mothers' plans for their future—to which the discussion turns.

From Migrant to Citizen: Intergenerational Hauntings

To remain affiliated in neoliberal societies, Rose argues, "one must 'enterprise' one's life through active choices." The "included" are those who "calculate their actions in terms of a kind of 'investment' in themselves, [and] in their families."[71] Those who fail to capitalize on themselves through responsible initiative, risk assessment, and thrift—the lone parent, the juvenile delinquent, and the school truant are among the 'usual suspects' Rose identifies—are marginalized and subject to different, increasingly punitive technologies of government, often administered by para-governmental agencies such as charities and voluntary organizations supported by grants and foundations.[72] Our research suggests that the LCP produces many of the families that come through the program as among these usual suspects. Rather than making good on their mothers' sacrifice, many domestic workers' children experience the same issues their mothers faced during and after the LCP, and the LCP plays no small part in producing them as marginalized Canadian citizens. Although their mother may have earned her family's entry into the realm of the governed in Canadian society, her experiences under the press of sovereign power live on in her own and her children's lives. The border continues—in an *enduring* way—to follow them inside.

We have documented the effects of the LCP on children by stitching together a patchwork of official statistics and by interviewing twenty-seven families who have lived through the experience of separation and reunion. These were difficult interviews to arrange, despite our capacity to draw upon the networks developed within the Kalayaan Centre, personal networks of the community researchers involved, the help of a settlement worker who provided further contacts, and contacts of Filipino Canadian undergraduate students at the University of British Columbia. The interviews were difficult to arrange in many cases because of the sheer number of hours that many of the adults worked; their schedules simply left no time. Beyond this, these were difficult interviews because they required families to tell stories of at least partial failure and pain; this was so even among immigrants who have experienced the most success.

Although there is no way of knowing the extent to which our sample of families migrating through the LCP is representative, some of its characteristics are in line with what is known about the population as a whole. Most of the families we interviewed arrived from 1995 onward (Appendix 1), reflecting the fact that the numbers coming through the LCP jumped dramatically in 1993, as did the proportion coming from the Philippines (92 percent of all Vancouver-based LCP registrants came from the Philippines in 1995 compared to 59 percent coming through a similar program in 1989),[73] and it is only since 1995 that significant numbers of family members have been sponsored through the LCP.[74] Families have been separated for many, many years: the median number of years is eight.[75] Certainly not all of these years are attributable to the LCP, because it is common for women to work first as domestic workers in another country in Asia or the Middle East. But for the majority in our small sample, they experienced at least six years of separation in Canada (Figure 1). A settlement worker at Immigrant Services Society, who reported dealing each day with twenty-five cases of Filipino women registered in the LCP or applying for permanent resident status, estimated that five to six years of separation through the LCP alone is the norm: "Five years, that's for the regular ones. For complicated ones [for instance, where the husband is also working overseas, or permission for children's migration must be sought from an estranged husband], it will take up to six to seven or eight years."[76] Given the length of separation, it is not surprising that most of the children are far from infants when they reunite with their mothers in Canada. Although there is a wide range of experiences among those interviewed, with the youngest child only 5 when they reunited with their mother and the oldest 27, the majority of children in the families with whom we spoke arrived in Vancouver in their teens: their median age was 13 (Figure 2). Some of the families interviewed were newly arrived; others were reunited for over a

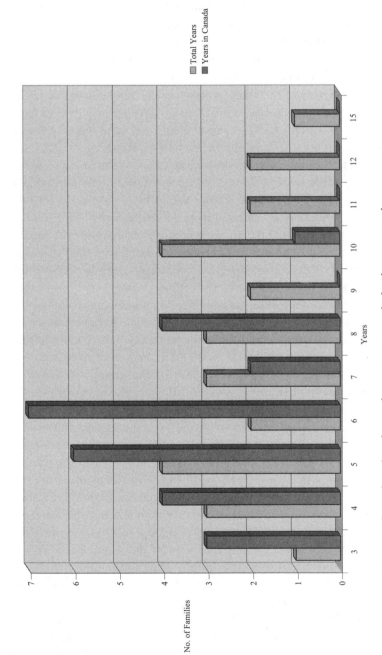

Figure 1. The total number of years of separation among the families interviewed.

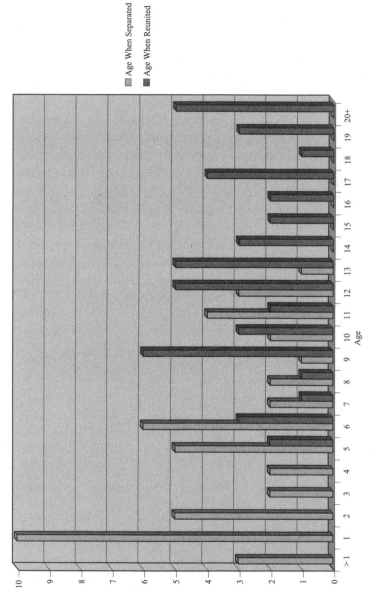

Figure 2. The ages of the children at their separation from and reunion with their mothers.

decade. But the majority of families had been reunited for at least six years and their experiences thus give a clear impression of the long-term effects of the LCP on the lives of family members.

Some of the children relive their mother's experiences, not indirectly but literally. This was especially so among the older youths arriving in their late teens and twenties. In the case of Liberty (who has "dreams, big dreams for [her] children"), her older children were 24, 27, and 28 by the time she could sponsor them.[77] One daughter had had a child in her fourth year of high school but continued to study and eventually completed a university degree with a business major in hotel and restaurant management. The baby, she told us, "was not a major obstacle" to her education. Her husband is now employed as a licensed civil engineer in the Philippines. Liberty, her daughter reported, was "angry" when she heard the news of her pregnancy and did not talk to her for several months. Fearing that this would disqualify her daughter's immigration, Liberty did not disclose to Canadian immigration officials the existence of her daughter's four-year-old child, nor did she allow her to be married. Coming to Vancouver, her daughter has left her own child in the care of his father: "My husband was a mama's boy. But now nobody looks after him because he is on his own with our child and I am not there. The baby was with me for a long time, so he is finding it a little bit challenging with the baby. It was hard for me to leave them. But I thought that I have to do this for the future of our baby because there is not much future for the child if we just stayed in the Philippines."

Two years on from our first interview, Liberty's daughter works at retail jobs, unable to get a job in hotel management until she upgrades her degree. She has returned once to the Philippines to marry her husband in a civil ceremony and hopes to sponsor her husband and child someday. In her mother's words: "She is a little bit disappointed because she has big plans for her son." Rather than bringing the cycle to a close, family reunification in Vancouver has opened a new chapter—a new generation—of family separation. Liberty says of her daughter: "That is what I told her. Now, you also experience what I experienced. The only thing is you have a fiancé who is taking care of your baby [in the Philippines] and your mother is here." This may seem like an unusual case, but it is by no means unique: a settlement worker at Immigrant Services Society happened to be working on a different but similar case when we interviewed her in 2006.

Liberty's eldest son (the one, you may recall, whose success on the private high school entrance exam propelled her migratory experiences), in contrast, could not be sponsored because he failed to register for one term of university and consequently lost his status as a dependent: "He was crying at the airport [when Liberty's other children left to come to Canada]. Both my son and my daughter's husband were crying at the airport. When I finally broke the news that he's not coming, he stopped from school. He was depressed. In his mind, he was thinking he will come and find a good job and help me." Liberty's son is now 30 and works as a waiter in Manila, and also is enrolled in a university course in hotel management. Liberty persists in her hopes that he will join her. "Even now, it's very stressful. I always think about that. And there are times I feel very sad and I cry. Because you see, he is the one who can help me. And every time we talk on the phone I am telling him, 'Just hang on. I'll do something.'" It is not too far-fetched to suggest that coming through the LCP is his best option.

Maria's family has used this strategy. Maria had lived in Canada for ten years before she was able to sponsor her husband and youngest son. After spending the processing fee for each child, she learned that her oldest children were too old to be sponsored as dependents and must find their way on their own as independent immigrants: "So I encouraged them to go to Hong Kong to work as nannies, and then apply under the LCP. With God's help, one of my daughters [who is a nurse in the Philippines] did manage to get to Canada under the LCP." After fourteen years of separation, at the time of the first interview in 2004, the second daughter was soon to join her family, again by coming through the LCP. This is a process that is referred to acerbically by activists at the Philippine Women Centre as "a package deal."

If Maria's two daughters have directly repeated her experience of immigrating through the LCP, her sponsored son knows firsthand some of his mother's experience of being deskilled. Enrolled in the first year of a Bachelor of Sciences program in industrial engineering in the Philippines, he came to Canada "to be a student and not to forget the things I learned in school." But his English was not good and he was placed at level 2 within the adult education system, the equivalent of first-year high school (or grade 8). At first he took courses at night school: "Math 3 and Grammar. I took other courses, step by step," while working during the day as a janitor. But soon he stopped taking courses. He told us: "We looked for ways to be able to go to school, but there were not enough funds. So we looked for ways to look for jobs. And the plan for education was forgotten. We also have to work to help my siblings back in the Philippines." He hopes that when his other siblings arrive in Canada, "they can help and I can study." His assessment is that it is too difficult to finish an engineering degree in Canada: "I'll just finish a technical course. It only takes eight months." He works with mostly Filipinos and speaks Tagalog on the job, which makes it difficult to improve his English. Given that his father died after our interview and within just a few years of migrating to Canada, the challenges of returning to postsecondary education have only increased. Consider: ten years of separation from her family, with all of the remittances dedicated to her children's education, weighed against two daughters in the LCP and a 20-year-old son resigned (for the moment) to a job doing janitorial work. When asked, "What is the best thing about Canada?" Maria's son answered: "There is work." When asked, "What is the worst thing in Canada?" "It's the kind of work one gets. Like the job I have."

Maria's son focused on the financial barriers to finishing his high school certificate in Canada; a settlement worker at Immigrant Services Society drew attention to important psychological barriers as well. In the Philippines, students graduate from high school after grade 10: "So sometimes if they are 16 years of age [or over], they come to Canada and they feel graduated" and find it very difficult to return to high school. This seems to have been a factor for one of Anna's children, who was 18 when she joined her mother after nine years of separation. Anna began her time as an overseas contract worker, first in Hong Kong and then in Vancouver, after separating from her husband when her children were 9 and 11. When the opportunity to come to Canada arose, "My father did not like it. Because he said, 'You know, your children are your only treasure. And you want to leave them? They are growing. They need your attention. They need everything from you.' I said I can still do that if I am there in Canada."

With her earnings as a domestic worker in Canada, Anna sent her children to private schools. Her daughter recalled: "Every year, every school opening, we would have new bags, new pencils, new clothes. Of course we were happy." By the time Anna was able to sponsor her children to Canada, both were attending Central Philippine University in the City of Iloilo. The youngest, Joy, was studying business management at the university; her son, physiotherapy. In Vancouver, neither her son nor daughter was recognized as having a high school diploma. In the case of Anna's son, his sister reported that the "assessment [by a counselor] was that: as long as your English is good, and you understand English, a high school diploma is not really needed." He eventually took a six-month nurses' aide course, so familiar to domestic workers who are trained as nurses and choose to upgrade quickly in Canada. In the case of Anna's son, however, the path from physiotherapy (student) in the Philippines to nurses' aide in Vancouver happened in a more compressed period of time.

Joy's downward educational mobility has been more decisive. Her English was assessed at a grade-10 level when she arrived in Vancouver at age 18, and she required both English and math to finish high school in Canada. Her age put her beyond regular high school, and she was enrolled for six months at an adult education learning center. She then "lost interest" and got a full-time job at McDonald's, where she has worked for the last decade.[78] "I said, 'What, back to high school again?' Of course, you feel sad about this. And then I said, 'Back to high school again. All this paperwork.' I just lost interest. What's the point? I was already working [at McDonald's]." Her friends are mostly daughters of mothers who have come through the LCP and, like Joy, they have not completed high school. "Some of them think of their future. Like some would like to go back to school. For me, it's different. That's it for me. I don't want to go back to school anymore . . . I have friends at work who were born here. Most of them are really focused on finishing college. But for us, it doesn't matter. You have a full-time job. You don't need a diploma, and it's not a big deal. But of course the jobs that we can get are lower jobs. It's not like office jobs, or computers."

At the time of the interview in 2004, Joy envisioned herself working at McDonald's for at least another three to five years, by which time she would be almost 30 years old. She recognized that she has not "fulfil[led] her] priority, which is finishing school. I did not finish it." Later in the interview, she speculated that at some point she might take a six-month course, one with a diploma. Only her former prediction has thus far turned out to be true: six years on from the interview, she currently works as shift manager at McDonald's and Starbucks. Of her mother, she said, "She always wanted us to finish school. This is the number-one priority. But because I changed my life to be like this, there is really nothing that she can do about it. Of course, she might say that her daughter is only a high school graduate [in the Philippines]. But you also learn from your experience. You don't have to be a college graduate. We are not illiterates, you know."

The choice to give up on the prospect of finishing high school in Canada is not always a choice, and children arriving at ages 16 and 17 are literally caught between worlds. Arriving in December at 17, Rosita's son was directed by his local high school to an adult education center. The adult education center sent him to his local high school: "The school board said I was too old. At that time I was 17. So I went to South Hill adult school. They said I was too young. . . . They told me I have to wait. So I [now] work [in construction] to help my mom."[79]

But what of children who immigrate at an age that allows entry into the regular school system? A Vancouver School Board multicultural worker, who has worked with the Filipino community in this capacity since 1979, judged that a more successful transition is possible when children are reunited by age 12–13.[80] However, analyses of government statistics do not give much cause for optimism. Information collected for each child enrolled in public and private schools by the BC Ministry of Education allows one to "track" children as they move through the school system. We identified and tracked ten cohorts of children: those who began high school (grade 8) in the Vancouver region from 1995 to 2004.[81] We have compared those who speak Tagalog at home with a selection of other Asian language groups,[82] as well as those who speak English at home. Children who speak Tagalog at home tend to have grade-point averages at the lower end of the continuum and perhaps most disturbing have a relatively low likelihood of graduating from high school (64 percent for boys in the City of Vancouver) (Appendixes 2 and 3). This is true for both boys and girls. Certainly, other language groups approximate the Tagalog-speaking children on specific measures. For instance, those who speak Punjabi at home have lower grade-point averages. The "dropout" rates for those who speak Vietnamese at home are worse than for Tagalog speakers. But what is particularly striking is that Tagalog-speakers living in the City of Vancouver (who are more likely to have migrated through the LCP than those who live in suburban areas) are at the low end for *both* of the measures.[83]

One weakness of the BC Ministry of Education data for our purposes is that it is impossible to know how many of those who speak Tagalog at home are children of the LCP. We have turned to the Canadian census in an attempt to determine more closely the effects of the LCP on children's educational outcomes (Appendixes 4–6). Again, those who came through the LCP cannot be identified, but we can distinguish children who were born in Canada from those who immigrated and assess how the timing of immigration has affected educational outcomes.[84] We have tried to prise children of the LCP from other Filipino immigrants by deducing that at the time of the 2001 census only youth who were aged between 15 and 22, and who immigrated between the ages of 12 and 16, are likely to have mothers who came through the LCP and could be expected to have graduated from high school. Fifteen- to 22-year-old youths who immigrated before the age of 12 are unlikely to have mothers who migrated through the LCP and thus form a quasi-control group for purposes of comparison.[85] The high school dropout rates do appear to be much higher for the LCP-identified group compared to other Filipino Canadians. The percentage of 15–18-year-old Filipinos in Vancouver not attending school in 2001 is 24 percent for LCP-identified boys and girls,[86] as compared to 16 percent and 17 percent for Canadian-born boys and girls, respectively, and 19 percent and 13 percent for non-LCP identified immigrant boys and girls. For Filipino boys in Vancouver aged 19–22 in 2001, the percentage without a high school degree is much higher among the LCP-identified group: 24 percent compared to 15 percent for Canadian-born and 12 percent for non-LCP identified immigrants. In Vancouver, fully 54 percent of males who immigrated between the age of 12 and 16 from 1991 to 2001 had completed just high school (or less), as compared to roughly one-third of nonimmigrant Filipinos or those who immigrated at a younger age (see Appendixes 4–5). The same pattern is repeated for both young men and women in Toronto, Montreal, and Winnipeg, suggesting that the LCP has generated a national—and not just a local (that is, Vancouver-based)—problem of low educational attainment among a large segment of Filipino youths (Appendix 6).[87]

The lone Vancouver School Board Filipino multicultural worker judged the challenges of children separated through the LCP to be specific to their circumstances, and to go beyond those experienced by other Filipino immigrant children:

MULTICULTURAL WORKER: I think the challenges have changed [since beginning her job in 1979]. At the beginning, when I first started working it was mainly adjusting to the new culture, new way of life, new ways of disciplining kids. So there was the cultural clash between these two cultures. But lately with the influx of families from LCP, I think there's this reunification problem because of different expectations from both sides . . . so it's not simple . . . it's not an easy problem to solve because sometimes there are really some very, very sad stories. Although they have reunited when they come here, other problems come in that [cause] the family unit to just [break] down . . .

GERALDINE PRATT: So when you began, that wasn't a part of your . . .

MULTICULTURAL WORKER: No, no. . . . When I started the main focus
was to facilitate communication between home and school.
GERALDINE PRATT: And now it's between parent and child?
MULTICULTURAL WORKER: Yeah, to some extent. But like I said, [with
government cutbacks] we do not get to know these things unless a
crisis has come up or there's really a serious problem that is affecting
the child's study.[88]

When guidance counselors and principals working at some of the high
schools in Vancouver with the highest proportion of Filipino youths were
interviewed, they described "a very quiet drifting off."[89] "In the classroom
they're probably some of the quietest." From the School Board Filipino
multicultural worker: "Somehow the Filipino kids are always able to blend
into every part of the mainstream. They are not the ones to stand out. Even
if they have problems, they do not stand out."

Incalculability, Truth Claims, and Counternarratives

What does it take and what does it mean to make Filipino kids migrating
through the LCP stand out from the mainstream? The school multicultural worker quoted above indicated that her knowledge of individuals'
experiences has been compromised by government cutbacks; even so, stories of individual experiences are typically discounted by government
experts as merely anecdotal, reflecting a governmental focus on the population. "Numbers," writes Rose, "are integral to the problematization that
shape what is to be governed, [and] to the programmes that seek to give
effect to government."[90] And yet the numbers that we can produce cannot
fully convince, given the ordering and bordering of temporary work employment as distinct from immigration and settlement programs.

This is for two reasons. Our numbers fail on technical grounds because
we are using numbers gathered by the state with other problems in mind.
The BC Ministry of Education collects information on ethnicity by language spoken at home, likely reflecting concerns about English-language
competency as it affects learning "readiness" and resource allocation for
language instruction and ESL (English as a Second Language) classes. The
census also offers no way of specifying those who have come through the
LCP. In other words, we are able to cobble together only circumstantial
evidence to assess LCP children's educational outcomes precisely because

the fate of families coming through the LCP has not been problematized by government. The extent of the lack of problematization is striking: noting that two-thirds of the households in our (nonrepresentative) sample was headed by lone female parents,[91] we approached Citizenship and Immigration Canada (CIC) for confirmation. What government could provide is information on numbers of sponsored persons classified in terms of their relationship to the LCP sponsor (such as daughter, son, spouse or equivalent, or older relative), with sponsors broken down by marital status. In 2005 (the only year for which we could obtain data), 68 percent of the 151 children sponsored through the LCP had been sponsored by a married mother (as opposed to a single or widowed or separated or divorced mother), a substantially higher proportion than is the case in our small sample.[92] (Although note that separations taking place soon after reunification in Canada, which are evident in our small sample, would not be recorded in these government statistics.) A data analyst for CIC cautioned, however, that the data file for permanent residents coming through the LCP is organized by sponsorship cases and not by family (that is, a woman could sponsor her partner and each child in separate applications). It is "an administrative" and not "a research" data set and would require "significant restructuring" to answer our question about family composition. That the actual family composition of those immigrating through the LCP remains unanalyzed is fascinating and reflects the second reason why our numbers are not entirely persuasive: the fate of Filipino families coming through the LCP is categorically distinct from the LCP. The LCP is a temporary work-visa program conceived within the needs of the Canadian economy for certain kinds of workers; it is not an immigration program, and the fate of those who eventually settle through it is—quite literally— irrelevant within the terms and objectives of the program. Our failure to convince, in other words, is also discursive or categorical.

There is an entirely different reason to question the efficacy of numbers. Numbers "turn a qualitative world into information and render it amenable to control." By their very nature, they simplify. They render groups as objects of governance, "made visible by being judged against an institutional norm."[93] When we claim that Filipino youths in Vancouver high schools have higher dropout rates and lower grades than other groups or that the majority of families coming through the LCP are led by a lone female parent, we judge these youths and families against what we are implicitly defining as a Canadian norm. We are ourselves engaging in the "actuarial imaginary of biopolitics."[94] We risk the naturalization of marginalization and injury. As Cheng puts it, "It can be damaging to say how damaging racism has been."[95]

Recognizing this, we follow two strategies to lay causal claim to the long-term destructive effects of the LCP on Filipino children's lives: refusing, on the one hand, a kind of abstraction; on the other, the categorical divide between the LCP and immigration. The first calls up Foucault's observation that resistant struggles in contemporary society typically involve a refusal of "abstractions, of economic and ideological state violence, which ignore who we are individually, and also a refusal of a scientific or administrative inquisition which determines who one is."[96] Speech, individual stories, testimony, bearing witness—these all work differently than the inscription of experience in numbers, returning complexity and, most important, proliferating the grounds for expertise. A second strategy works away at the categorical distinction (if we follow Agamben) that founds sovereign power: this is the distinction between politically qualified life (in this case, as an immigrant permanent resident) and those excluded from it (living in conditions of servitude defined by the LCP). Refusing to draw this line, by insisting that domestic workers are always already political subjects inserted in family relations, "takes away," Edkins and Pin-Fat argue, "the ground upon which sovereign power is constituted. It insists instead on the politics of [sovereign decisions] and demands that specifics of time, place, and circumstances be attended to."[97] The lives of domestic workers and their families are not and cannot be segmented in time and place by sovereign fiat, and the problems we detect at the point of family reunification have everything to do with what has come before. We note in particular four lines of continuity. These are: mothers' sacrifices during the LCP provide the grounds for family strife, are bound up with children's difficulties adjusting to life in Vancouver, leave mothers with a diminished capacity to support their children at school, and propel children into the Canadian labor market as unskilled workers. We take each in turn.

A discourse of sacrifice circulates within stories of family conflict, and many children of the LCP have been witness to and participate in a great deal of family conflict. One of our interviews was stopped short because husband and wife became embroiled in a serious argument. Without raising this issue, in four other households we were told that the police had been called to mediate a domestic dispute, between husband and wife or mother and child. Certainly LCP families have no monopoly on marital discord and family violence, but there are common themes that anchor this discord and violence in the LCP, in particular a dynamic of sacrifice, debt, and actual or perceived ingratitude created by staggered family migration. In the case of Victoria, she describes her 5-year-old son's reaction when his father was removed by the police. Victoria had left her son when he was just four months old in the full-time care of his father, and they had been reunited in Vancouver for five months at the time of the assault.

> VICTORIA: And then that time when we had an argument, my son is so sad, that his dad was being picked up by the police. "I miss my dad. I miss my dad. Where is he? I thought they will return him back right away that night." That's what my son was thinking. But then, because of what he did to me, [her husband] was charged with assault. They restrained him from getting too close, to coming closer to us. I think that was for two weeks that he had that restraining order. So it's a hard thing for my son to accept that time, and that's why my son is crying all the time. "Where is my dad?" He kept looking for his dad, and kept asking me. And even though I explained, "Why are you still defending your dad when I'm the one who is the victim here?"—I said this to my son—I can't blame my son for those emotions. He was close, attached emotionally to his dad because they lived together [in the Philippines].
> INTERVIEWER: Was your son present . . . ?
> VICTORIA: Yeah, he was sleeping and then he was awake when the police came. That's why he saw his dad being taken. . . . After I dropped the charges against him.
> INTERVIEWER: Why?
> VICTORIA: Because I pitied my son's emotions. That's why I dropped the charges and gave him—what do you call this?—a second chance.

For Victoria, the debt that structures the conflict with her husband is monetary:

> The main argument that we are always fighting is money. Money and debts. . . . And then I said to him, "I have all of this debt just for you guys, in order to be ready and prepared for having a family [join me in Vancouver]. And now you're blaming me! You should help me and support me paying all of these debts. But what do you

do? I have to pay all of this on my own." . . . The same arguments.
Even in the car, even there we fight. I will tell him, "Get out! Get
out of this car!" And he will say, "Why would I get out? I'm also
paying the insurance on this car."

Maria and her husband could not recognize each other's sacrifice, and being
separated, they had never actually seen it. Her husband remembered
becoming a single parent of four children when she left for Singapore:

I became a father and a mother to my children. It was tough for
the children. Especially for my youngest son. He was only 6 years
old. . . . My workplace was 8 kilometers from the *barangay* [village]
where we lived. So I had to travel each morning. I had to prepare
the kids before they go to school. . . . I put the youngest where I
could be with him most of the time. But the elder one had to stay
in the *barangay*. And my older daughter was with me in the high
school [where I taught]. And the other boy was also in high school
but in the *barangay*. So that's how it works . . . [INTERVIEWER:
You have no other relatives to help you?] My in-laws are around.
But they are busy with their own family, especially my mother-in-law.

But from Maria's perspective:

My husband was telling them that, because you have been away
from your mom for a long time, I don't know if you can manage
to deal with her. I think that this is a negative way of putting it.
Instead, I would like him to tell them that, because we have been
separated for a long time, they should understand her, and that she
did that [came through the LCP] because she wanted us to be
together. But he is different [in what he says to our children].
Instead, I feel that he is helping to alienate the kids from me. So
we could not agree. I always think that I am right, while he thinks
that he is also right. He says that I don't listen to him. . . . I am very
independent and I can manage alone with myself without my kids
and husband. I told them that I did these things for them. [Inter-
viewer: But at the same time, he was also doing much there in the
Philippines, taking care of them.] But I send them all the money
that I make here. And this helps in their studies. And also our

house there is close to my mother. It is only a block away. . . . We always have different opinions and decisions from each other. He has different views and I have different views. So, it is difficult. Although we live in the same place [and have sought counseling], the relationship is not good.

Some of the children spoke of their experience of this conflict. In Michelle's case, her father's unfaithfulness to her mother caused considerable conflict, which affected her commitments to school:

At the same time [though he continues to live with his wife], he's got a girlfriend here [in Vancouver], so probably some part of his salary was going toward the girlfriend. So it really creates a lot of conflict inside the family. So having that problem, which started from the separation of my mom and dad [while she was registered in the LCP], it kind of creates a hell inside your house. Like you don't want to go home anymore, which motivates you to go out [quit school and get a job], just pay rent all by yourself.

When John came to Canada with his mother and siblings, they were picked up at the airport by "some random guy" who turned out to be his mother's boyfriend. He describes the scene when both mother and father (who has lived away from his family for thirteen years as a migrant worker in London) revealed their respective boyfriend and girlfriend:

He called and we hear this whispering on the phone and then my mom started crying out of nowhere . . . then my dad was talking to her . . . and this girl talked to my mom telling bad things . . . and then of course my mom cried, right. . . . I talked to this girl, too: "Why are you talking like that to my mom? You don't even know my mom." . . . Everyone's crying now because it's on the speaker-phone. My mom put it on the speaker-phone. So my little sister is crying, my brother . . .

He spoke of remembering "when your parents, your family is still complete . . . it's happy . . . you want that back, right? It's really hard. . . . You know what's happy, right? You've felt it before." Of the Philippines: "I notice it's happier there."

Family conflict is not the only issue that emerges from the staggered family migration instituted by the LCP: the LCP creates a situation in which different members of a family are simultaneously living within different economic circumstances. This is because women who come through the LCP not only pave the way for their family migration; through their remittances, they improve their family's situation in the Philippines. As Rhacel Parreñas has pointed out, it is often middle-class families who send family members overseas as contract workers, precisely to maintain and enhance their middle-class standing in the Philippines in the face of the privatization and deterioration of public services, especially education and health care.[98] One of the women interviewed revealed that her husband did not want her to leave the Philippines to work as a domestic worker. But when she sent home her first paycheck, her family radically reassessed the situation, and said, "'Oh, it's a big amount. Okay. Just stay there and don't come back. Just send the money.' That's what they said to me." Certainly few families are as outwardly calculating, but the remittances are significant, and there can be a stark disjuncture between the life circumstances of women in Vancouver and those of their family in the Philippines. Many of the children went to private school in the Philippines, and a number had nannies of their own.[99]

Susan, for instance, described her daughter as being extremely angry for almost eight months after arriving in Vancouver in 2003 at the age of 12, following a separation of over ten years. "The first couple of months," Susan said, "every time I would speak out, she would not allow me to finish because she would scream at me." Part of this was tied up with her daughter's belief that her mother had abandoned her father. (Susan had chosen not to sponsor his immigration to Canada.) But her daughter was also distressed by Susan's economic situation in Vancouver. In the Philippines, the daughter lived in a house Susan had purchased, in the care of a nanny. When her daughter arrived, Susan was still sharing an apartment with a roommate. After two weeks, she found a one-bedroom apartment for herself and her daughter. Initially they had no bed and slept on the floor in sleeping bags. Susan bought a secondhand bed, and her friends helped her find things for the apartment, including another bed. Susan bought things for the apartment slowly:

I just cannot afford to buy all the things that we need at once. I don't want to max out my VISA because I wanted to use it for

other more important things. I did buy a television because I know
that she would need to have something to watch and entertain
herself. . . . Back in the Philippines she had everything—her room
and her nanny. So her new situation must be quite a shock to her.
I was still saving up to be able to buy our needs. . . . I started to buy
things slowly for us. My daughter was still surprised. She asked
why I was poor here. Of course, in the Philippines she had everything, since I was sending money every month to take care of her.
Back there she had a nanny, and maybe a middle-class lifestyle.
But now here, there is a kind of leveling off. . . . But sometimes she
thinks that it is just like in the Philippines, where she can buy any-
time and eat out. I told her that we should instead just cook in the
apartment and not spend money. When she buys her dress, she
thinks that spending $150 for her dress is cheap. I don't think that
she knows the value of money. She would tell me that in the
Philippines she often gets nice dresses. . . . I checked out the food
bank just in case we run out of food. When she saw a candy from
the food bank, she asked me where I got it. I told her it was from
the food bank. She was disturbed by this and told me not to go
again. I told her that I checked out the food bank so that, in case I
could not find a job after my EI [Employment Insurance] has run
out, at least I know where to go. That was my first and last trip to
the food bank. I wanted to show her how tough life could be here.
She was embarrassed by this. But I just wanted her to know that
there is someplace that we can go to if there is nobody who can
help us.

Susan is close to the family for whom she worked as a domestic worker for
four years in Vancouver and feels they respect her: their children are the
age of her daughter, and when her former employer invites her over, they
pick her up and "those kids would open the car's door for me." But her
daughter will not join her on these visits. She says that she is embarrassed
to come.

Susan's sense of vulnerability, which drove her to familiarize herself
with the food bank, comes from her experiences of deskilling in the Vancouver labor market, so familiar among women who have come through
the LCP. Mothers' deskilling has two important implications for how their
children will fare in school.

First, in many cases, these women have been little more available to their children and husbands in Vancouver than they were in the Philippines. Violet relates:

> I was working two to three jobs just to be able to provide for ourselves. So it is still the same. I don't have much time for them. The only thing that has changed is that they are here instead of being in the Philippines. But we are still separated because of the work. They wanted me to stay with them longer. But we cannot. We have to work in order to survive. I hate to think that this is happening to us."

Albert's mother works at two jobs during the week and cleans houses on the weekend. Reflecting on his time—not in the Philippines but in Canada:

> And [my mother] has to work two extra jobs. And for what? For us to get food, shelter. And we don't even get to see her. I only see her a couple of hours and then she goes back to sleep. I see her the next morning, and then she goes back to work. It's like someone stole my mom. That's what it's like."

John's mother has three jobs: "We don't really see her that much. Only at dinnertime, when she cooks. Every morning too." In a focus group held with youths in August 2006, a number confirmed this experience: "My mom works at night. I only see her in the early morning if I can." "Yeah, that's like my mom. Because my mom has two jobs. She leaves at six and comes back at four. And then at five goes to another job until one in the morning. So she only has five hours of sleep. So sometimes we see each other on Saturdays. But she picks up some other work on Saturday, too." A third youth chimed in: "Oh yeah, that's the same for me."

Consequently, there is little time for many mothers to monitor their child's progress at school, something noted by guidance counselors with whom we spoke. Commenting on a parent night for grade-10 students, a guidance counselor from the high school with the third largest Filipino population in the city noted that "with the Filipino kids, I don't think I saw too many [parents] come out. But that's sort of representative of our area." Certainly some youths credited their mothers with the fact that they finished high school. Carlos, for instance, remarked that, even though many of his friends had not, "I decided to finish high school. My mom helped me a bit." Asked how she helped, he replied, "Yelling at me to go to school." Carlos's mother, Coretta, clearly values education: she has a Bachelor of Science and Education degree, worked for four years as a teacher in private schools in Manila, and in Canada has worked very hard to obtain her credentials in early childhood education, on a part-time basis at night, after a day's work. And yet she rarely attended parent meetings: "Even though there's a parent meeting, orientation, or that kind of thing, I just ignore them because I'm more [focused] on my job. Because that is the only source for us to live. For us to make our day-to-day living." She monitored her son's progress through his report card: "He's fine because his grades are okay. Although there's hundreds of lates, really hundreds of lates. And some absences, too."

In other cases, youths assessed their parents in less kindly terms. Mai ran away from home at 14, two years after reuniting with her mother, and moved in and out of group homes and friends' houses until 18, when she returned to her mother's house to give birth to her baby. She spoke of her sense of neglect from her mother, who worked seven days a week housecleaning: "We [she and her sister] were always by ourselves.... My mother didn't really care what I'm doing at school. She just couldn't take it." Mai got "kicked out" of high school in grade 9: "I got attention. Even though it's negative attention. As long as I got attention." "And my mom didn't know what's going on. But she would yell at me and told me: 'You're stupid. Why did you drop out?' Obviously she didn't know what's going on. She doesn't even come with me to the meetings." Three years after the birth of her baby, at 21, Mai, still living with her mother, completed high school through adult education, but as she observed: "I still can care about school, but I already have a child and it's going to be very hard if I do this."

Witnessing the numbers of hours that their mothers work in the labor force has a second effect on children's education: some children feel the responsibility to contribute to household income. Interviewed when he was in grade 11, John worked forty hours a week at McDonald's and "helps out at home" by "paying a share" of expenses. In a focus group with youths, several lamented the fact that, in comparison to in the Philippines, it was common for high school students in Canada to have part-time jobs: "Yeah, if you're 17 or 18 in the Philippines, you don't have to work. You just study. ... Of course, if you work [in Vancouver] you have a reason. You have to help. And you need to have something if you want to go out."

Or buy clothes. And also your parents don't pay for school and books. Of course, you have to think of that and help out even as little as you can."

In the case of Rosita's sons, 17 and 19 when they arrived in Canada in December 2006, neither was able to enroll in school, despite the fact that education is highly valued in their household. As discussed earlier in the chapter, Rosita was a high school teacher in the Philippines and immigrated in large part so that she could send her children to good private schools. Her younger son had not completed high school when we interviewed her, and she wept when she told us that her two sons were working in Vancouver as laborers:

> At this point, I don't know when they are coming back to school. . . . When school started this year, my eldest son [who was studying computer science at a university in the Philippines] told me: "Ma, age doesn't matter in education. So I'll help you with all these bills and things like that. . . . I was crying but I don't know [what else to do]. . . . I'm pretty much open with what is happening with the expenses. . . . And the reason that they stick to their [construction] jobs is that they can see that I cannot afford to pay the rent."

Four years later, her younger son was working to complete his high school degree; her eldest son had lost his job in construction and was working in low-level service employment.

Jhimmy's case is also disturbing because his mother seems to have done everything to prepare him for a university education in Canada. He was enrolled in private school in the Philippines until he joined his mother at age 11. Although his mother was able to buy a house in East Vancouver, she used her employers' address (where she continued to work as a domestic worker) to enroll her son in a public school on Vancouver's affluent west side. Asked why it was that he went to this school, Jhimmy quipped, "Because I was too smart for the east side. [heh, heh] That's what my mom said. She said that there's less chance for me to graduate if I was on the east side." He graduated with B's and A's, English as his best subject. He experienced some racism at school at the hands of recent immigrants from Hong Kong and Taiwan, but he dealt with this by banding with second-generation Chinese and Caucasian students. He participated on school sports teams, including rugby and basketball:

My school experience was actually pretty good. My counselor . . .
I'm the only Filipino guy [in the entire school], right . . . so the
counselor just called me and checked up on me once in a while.
We actually kind of bonded over the years because she helped me
a lot. Because when I was in grade 8, I remember some Greek girl
picking on me. It was my first week in high school, and I got really
mad and she called me in to try to talk me down. So we got close.
She helped me out with my courses, and I actually graduated when
I was 17. So I actually did pretty good because of her.

He remembers—in some detail—that his school friends went to college or
university: "Most of them went to Langara. Some of them got into UBC.
Other people, there's one friend who's going to Washington State. And
then to U Vic and the University of Toronto." And yet Jhimmy did not:

After high school my mom asked me to get a job, but she still
wanted me to go to school. Then after a while it got hard, because
I work eight hours a day, and just to help my mom out, because she
can't carry the whole load. Because it's just the two of us, paying for
the house, all the food. So I want to give my share, too. ["So it was
at 17 that she wanted you to start paying your share?"] She didn't
want me to pay. I just wanted to help her out. So I just give her
paychecks, whatever I can give her. And [so she does] not worry
about me having money. So I don't get an allowance or anything.

Jhimmy's pressing need to contribute financially was no doubt tied to witnessing his mother's daily pattern of overwork at three different jobs: one
as a full-time housekeeper, another cleaning houses, and a third cooking
for a singer, retired from Hong Kong. Despite his mother's well-planned
strategy, his close connection to his guidance counselor and a cohort of
peers who attended university, nine years after high school graduation,
Jhimmy has completed a short course at Vancouver Community College
but continues to work full-time as a cook at a fast-food restaurant.
    And finally, the tug of youths into employment in low-skilled, readily
available jobs comes not only from immediate family responsibilities but
also from felt obligations to remit money to extended family in the Philippines. Just as their mothers are often unable to invest in their own retraining in Canada because of responsibilities to remit money to relatives in the

Philippines, some immigrant children feel the same obligations, with the same result. Rosita spoke of the pressure that their cousins place on her sons: "Whenever he [her son] calls, of course, they would always talk about money, money, money. Like the cousins would say, 'It's my birthday. [Can you send me money?].'" But she also recognized that there are family problems "that we cannot really just ignore"; her eldest son, now in Vancouver, had recently contributed substantially to the purchase of a car in the Philippines, which family members use to drive his grandmother to needed medical treatments.

Concluding Remarks

Not so long ago, a CEO of a large energy corporation was quoted as saying, "We don't lack jobs in Canada, we lack people. We've got thirty-year civil servants who've spent their whole lives saying, 'How do I create a job?' And now they should be asking, 'How do I create a skilled worker'—and, quite frankly, an unskilled worker."[100] It appears that the LCP accomplishes the last task, very efficiently, for two generations in many families. Many women coming through the LCP are deskilled in the long term and, while many mothers were able to purchase good private school and sometimes university educations for their children in the Philippines, these educations have not worked very effectively for their children in the Canadian context. In some families, a second generation of university-educated daughters is coming through the LCP, and/or the separation of mother from children continues, because either older children have "timed out" of the sponsorship program, or they have been forced to leave their own child behind in order—once again—to realize their "big dreams" for their child. It is common for youths coming in their late teens to become trapped in low-level service jobs, and relatively high dropout rates from high school ensure that Filipino youths are qualified only for low-skilled work. Edkins and Pin-Fat argue that we "need to show that sovereign power does not willingly enter into power relations but survives through relations of violence."[101] We have shown that even when sovereign power enters into such power relations—in this case, answering criticisms of the LCP by trading citizenship for a stint of indentured servitude—the violence persists. Liberal ambivalence does not erase the violence of illiberal practices. The threshold question of citizenship (and sovereign power) cannot be separated from the question of inclusion. For guest workers and other resident noncitizens, these questions are neither practically nor analytically distinct. We have shown that in the case of the LCP the threshold question continues to structure immigrant lives long after formal inclusion in Canadian society.

In a neoliberal society that highly values social capital and individual entrepreneurialism, low high school completion rates among LCP children is a very real catastrophe.[102] That this should be the outcome of their mothers' adventurous and courageous entrepreneurialism, aimed precisely at their educational success, is almost beyond reckoning. Contemporary Canadian immigration policy, Xiaobei Chen argues, has decentered race and ethnicity to prioritize age and vitality as criteria for entry into the nation.[103] She is critical of what she terms a child-centered immigration policy that covets the young, productive, and adaptable over other kinds of citizens. If this is so, the LCP, a program that seems oblivious to the human capital of generations of Filipino citizens, fits oddly within this matrix of calculation and has the effect of structuring new and enduring forms of racial hierarchy within Canada.

Freedom, Rose notes, is not "a sham," but we must ask "the price that modern freedom exacts from those who lack the resources to practice it: those "others" in relation to whom our freedom is always defined."[104] In the case of Filipino migrant workers, the geographies that produce them as "others" are complex, and a lack of resources is produced within and alongside—not outside—modern governmental freedom. Overseas Filipino workers are caught between colliding and colluding neoliberal projects. The LCP answers both the economic crisis in the Philippines and a labor market and child-care crisis in Canada. Both governments speak in the language of choice and freedom, but it is almost impossible for domestic workers to negotiate the freedoms offered and required by the competing citizenship projects of the Philippines and Canada: sending remittances strips domestic workers of their opportunities to build their human capital in Canada, and the period as noncitizen in Canada has an enduring impact on the young and middle-aged alike. Miller and Rose have observed that "while governmentality is eternally optimistic, government is a congenitally failing operation. . . . 'Reality' always escapes the theories that inform programs and the ambitions that underpin them."[105] How much more so when this reality exists within and between competing national projects of government.

And so what can be done? Wendy Brown has observed that what puts the "neo" into neoliberalism is a refusal of liberalism as a political and not just economic doctrine. Neoliberalism involves a radical submission of the political sphere to economic rationality. "A fully realized neo-liberal citizenry would be the opposite of public-minded; indeed it would barely exist as a public. The body politic ceases to be a body but is, rather, a group of individual entrepreneurs and consumers." Brown reminds us that historically liberalism has been a political and not just an economic doctrine, one that has itself functioned in contradictory ways. Certainly it has been a mechanism to legitimate and mystify social stratification and racial, gender, and other subordinations. But it has also functioned as a mechanism to challenge these forms of stratification. This is, she writes, the "Janus-potential of liberal democracy vis-à-vis a capitalist economy." It provides "a modest ethical gap" between economy and polity.[106]

But how to occupy this gap? To focus on educational and labor market outcomes alone is to instantiate a neoliberal reduction of questions of justice and politics to the economic. In formulating the LCP as a political problem by tracing its long-term effects on children's educational attainment, we risk further marginalizing the Filipino community. To claim that two-thirds of the mothers coming through the LCP are lone parents risks pathologizing the Filipino family. We want to insist, however, that university-educated, professionally accredited women taking responsibility for their children in the only way that they see possible is not in and of itself a problem. Individuals seeking a living wage across national borders is not in itself a problem (although the *necessity* to do so certainly is). Parents' separation for almost the entire lives of their children, and deskilling single mothers to the point that they must work in two or three jobs in order to survive, these do—most definitely—pose problems for families. These problems go far beyond economic marginalization within Canadian labor markets in ways that we have begun to elaborate through the astonishingly frank, generous, and painful revelations of the conflict and disappointment experienced by many families who have migrated through the LCP, parsed against their "dreams, big dreams" for their children. To understand the full impact of the LCP, we must slow down, listen closely, and engage with the complexity of families' lives, both in Canada and in the Philippines, to weigh the affective costs to Filipino families along with the more evident economic ones.

CHAPTER 2

Waiting and the Trauma of Separation

IN RESPONSE TO A CALL TO PRODUCE a short five-minute film to reflect on the Philippine nation twenty years after the overthrow of Marcos, Filipino filmmaker Lav Diaz created *When the Rain Stopped,* described in film notes as "poetry in a doorway."[1] In this film, the camera is stationary, located just within the doorframe of a home at a child's eye level, looking out into an unkept field, jeepneys occasionally passing on a distant road. Rain pours down. Time passes. The back of a woman appears. Carrying a suitcase, she walks across the field. A disembodied male voice says, "First I saw my mother leave." We wait and we watch. After several minutes, the back of a man appears, and he too walks across the field: "Then I saw my father leave" (Figure 3). We wait and watch: the rain, an occasional jeepney in the distance. In the final moment, a young child faces the camera: "And then I saw myself." The film invites us to do some of what a child can do when their parents leave—for years at a time—to work overseas: this is to wait and watch, and to feel the tedium and emptiness of this pursuit.

"Waiting" is the title of Mildred Grace German's installation, part of the *Maleta* exhibit (which translates as "Suitcase"), put together by the *Sinag Bayan* Cultural Collective (a Filipino Canadian arts collective in Vancouver) and displayed at Gallery Gachet in Vancouver in October 2007 (Figure 4). A cluster of suitcases, an open sky, a bench, a ship in a bottle, a clock; and again the invitation to wait. In the text that accompanies the installation, German writes:

What is it that a person is really waiting for? Waiting for a bus, a train, flight schedule or airplane, time passes by. Waiting for your travel documents to get approved, saving enough money to book that plane ticket, and packing your suitcases, time passes by. Waiting for the moment to see your family you've never seen for years, to kiss your mother and father hello, to hug your child you've been

Figure 3. Film still from When the Rain Stopped *by Filipino filmmaker Lav Diaz.*

separated from, to cry in someone's arms while she is hugging you—before these moments, there is waiting. Waiting also conveys the notion of "When?" and the notion of "Will."

Questions such as "When will there be a chance for the good life?" "When will this pain go away?" "When will the justice come?" The questions are never-ending . . . and the answers demand waiting.

But what is waiting? For migration, waiting is either for a green pasture or a torture chamber.

Feel free to take a seat on the bench.

Both the film and the installation work in similar ways. They do not so much describe the separation of so many Filipino children from their parents as work affectively by inviting us to experience the tedium of waiting, and the emptiness of longing in the absence of a mother, and sometimes father.

This chapter is another kind of invitation to witness the experiences of Filipino families waiting to reunite after being separated for many years. The invitation emerges from a desire to alter what Rothberg has termed the "conditions of visibility in which the state performs its dirty work."[2] Because, as noted in chapter 1, domestic workers are navigating their course through two national contexts, we might ask: Which state, and which dirty work? Here the chapter focus is on Canadian state policy and the dirty

Figure 4. "Waiting," an installation by Mildred Grace German, was included in the Maleta *exhibit displayed in the Gallery Gachet in 2007. Photo courtesy of Sean Parlan.*

work of importing mostly university-trained mothers to care for Canadian children under labor conditions intolerable to Canadian citizens, mothers who are compelled by low wages and high costs in the Philippines to care for their own children by leaving them to work abroad. Writing about state violence displaced onto "sacrificial victims," often racialized and/or chosen from outside the community, Jenny Edkins argues that "the success of this 'sacrificial substitution' depends on a concealment of the displacement of violence."[3] It seems possible to say that mothers entering the Canadian nation to care for Canadian children while their own children remain in the Philippines are sacrificed for the benefit of Canadian families, and that a sense of Canadian benevolence and liberal universalism depends on concealing this fact.

Chapter 1 explored how invisibility is conditioned by the timing of Canada's Live-In Caregiver Program (LCP): domestic workers come as individual workers under a temporary work-visa program and only later are admitted as immigrants. The structure and timing of the program conceal one of its most pernicious effects: the marginalization of domestic workers' children as many fail in Canadian schools. Teachers spoke of the invisibility of Filipino children drifting away from Vancouver high schools, and there is a danger that children's failure at school will be individualized or lead to the pathologization of Filipino families and doubts about their capacity to integrate. This chapter exposes a prior source of invisibility that equally screens Canadians from the violence of the LCP. This is the geography of separation: a mother here, a child there, this geography shields many Canadians from the violence of separation. Filipino mothers may cry in the basement rooms or nanny quarters of middle-class Canadian homes, but they are unlikely to make visible their feelings to their employers, not simply out of modesty but from literal fears about losing their jobs: no employer wants a grieving or depressed nanny. The issue goes beyond what domestic workers choose or are able to reveal to their employers. The invisibility of separation is structured by Canadian law and immigration policy: domestic workers under Canada's LCP are not immigrants and certainly not (yet) citizens.[4] As Ann Cvetkovich (*Archive of Feelings*) notes, not everyone's feelings matter in the national public sphere, and there are often significant gaps in what she terms a national archive of feeling. As guest workers in Canada, we venture that the feelings of domestic workers and those of their children in the Philippines matter very little. We might think of our project as one of assembling this missing archive to animate a more inclusive national public sphere.

Invisibility of the experience of separation to Canadians is not the only issue: a child looks into an empty field, a mother cries in a basement; for many Filipino families, the experiences of children and parents are invisible, one to the other. If, as argued in chapter 1, the difficulties experienced by youths at the point of family reunification in Canada are intimately tied to the experience of separation, we need to make visible this period of waiting, to better document and understand the process of estrangement. Our objective has been to counter the invisibility of family dislocation resulting from overseas contract work and to communicate across the emotional distance that often persists between mothers and children even after they reunite.

If this has been our objective, it has been difficult to execute. Despite activist community commitments to the research, the process of gathering interviews was slow and halting, and we have waited hopefully for a kind of transcript that rarely came: one that provides full and vivid descriptions of family separation and reunification. Rather than being in-depth, in many cases, especially for youths, the details given in interviews are vague, thin, and therefore unsatisfying. We tried focus groups, but the results were little different. Over the course of the project, we schemed about new methodological strategies that would unveil—finally—the full story. If youths held a photograph or a childhood object in their hands, would the stories flow more easily? If we asked them to remember specifically and contextually, perhaps a particular long-distance telephone call with their mother or her first visit home, would they be able to give us a more satisfying level of detail? We returned to reinterview three mothers and eight youths in an effort to achieve the desired wholeness, completeness.

Slowly, we have come to recognize this quest for plenitude—and its failure, perhaps especially its failure—to be at the heart of, and not an impediment to, the research project.[5] Trying to remember if his mother left when he was 12 or 9 or 10, one youth, Eduardo, put the matter simply: "Well these are moments I don't want to remember . . . for my mom to leave, right." Difficulty remembering goes beyond the desire to forget. The experience of separation was traumatic for at least some youths, and so memory takes a distinctive, uninterpreted, and fragmentary form. The experience of separation itself was often vague, thin, and unsatisfying. Words cannot easily fill these spaces of absence and loss.

Documenting the limits to transnational mothering is not a criticism of women's efforts to care for their children from afar. In her research on children left in the Philippines by migrant parents, Rhacel Parreñas counters negative stereotypes that circulate in the Philippines of maternal abandonment by migrant mothers; she does this by demonstrating the extensive efforts of migrant mothers to maintain intimacy with their children.[6] Their diligence is such that they often, in her view, "over compensate" or "over perform" their mothering role. A number of researchers have found, however (including Parreñas herself), that children left by migrant mothers nonetheless are more likely to feel abandoned than those left by migrant fathers (who do relatively less to care from a distance).[7] This reflects, Parreñas argues, not actual neglect of children left by migrant mothers, but "unrealistically high standards of care work placed on migrant mothers," which "are so difficult for them to meet that even the most cared for children . . . still question the love of their mothers." Parreñas reasons that children fail to recognize their mothers' transnational care and the extent of care provided by extended kin because of the "ideological stranglehold of the modern nuclear family among members of the transnational families of migrant mothers."[8] Maternal ideology dictates that only a mother— close at hand—can properly and fully nurture a child. This is a convincing and important argument; however, the purpose and target of our critique is rather different. While Parreñas is rightly concerned about a stigmatizing discourse of abandonment that has arisen around migrant mothers in the Philippines, our concern is with a silence about this issue in Canada and a complacency around what Shellee Colen has called "stratified reproduction," whereby different groups of parents have unequal rights and capacity to care for their own children on a daily basis.[9] We take migrant mothers' and their children's experiences at face value to consider what they tell us about their experiences of separation. We understand their memories, though no doubt inscribed by maternal ideology, to be their "felt experience of history."[10]

We emphasize, then, the failure of mothers and children to connect and the destructiveness of distance, not as the only but as the majority experience. In this we are susceptible to Deirdre McKay's cogent argument that such readings potentially betray Eurocentric, middle-class norms of family and intimacy.[11] Arlie Hochschild's influential care-chain analysis, which posits the exploitative extraction of emotional surplus labor from the global South by families in the global North, relies too heavily, McKay argues, on the primacy of the nuclear family and the authenticity of face-to-face intimacy, such that mothers' absences can only be seen to deplete care resources and leave emotional voids for children left in the care of extended families.[12] In a rich ethnographic account of one family from rural Ifugao, McKay argues that in this region of the Philippines there is nothing particularly new or damaging about parents leaving their child in the care of extended kin, and that money earned by migrant workers can thicken intimate relations among extended kin, maintained by steady flows of remittances, gifts, and daily text messages. The migrant parents who are at the center of her narrative weigh the emotional costs of separation from their son to what they perceive to be the alternative if they were to stay in the Philippines: "a life of poverty and malnutrition with quarrelling parents."[13]

What follows is not a description of a care deficit in the Philippines or of the attenuation of intimacy among extended kin in a transnational field of relationships. Rather, we listen to what mothers and children reunited in Canada are telling us about their difficulties maintaining intimate relationships between each other across space and time, and the sense of loss that this entails. The politics of this gloomy perspective, of writing about the failure of emotional attachment and irreparable, irretrievable loss are this: "Loss [can be] productive for politics."[14] Loss, Judith Butler notes, cannot be represented, but it must be marked. It is not something that you "get over" or "work through." Precisely because of this melancholic quality that forecloses closure, marking loss can be an animating "resource for the future" by stimulating critique and gathering community. "It becomes," Butler writes, "the condition by which life is risked, by which the questions of whether one can move, and with whom, and in what ways are framed and incited by the irreversibility of loss itself."[15] We tell stories of loss—irreversible loss—with the hope of animating a different future.

Communicating across Distance

Like many mothers, when Rosita came to Canada in 2000,[16] she made careful plans for her children: she arranged for her three children to be cared for by two sisters close to appropriate schools and made a detailed budget to ensure that her children's needs would be met. She called her children on the telephone and sent letters as often as she could: "I just wanted to be sure that we are communicating among ourselves as often as possible." It was almost six years before she went back to the Philippines and could speak to her children face to face that she learned that the sister caring for two of her children had ignored the detailed budget and taken for herself much of the money that she had sent for her children's care, along with the savings that she had deposited in a Philippines bank account for her children's airfare to Vancouver. Her children were sometimes hungry, they slept on mattresses in the living room, and gifts that their mother sent at Christmas and on other special occasions had not been received. Rosita's efforts to communicate with her children "as often as possible" clearly were not enough.

Most Filipina domestic workers we spoke with were able to visit their children in the Philippines very infrequently. It was common to visit them for two weeks once every three years; some mothers we interviewed did not see their children for five, six, in one case even ten years at a stretch. The airfare between Canada and the Philippines simply costs too much when mothers, especially single mothers, are saving both to support their children in the Philippines and to bring them to Canada. Mothers spoke of their efforts to keep in contact with their children through letters, cards on special occasions, photographs, tape recordings, in one case webcam, and, most common, telephone conversations and text messaging. But there are limits to these media for communication, such that Rosita's experience was possible.[17]

Our analysis of these limits needs to be qualified with the recognition that the experiences of separation of many with whom we spoke predate widespread use of the Internet and mobile phones: the median year of family reunification in Vancouver was 1999. By far the most vivid and happiest communication story was told by a woman who was separated from her family from 2003 to 2007 and purchased a computer in 2005 after she had finished the LCP and moved into an apartment on her own:

Everyday we webcam! . . . There are even times that the webcam is turned on and they're just about. It is me who sits down in front of the monitor, listening to what they are doing. . . .When I get homesick, I just listen to the little noises they make, what conversations they are having. When the kids are playing, even if the camera is not focused on them, I could still hear what they are doing around the house. . . . So they are all about, doing this and that, whatever they like. That's all. I just listen. That's how I spent my day, my time.

The computer offered more than passive comfort to a homesick mother, however, and Tita described the ways that it allowed her to participate in her children's daily life, in ways that she felt eased their eventual reunification in Vancouver.

> I think it plays a really big part—the consistency of the communication—because even if you're not there physically they know that you are there and they know what's happening. And they know that you know what's happening to them. So little things like homework. "Mom, I have homework! I don't know how to do it!" "Okay, let's do it together." Or: "Mom, can I go on this field trip?" "Okay, what are you going to do there?" "This and this and this." "Okay, you can go. Ask your papa." Or: "Mom, can I eat this?" "Are you coughing?" "No." "Okay you can eat it. But not too much." Little things like that still make you part of their life even if you're not there physically.

These comments lend support to a number of commentators' optimism that the Internet provides "a new space for maintaining intimacy" and "alternative contexts of care" for transnational families who must live apart. "In particular," writes Valentine, "e-mail allows absent parents to provide emotional care for children from whom they are separated. Both parent and child can also build up a mutual knowledge of each other's everyday life such that the child might still be expected to use online communication to negotiate his or her autonomy/independence by asking permission from his or her parent to do particular things, while the parent can use technology to discipline the child."[18]

There are, however, dangers of overgeneralizing this enthusiasm for "cyborg mothering"; to do so would be to ignore the economic constraints of the women who migrate through the LCP and gloss the fact of separation. In 2003, roughly 1 percent of the population in the Philippines owned a personal computer.[19] While a larger proportion of the population has access to computers at Internet cafés, in 2000 only 2.6 percent of the population in the Philippines used the Internet. (By 2006, this proportion had increased dramatically to 16 percent, but by 2009 still only a quarter [24.5 percent] of the population used the Internet.)[20] Rosita's comments are telling. She reunited with her children relatively recently, late in 2006, and her eldest son was studying computer science at a university in the Philippines.

But Rosita estimated that it would cost one month of her salary to purchase a computer. Weighing these costs against her determination to save to bring her children to Canada, she decided against the investment. There are, in other words, some serious blockages in global flows of information tied to inequality of access.

By far the most common means of communication among participants was telephone,[21] and many women spent hundreds of dollars a month on long-distance charges. In 2002, for their political fashion show, the Philippine Women Centre of BC crafted a dress out of used prepaid overseas telephone cards. In a matter of days, they had collected enough to construct both a dress and accessorizing handbag (Figure 5).

Figure 5. A dress constructed from used telephone cards, featured in the Philippine Women Centre of BC political fashion show in 2002. Photo courtesy of the PWC of BC.

But there are limits to the telephone as a medium of communication, not the least, cost. Before purchasing her computer, Tita called the Philippines "everyday, [spending] maybe ten dollars. Everyday! It's all phone cards. Oh my gosh, I should've been a millionaire by now if I saved all that money." Most other mothers made this calculation very quickly and began to portion their telephone calls to at most once a week. Rosita, for instance, called her children every night during her first weeks in Vancouver in 2000: "I will just be crying on my bed, [missing them and] not being able to ask them how they were in school." But she soon recognized that this was too costly and moved to a schedule of phoning once a week. In her first weeks in Canada, her children also called her employers' house "in any time of the night" wanting to speak with her. But, aside from the disturbance to her employer, this was too expensive: "So I stopped them from doing that, and I just set a time to call them. And they kind of accepted" the discipline of this regime. A number of mothers told us of their arrangements with other domestic workers to call among themselves, to stave off loneliness and save the money to remit home: "You have nobody to talk to in the [employers'] house. You feel so isolated. So the tendency for me is to call the kids. Especially when I am lonely. . . . In order to reduce our long-distance telephone calls, we would call each other and talk among ourselves." This talk built friendships among domestic workers in Vancouver but left mothers and children to communicate across longer periods of silence.

At any expense, the telephone is a constrained medium for communication. Despite the fact that they were text-messaging each other frequently, it was not until she returned home to visit that Rosita detected her sister's neglect. This is because the messages she exchanged with her children were short and decontextualized, what communication specialists term "phatic" communication (in which the act rather than the content of the communication confirms the relationship). "I would receive a text message that [said], 'Ma, I haven't paid my tuition yet.' I [thought] . . . maybe . . . because of the hardship or other needs of my [extended] family, [my sister] wants to help others, too. . . . My kids were sending me a text that says 'Ma, can I buy this?' Because they would ask me first. I said, 'How come [you're asking me]? The money is with auntie, you can just ask her.' Because everything is there in the budget. 'No, I don't have this.'"

The issue goes beyond the limits of the technology; Rosita's children were monitored and censored. Her daughter told us: "Cuz, every time we

talked to [our mother], my aunt was, like, in front of us. And dictating
what she wanted us to say. So we couldn't tell her. We couldn't really talk
to [our mother] privately." When they wrote letters to their mother, their
aunt would tell them to add more "stuff, like the good things that happened there." She pressured the children to say only positive things: "[My
aunt] said you should say this and that, so your mother won't cry, won't
miss you. Say you're okay and she won't worry" (Figures 6 and 7).

Youths with whom we spoke tried to grasp the unsatisfying nature of
the telephone conversations with their mothers. For Michelle, as time
went by, there was simply less to say and conversations became formulaic
because the meaning of what was said could not be anchored in either her
or her mother's worlds:

> I don't stay on the phone that much because after a few years
> being separated from my mom, all I could talk to her about is my

Figure 6. A child's letter to its mother, included in the Maleta *exhibit. Photo by the author.*

accomplishments, and then after that I don't know what to talk about anymore because I've got no connection anymore. . . . I wasn't really that emotionally attached to her anymore. . . . I couldn't connect because I'm not really open with my love life. I'm only open with what I'm achieving in school and stuff and she can't really relate to what I'm saying because she doesn't know the people that I'm talking about and she changed in a way that she talks about people I don't know about. And I end up just saying, "Ha? Ha ha, oh yeah, heh, heh, heh." I'm laughing, but I don't

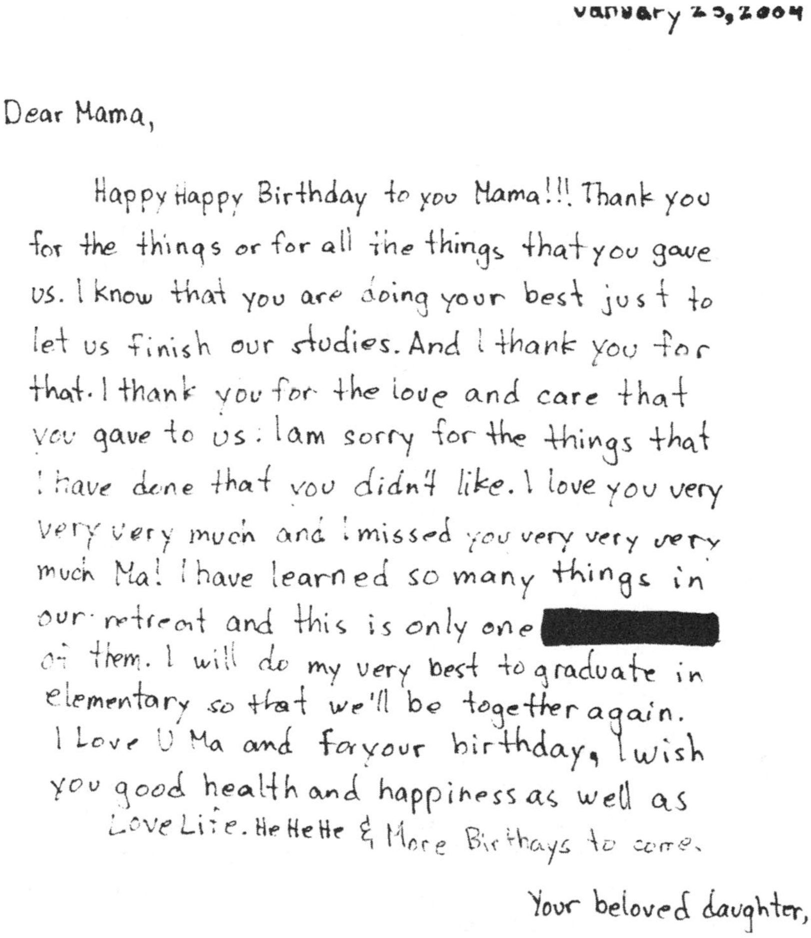

vanuary 23, 2004

Dear Mama,

Happy Happy Birthday to you Mama!!! Thank you for the things or for all the things that you gave us. I know that you are doing your best just to let us finish our studies. And I thank you for that. I thank you for the love and care that you gave to us. I am sorry for the things that I have done that you didn't like. I love you very very very much and I missed you very very very much Ma! I have learned so many things in our retreat and this is only one ██████ of them. I will do my very best to graduate in elementary so that we'll be together again. I Love U Ma and for your birthday, I wish you good health and happiness as well as Love Life. He He He & More Birthays to come.

Your beloved daughter,

Figure 7. A child's letter to its mother, included in the Maleta exhibit. Photo by the author.

know what I'm laughing about, right? She talks a lot about other children, which I'm not interested in hearing about. A lot of things going on that I cannot relate to, so I can't talk to my mom for long on the phone. Since she's separated from me, she doesn't know me that much, so all of the advice that she could give me whenever I tell her my problems is the usual things that a person would give when they're watching teledrama. What you just see on TV, but it doesn't really help because I know what was going to come out of her mouth already.

Rosita's younger son (who, like Michelle, was 11 when his mother left) remembered the phone calls more fondly but also spoke of their unsatisfying quality: "When [my mother] called, I was so happy. When the call was over, I wish she would call back a second time." The infrequency of phone calls was no doubt a factor, but a second call possibly would not have satisfied. Phone calls are always finite in time, and they do a poor job of communicating context and producing nonlinguistic, sensate, bodily forms of meaning. Two brothers, Jack and James, whose mother left to come to Canada when they were 2 and 7, described talking on the phone to her as "scary, because you are almost talking to a stranger. And she is asking us all these questions, like 'How are you?' I would say, 'I'm okay.' It's weird because you cannot see the face." Interviewed three years later, in 2007, the youngest repeated the same sense of disquiet about the absence of visual information and the disembodied nature of the communication: "Yeah we talked on the phone and it's really hard when you don't see the person. And you're just talking. And it's just a voice in the phone. . . . She would say a lot of stuff and I would say, 'Yeah'. It's like a one-way conversation. I would just say, 'Yeah'. I didn't know what to say to her. It's hard to say, 'Guess what? [This happened to me today.]'" Asked whether he saw his mother as his mom, he replied, "When she came home, yes. But if I'm just on the phone or writing, no."

Without a face and body, this was not his mother. Without a face and body, he felt no responsibility to enter into a two-way conversation with "the voice in the phone." Overinterpreting these remarks is a risk (beyond the risk of Eurocentrism noted by McKay), but it seems worth noting that the face and faciality has been the site of so much theorizing about the moral claims that one human can make upon another.[22] Seeing and being seen call up a different kind of relation than does the voice; certainly face-to-face seeing engages a wider range of senses.[23] The forms of communication available to most mothers who attempt to care at a distance—tape recordings, phone calls, letters, text messaging—are all of necessity disembodied, decontextualized, and partial. Remembering the tape recordings that she used to receive from her husband and young son when working in Hong Kong from 1988 to 1994, one woman, Coretta, spoke to the disconnect between her body, her letters, her face: "So I was hearing [my son's] voice saying, 'Where is mama? Why can't I see her? Is that her letter? Is this her picture now?'" Her husband attempted to insert her into her son's daily life by answering: "Yeah. And you know the clothes you are wearing right now, that we bought yesterday? She sent the money for that. [And for] your milk, and shoes, and your toys." Inserted thus, Coretta is still not embodied; she comes to life and gains substance as a stream of commodities.

Some families struggled to embody the forms of communication available to them by sending traces of their bodies through the mail. A detail from another piece of the *Maleta* exhibit—a collage of actual letters sent by family members to domestic workers, entitled *Malayo* (which translates as "Far Away")—shows the tracings of children's feet in paper, which they posted to their mother in Vancouver (Figure 8).[24]

Mothers' Visits and the Shock of Nonrecognition

In another piece in the *Maleta* exhibit, a family photograph is held up for inspection. If the mother in the photograph is smiling, we will never know it: her face is blank. The text reads: "Family ÷ LCP = Reunification with an estranged mother. We shouldn't have to learn this the hard way" (Figure 9).[25]

Both mothers and children we interviewed spoke of this erasure and the shock of nonrecognition—literal nonrecognition—when mothers returned home for visits, especially when children had been left when very young.[26] Jack, whose mother left when he was 2, said plainly, "No, I didn't remember her. When she came back [to visit the first time], I didn't recognize her." We present several accounts of the shock of nonrecognition to underline that this is a community, and not just an individual, experience; indeed, through repetition, the stories begin to take on the quality of a genre.

Tita described the moment at the Manila airport when she returned after being in Canada for a year and a half. She waved at her 4-year-old, who "kind of just looked back at me, like 'Okay, who are you?' 'Oh my gosh

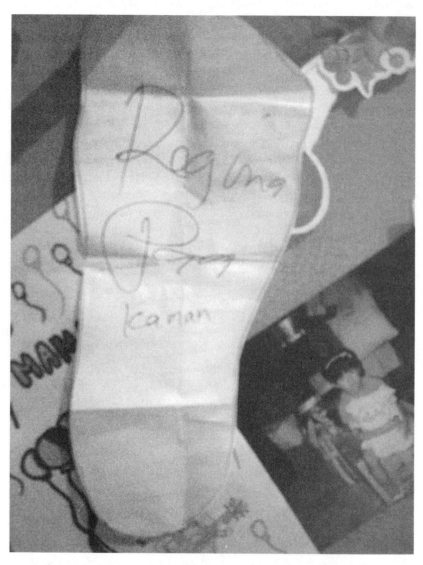

Figure 8. A paper footprint included in the Maleta *exhibit. Photo by the author.*

Figure 9. The project Equations *by Mary Castellanes, with help from Denise Valde-cantos and Niki Silva, consists of two posters with accompanying petition booklets. Photo courtesy of Sean Parlan.*

[I thought], my baby doesn't know me anymore!' Then I said, 'Hi baby!' '[Gasp] Mama! Mama!' It's the voice that she recognized. I was thinking if I'm not calling frequently [she was calling every day], I might not be known anymore, not even the voice. No face, and no voice."

Manila airport was also the scene of Coretta's disappointment. Returning from Hong Kong after three years, she worried on the plane: "'Will he [her 4-year-old son] still know me? Will he still come to me?' Before [I left] we're really close. The bonding is there. The attachment is there." When they met, "It was no longer the same. He knows me as mom but the attachment is no longer there. . . . My late husband said, 'Oh, she's coming. She's coming.' But he is turning his head away. And he's really clinging to my late husband. 'Oh, that's your mama.' And he just looked at me . . . and nothing . . . there is no sign of knowing any more. . . . It's just a dream for him: 'Oh, I have a mama, but how come now she's here?'" Coretta's son remembers: "She left me for wherever she went. I didn't see her again until I was 5 years old. But she was like an aunt to me. I didn't know she was my mom."

Michelle (whose mother left in 1998, when she was 11) remembers her mother's failure to recognize her: "She didn't even recognize me. She walked past, by me and then I said, 'Mama. It's me!' And then she cried. And I cried, too. Because it was a long time [four years since she had been home for a visit]. I got emotional. But I didn't really miss her that well. That's the thing. Because I don't have that connection with my mom anymore. It was broken, right. . . . She's no more to me at that time than a drawing."

Violet described her first return after two years working as a domestic worker in Singapore:

It's funny or sad because when I got home, my kids could not even recognize me. I went home and surprised them. . . . My daughter was 7 years old and the other was 5½. This was in 1993. They were still quite little. It was a surprise when I came home. . . . I told them that I was coming home, but I didn't give them a fixed date. I arrived at around six o'clock in the evening. It was already dark. I rented a jeepney from General Santos [city] to drive me to [our village]. I told the driver to shut off the light when I arrived because I wanted to surprise them. They were there in the village. It was a small village. The next morning was to be the village fiesta. And people were preparing meals like butchering pigs for the following day. And people were asking who was that who arrived. And my sister hollered at my youngest daughter: 'It's your mom. She's home!' My daughter just stood there. She hardly recognized me. I had to pull her up and embrace her. And I really missed them."

A number of women judged that their children's recognition came only from the photographic evidence. From Jeanette: "[my youngest daughter who was 2 when I left] recognized me because of pictures that I have been sending home." From Marie: my son recognized me from "the pictures we used to send to each other." But for some of the children, this photographic evidence was not enough. At 3, Judy was left in the care of her father, "a heavy drinker," who for the most part passed the responsibility of Judy's care to his siblings. "And they also drink," Judy remembered:

"And I don't remember hearing much from mom or seeing a lot of her since she went abroad [first to Singapore for four years and then Canada for six]. As I mentioned before, I cannot even remember what she looks like. I remember my dad showing my mother's picture to me and telling me that that was my mom. I said that that was not my mom. I was thinking at that time that he was introducing another lady and he was trying to brainwash me that the woman in the picture was my mom. That's why I said, 'No, that is not my mother.' Because my mother looks Chinese and she was thin [in the photograph] and that was not the picture that I saw when she was still in the Philippines."

Beyond the issue of nonrecognition, many of the youths described their mothers' visits as quite stressful. Jack and James, whose mother left for seven years when they were 2 and 7, felt that

the hardest part [of the separation] is when she comes home and leaves again. It is very distressing for us. She visited us, I think, five times before she finally sponsored us and got us. We would be scared [during these visits]. We would usually try to avoid her in the first week. It's just weird for us. We were little when she left, so we don't fully understand these things. [They were asked, "Was she a bad mother? Because you were scared of her?"] Not really. [But it was traumatic for both of you?] Yes. I don't know. We cannot figure it out, why we would feel this way.

In a second interview three years later, the two brothers again recounted the difficulty of their mother's visits. From the younger brother, we heard: "I think I stayed away from her [during the visits] because I didn't know who she was. It's hard. Like I know our neighbors more than our mom." From the older boy: "I guess what's the hardest was when we were still home [in the Philippines] when she comes and visits and leaves again. It's very sad."

In some households, the parents attempted to protect their children from the sadness of their mother leaving. In Coretta's case, she followed her late husband's suggestion that she let her [4-year-old] child sleep without saying goodbye, "because otherwise it's so hard. 'He will cry.' 'You will cry.'" Other families used this strategy as well,[27] and a number of youths described what it was like to wake up and find their mother gone. Raphael's mother, Maria, left when he was 6 years old, first to work in Singapore for two years and then in Canada for a further eight years before reunification. He did not see his mother for five years when she first left. He remembers his mother leaving in this way: "But when she left, I did not see her boarding the plane. My sister [who was then in high school] brought me somewhere because they did not want me seeing her go. They did not want me to know that she left because I was still little at the time. They did not want to see me crying. . . . She did not say that she was leaving. I do not know [what she told me]. And I did not understand it at that time."

Jhimmy's father left for Saudi Arabia when he was an infant "and never came back." His mother left for Hong Kong when he was 3, and it was ten years before they were reunited. While in Hong Kong, she called daily. When she came home to visit, he remembers crying when she left: "Once she leaves, they make me sleep first. And when I woke up she is already gone. Because I won't let her leave. They would let me sleep before she leaves, and she would leave a recorded tape for a message." In a later interview, he repeated the memory: "It's really painful, someone else [his mother's sister] raising you when you were a kid. It's family too, but then it's different not being with your mom. I remember they had to put me to sleep before my mom could leave to go, because they know I wasn't going to let her go if I was still awake. You know, I was a little kid."

Asked "What do you remember most when your mom was leaving," Rosita's daughter, 7 when her mother left for six years, said simply: "I don't remember. The second time we dropped her at the airport, when we went back to the house, I cried. I realized she wasn't with us anymore." Feelings of bewilderment, of inexplicable fear, of not understanding the sudden departure of one's mother, the repetition of the same memory ("as I mentioned before"; "they put me to sleep before my mom would go.... I wasn't going to let her go"), an incapacity to remember: these resonate with accounts of symptoms of trauma.[28] Traumatic events are repeated because they "resist meaning. Traumatic events are so shocking, so outside our expectations, that we do not know what happened.... What happens just does not make sense. When traumatic events are remembered, it is not a question of remembering what we thought happened. We can remember what we saw: there is nothing else to remember. We did not interpret what we saw at the time. We could not."[29]

From a psychoanalytic perspective, the magnitude of the shock is not the issue: it is "the lack of preparedness to take in a stimulus that comes too quickly," not the literal threat, "but the fact that the threat is recognized as such by the mind *one moment too late*.... [N]ot being fully experienced *in time*, it has not yet been fully known."[30] It is the lack of direct experience that leads to both the repetition in memory and the difficulty of retrieving memory in other than fragmentary form. What could be more traumatic to a child than the unexplained departure of its mother? And what could prepare a child less than a departure while it sleeps?

Moreover, children's waiting typically is not anchored in a fixed temporal framework: for some it begins in sleep, for most there is no clearly defined endpoint. When asked, "Did you know when you would see her again?" Rosita's daughter said simply: "No, we didn't know." If children did not know when their mothers would return, they were also confused about the timing of the bureaucratic process that would lead to their own migration and reunification with their mothers in Canada. Rosita, whose children were 7, 11, and 13 when she left, remembers them asking, "Why are we still here? What's going on?" The confusion was even more profound for younger children. It was Coretta's impression that her son, just 1½ when she first left for twelve years, "couldn't really understand why I'm coming and going away again.... He can't really foresee what is going on, and understand fully. He was confused." When he was 12, she returned home (her third visit in ten years) and told him that she was preparing to sponsor him to Canada:

I'm saying, "Oh, I'm flying tomorrow." And [he said], "So I'm coming with you?" The excitement of the snow and ice. I [tried to] fully explain to him that "I am going back to Canada to prepare your papers there for you to come over there." But his understanding is [that he would come] right away. Like that afternoon. I said, "Hm, it takes a while." I said, "Maybe a year, a month." And then he just said again. . . . You can see in his face that the confusion is there. That: "I don't understand. I don't get what you mean. What are you talking about? Is this reality? Or do you know what you are talking about?" Something like that, in his mind. [No matter] how many explanations you make, still the child is in confusion because he doesn't understand why I went to Hong Kong and left him. Looking after other children. Why not him? And why am I sending letters, sending pictures, money, and those kinds of things? Why am I not there? Truly, physically, personally there to assist him. And be there in his growing years.

Family Dislocation

All of Coretta's questions focus on her own absence, but the extent of dislocation in many families is more extensive and complex. At least half of the children in our sample changed homes when their mother left, usually to live with grandparents or aunts. In the case of ten households, there was no father to take over their care; their mothers were single, separated, or widowed. In five other households, the father was present, but the children still moved to live with other relatives, in most cases because the children's mothers decided their husbands would not provide for them or had not demonstrated adequate care. In the case of Lisa and her husband, Lisa told us that "I just left my kids to my family just in case. . . . It was my woman's intuition that just in case [he] would have another woman when I am away, at least the kids are taken care of. . . . But nothing happened. We are still together." Her husband visited his children very infrequently: "That was my mistake. I admit that I did not see them often. I would only see them once a year. [They had been relocated from Manila to Lisa's sister's house in Iloilo.] That's why the kids got mad at me. They were thinking that I might have another family in Manila."

Even when children stayed with their fathers, only rarely did their fathers take over their care. Raphael's father, who stated, "I became father and mother to my children," was an exception. In her study of ninety-four children left by migrant mothers in the Philippines, Parreñas notes a tendency for fathers to pass the care of their children to other women, either extended kin or nannies, and to maintain emotional distance from their children.[31] With some exceptions, we found this as well. Albert, who lived with his father and siblings, was mostly taken care of by his grandmother because his father "worked all the time." From John, we heard: "I did not know him that much. So I'm not really close." From Jack, who was raised by his father "with lots of help from relatives": "I wasn't really very close to him in the Philippines." Michelle describes the distance from her father more fully:

> When my mom was gone, my teachers and my dad were taking care of me. Emotionally my teachers were taking care of me. Financial-wise and physically, my dad was taking care of me. The routine was . . . back in the Philippines you kind of like work during the day and drink in the evening. So my dad would work and I would be in school and then he would cook food and I would eat in the evening and wait for him to come home drunk. So pretty much we didn't have that much time to talk because I was so annoyed when he comes home, and I just stay inside my room kind of thing. So I would just talk to my dad if I needed money or I needed a ride. Usually I don't because there's lots of jeepneys. So my teachers were the ones taking care of me emotionally because they would give me advice and all that. If I've got problems, I just talk to them. . . . One of the teachers that I had [in private high school] became my second mom. . . . My mom would take care of me in a way that she would send money and letters. But it's hard to connect when you're just sending letters, right? It takes a month before it gets to the Philippines.

Michelle's relationship with her father was complicated by the fact he had a girlfriend in the Philippines: "I was really against my dad having another girlfriend instead of my mom. And I knew my mom was working very hard here in Canada. So at that time, I would spend most of my time out. And then when I'd get home, I'd just eat and sleep and that was my routine at that time. Pretty much I had no connection with my parents. . . . I can't really listen to them. Basically my trust is gone."

Even in households where a girlfriend was not a direct threat, unfaithfulness to their mother lingered as a destabilizing potential. Leonard, a dedicated father who took over his children's primary care (with the assistance of a nanny) and described his children as his top priority ("The kids have always been my priority"), noted his young children's watchfulness and their worries about his loyalty to their mother: "My kids, especially [my youngest who was 5 when her mother left for five years], every time I pick her up at school, would watch me when I talked to other parents—especially the mothers of her classmates. She would insist that we should go at once. She did not want me to talk to those women. And sometimes, she would cry when she sees me socializing with other women. . . . She doesn't want any other woman to ride with us in the family vehicle."

As another kind of dislocation, in three families with more than two children, siblings could not stay together but were sent to stay with different relatives. Thus they were not only separated from their mothers but from their siblings as well. Rosita's daughter remembers: "I missed [my brothers] when we were separated, and I asked my auntie if I could stay with them." She described a kind of homesickness when separated from her brothers: "I didn't really feel at home when I wasn't with my brothers. So I asked, 'Can I stay with them?'" She could not.

Not all children stayed with the same caregiver when their mother was away. Rosita's eldest son moved between his aunt and grandmother, who lived in different towns. "They told me, I was an NPA. No permanent address."[32] After three years, Violet moved her children from one sister to another, from village to town, because only one sister had access to a telephone. When Susan assessed that her husband was doing a poor job caring for their daughter, she hired a nanny and bought a house for daughter and nanny close to her mother.

Finally, when the children are reunified with their mothers in Canada, most experienced another profound rupture of attachment; they were forced to leave the persons who cared for them in the Philippines in their mothers' absence. The Live-In Caregiver Program is a rarity among guest-worker programs for migrant domestic workers (worldwide) because mothers are able to apply for permanent residency after completing twenty-four months in the program, and then they may sponsor their families. This is typically seen to be its great benefit. But the situation is sometimes more complex. For Eduardo, coming to Vancouver meant leaving his father. His mother left when he was 12, and he was 20 before she could sponsor him to Canada. His father took care of him during this time, and Eduardo talks about the emotional care his father provided: "For my dad it was really, really hard. You notice it right away. It's really hard to be a mom and a dad at the same time. . . . Whenever we need comfort, which is the mom's—

not the mom's job but the mom more often . . . it's the mom . . . when you need comfort, you go to your mom. So we don't have one because my mom is back here in Canada and we are back in the Philippines. We were comforted by my dad." When it came to sponsor her children, Eduardo's mother filed for divorce:

> My dad just signed the divorce papers. And he asked us, do you, do you guys still want to go? We . . . me, I was undecided. I grew up with my dad, right? [My siblings and I] were really doubtful. Like it made us think we don't want to come because [he's] not coming. . . . It's very hard for us to decide right away. Especially for me because my dad was asking me. . . . Because you want to be there [in the Philippines]. But you are the one being sponsored and your siblings will go with you. So it was hard to decide if I wanted to go. . . . [Are you closer to your dad?] After what happened being separated right now, I can tell you I love my dad. My dad was there when we were growing up. That's a big factor. It doesn't mean I don't love my mom. And it doesn't mean that I am blaming my mom that she has another husband here or for what happened to our family. It became a broken family.

We have noted that many children whose fathers were present in the Philippines received most of their care from an aunt or grandmother and some youths mourned the loss of this attachment. This was the case of Lisa's youngest daughter, for instance, who lived with her mother's sister in Iloilo in the Philippines from the age of 6 to 11, while her mother worked in Vancouver and her father worked in Manila. As a consequence, "My youngest is very closely bonded with my sister in the Philippines who took care of her. My youngest grew up looking up to my sister as her mom. [Husband: And she calls my sister-in-law her mommy. She grew up like a daughter to my sister-in-law.] Before [when she first arrived in Vancouver], she would compare us to her aunt or my sister. She would say that she could get all of the things she wanted when she was in the Philippines."

Starting in grade 5 in Vancouver, this daughter was still on the honor roll in grade 10. By grade 11, her grades had dropped, she was late getting up in the morning, skipped classes, and lied to her parents about attending school. It was during this year that she slashed herself and took an overdose of pills:

The doctor who took care of her when she attempted to slash herself said that there is someone who is very close to her that she misses a lot. And she is in the Philippines. This is my sister-in-law. This is why, when she graduates this year, I would like my sister-in-law to come here to attend her graduation. [Interviewer: Does she still long for your sister and look at her as her mommy (six years after joining her mother in Vancouver)?] Yes. [Does she express this to both of you?] She does not really articulate it. But I could sense that she misses her a lot because she would often mention that life in the Philippines is much better than here.

The long-awaited reunion with their mothers often offers children few resources to mourn these losses, sometimes quite literally. Albert, speaking of his grandmother, who raised him from the age of 5 to 12: "When my grandmother passed away, I can't even [go back to] see her. We didn't have that much money to go back because we were struggling to buy a house [in Vancouver]." Later in the interview he stated again, "When she passed away, I couldn't even go back to visit her."

Family Reunification

Given the difficulties of maintaining intimacy over years of long-distance separation, it is hardly surprising that many mothers and children did not know each other when they reunited in Vancouver.[33] Coretta described an intensification rather than lessening of feelings of distance at the moment of reunification: "It's more difficult when they arrive because your expectations of being united . . . It's not back in the Philippines that [the separation] is so real. There's no division, or you cannot see any wall between you. But when they are here: it's like a tall building keeping you apart. . . . It's difficult to look at the reality, that the attachment and bonding is really . . . is . . . there's a division of that bonding . . . It's sort of . . . you cannot really explain the feelings." Interviewed seven years after reuniting with Coretta, her son spoke of missing his aunt and grandmother and the emotional distance from his mother. "I miss them. I miss them a lot, right. I grew up with them. They raised me. Of course it's kind of hard not seeing your mother for a long time. It's kind of weird. The separation is too long. You guys don't know each other. . . . You don't get each other." In a second interview, he repeated: "Of course, when you don't see each other,

WAITING AND THE TRAUMA OF SEPARATION   67

you don't know the character of your mom. And so you develop this conflict because you don't know her character." His comments are cryptic,
but perhaps there is little more to say.

Mothers spoke of reading their children's distance through their body
language. Jeanette left her family for "only" four years, one of the shortest
times of all the families interviewed. Of her youngest child (who was 7
when they reunited), she said, "But of course she was a bit hesitant to
come to me. She was more attached to her father. I could see and feel the
difference between the two [children] in their closeness to me. But I understand that, because I left when my daughter was still so young."

Marie described the same aloofness in her son, from whom she was separated for seven years and did not see from ages 5 to 9 (when he joined her
in Canada), and her efforts to read and repair the distance: "Emotionally,
there was some gap. He was kind of aloof. I think we were both studying each
other's reactions. . . . I had to show him how special he is to me. I gave him
extra care and attention so that he would realize that if I left him, it was for his
own good. . . . For the first few months I often found him quiet and in deep
thought. I guess he was thinking of his friends and relatives at home. I didn't
know what he really wanted, especially about the food and his clothing."

Violet described the much-awaited reunion at the Vancouver airport
with her two daughters, now 14 and 17, from whom she had been separated for eight years. "It took them four hours to go through customs. And
you know the excitement. My neck was already stiff waiting for them outside. And when they came out, I hugged them. But they were not used to
me because of the long separation. And this was the problem. My [14-
year-old] daughter Rachel would not hug me. I had to grab her and hug
her. It took them a while to warm up to me. It was April when they arrived
and it was still a little bit cold."

Susan also described the long, slow thaw of her daughter, age 12, when
they reunited in 2003 after ten years of separation: "For the first couple of
months, every time I would speak out she would not allow me to finish
because she would scream at me. She says that she does not want to meet
or talk with other people. I think it took about six months before she began
to thaw out. She feels insecure and cares much for her dad. She misses him
very much. . . . The problem is this separation between her father and me.
I think that sometimes she is blaming me for this. And when she was [in
the Philippines], my in-laws must have put this idea into her head that I
separated from her dad because there was another man in my life."

For some mothers and children, they were never able to enter into the emotional space—the tall building—that divided them. Asked whether she saw her mother as a mother, a friend, or a stranger, Joy replied: "She's like . . . this is the thing . . . a stranger as a mother." Jack and James, who have been reunited and living with their mother for eleven years, said: "We don't really know her even now." Asked, "Are you close to your mom now?" the younger brother replied, "We always fight." His older brother confirmed: "Yeah, [she and I] always fight too. Seriously. She's working a lot now too." Three years after reunification, Violet said of her relationship with her 20-year-old daughter (who now works at Burger King and is attempting to address a serious drug-addiction problem that developed in her first years in Canada): "Our relationship has not been very good. . . . Her priority right now is her boyfriend. I think it is a distraction. She is thinking that the thing that she could not find in me, she could find it in her boyfriend. . . . In my opinion, she is looking for something that she cannot find in me and she finds it in her boyfriend. But I know that her boyfriend cannot give it to her. So that is the problem."

But to say that separation is traumatic and that mothers' and children's losses are irretrievable is not to say that families are passive in the face of these challenges, or that new and positive mother–child relationships cannot and do not develop in Canada. Coretta described her tenacity rebuilding her relationship with her son by saying that she had been "through the hole of a needle," an expression that calls up both the difficulty of threading a needle and her capacity to strategize. As she put it, "You really need a magnifying glass so you can see the hole." Many families did describe a growing closeness—over time—after reunification. For example, after leaving her son with her parents when he was 3 months old, Liberty saw him only once, when he was 3, before sponsoring him to join her in Canada when he was 10. When they met, he said, "You're my auntie. You're not my mom. You're auntie." She had to say, "I'm not your auntie. I'm your mama." When her eldest daughter suggested that she share her bed with her son, Liberty described her reluctance: "I said, 'Oh, okay.' But in my mind . . . because I'm used to sleeping alone . . . And I'm not yet . . . you know. But then later I said, 'Yeah, okay.'" Developing a relationship with her son has been easier than reconnecting with her daughters, both of whom were almost teenagers when she left to work abroad: "You won't believe it, we [she and her son] have this bonding. Not like them [her daughters]: we have to adjust." Liberty described with immense pleasure her relationship with her 12-year-old son: "He is very helpful. When I am really tired, I say, 'I am tired.' And he says, 'Okay mom, you go to bed and later I'll do something for your dinner. I will wake you up.' Yeah! So I fell asleep for forty-five minutes. Then he did something, like open a can of tuna or salmon, or cook some eggs. He gives me a glass of milk. And he says, 'You cannot drink water. This will give you strength. Because the following day you'll go to work.' . . . He makes me strawberry smoothies while I watch TV."

For Michelle, too, the effects of separation were not uniformly negative. She joined her mother in Canada at the age of 17 after six years of separation. Because of the conflict between her mother and father (her father had another girlfriend in Vancouver), she described her home life as "hell." She spoke of coming to a better understanding of her mother at 19, when she began along the course familiar to so many Filipino youths who reunite with their mothers in Vancouver: working full-time at a fast-food restaurant. "That was the time that I began to appreciate my mom more because I could see how hardworking she is . . . I realized how much she cared about me when she was working seven days a week." But, equally, Michelle described integrating her experiences of separation and disconnection into her sense of self, and using it in creative and productive ways. "If you don't have that much connection with your parents and you just don't connect with them, you kind of rebel [against] everything they say and you just don't believe them. You don't have any belief in them. So you feel, even though you're not alone, you feel alone because you can't trust anybody. . . . So I can't really listen to them. Basically my trust is gone. It's because my mom was separated from me and at the same time my dad was kind of separated from me. . . . So there was no guidance at all and I had to rely on myself and my [older] sister."

This sense of independence structures Michelle's story of how she decided to complete high school in Vancouver:

And unlike other [Filipino] people—well, most of the [Filipino] kids here when they come here they kind of rebel against their parents—I have that thinking that if I rebel now and I wouldn't be able to finish [high school], that's actually my fault and that's not my parents' fault. My parents would be emotionally affected, but I'm going to be physically affected. . . . So that's why I wanted to finish school. . . . It wasn't really [my mother] that motivated me [to continue in school]. . . . What motivated me most is looking at myself in the future, whether I'll still be in the fast-food business or am I going to start having my own business or working in my profession. So having a sense of—being scared actually, whether you're going to be able to buy your own house later on or you're going to have to depend on your parents and stand that kind of atmosphere [of conflict in her parents' home] until the end.

Michelle has refused her future in the fast-food business, has completed high school and a medical technician course, and envisions her determination as "a ripple in the water that starts spreading out ... an example for everybody else, especially [Filipino] kids right now."

Conclusion

Transnational mothering cannot transcend distance. Cyborg mothering is a fantasy for most poor migrant mothers who cannot access the technology that many of us take for granted: a computer with an Internet connection. Communication with their children is often infrequent, and inevitably fragmented and stripped of the sensuality of day-to-day, face-to-face, embodied contact. Separation of mothers from children is profoundly disruptive, and it is just the beginning of a chain of dislocations that are genuinely traumatic.

Genuinely traumatic. What is at stake in such a claim? Against those who argue that invocations of trauma evacuate the political from public culture by individualizing, depoliticizing, medicalizing, and pathologizing social life,[34] we follow those who argue that testifying to trauma can be a form of agonistic politics and a means to build political community.[35] Jenny Edkins has claimed that testimony to trauma "challenges sovereign power at its very roots" because it makes visible the violences upon which liberal democratic state power rests. Those who experience state-induced trauma face the arbitrary and ungrounded nature of sovereign power and the "lack of guarantees" that state authority offers "for the self as a person."[36] Like all temporary migrant programs,[37] the Canadian government's decision to admit Filipino women under the LCP as individual workers rather than as immigrants with families is an arbitrary act of sovereign power that defines these women as less than citizens and temporarily strips them of their full personhood, including familial relations.[38] The trauma children experience when their mothers leave them for years at a time is one effect of this.

When children and mothers find ways of speaking of their loss and trauma, they are refusing "to take [their] place in history" as officially narrated, thus disrupting the smoothing over of state violence.[39]

Edkins writes about a tendency to "gentrify" trauma, to contain and control it through narratives of rescue, redemption, and overcoming; in this case, it would be through the immigrant success story or what is sometimes called "ethnic succession."[40] Immigrant success stories are typically tied to children because migration is so often done in their name, for their future. In this sense, children often bear responsibility for redeeming or making good on, and in the face of, their own and their family's trauma. Given the weight of this responsibility, it seems especially important that children's losses be marked and the impacts of these losses critically examined. Registering the effects of loss is not the same as claiming victim status; it can be a creative political response. The *Maleta* exhibit, which included work created mostly by Vancouver-based Filipino youths, is one such response, which found its way for a short while into official history when it was moved from a small Downtown Eastside art gallery to the Vancouver Museum in December 2007.[41]

But the will to forget is strong. When Deward Ponte, a 15-year-old Filipino youth who reunited with his mother in Vancouver 2005, was stabbed to death on January 28, 2008, Filipino activists used our research—some of which is reported here and in chapter 1—to draw the connections between the experience of separation and the marginalization of Filipino youths in Canada. An article appeared in a national newspaper with the headline: "Caregiver Plan Indirectly Linked to Her Son's Death, Mom Suggests."[42] The reporter who wrote this article had contacted me by e-mail for background to the story late Friday afternoon the week before the story appeared. I responded Monday morning but received the following: "Thanks for reply. In this business, it's now old news."[43] For those who have experienced separation, this is indeed very old news. But marking, and re-marking, and re-marking waiting, absence, and loss continue to animate the questions with which we began, those posed by Mildred Grace German. Waiting animates her questions and the pursuit of answers well worth waiting for.

· CHAPTER 3 ·

Listening to Mothers' Stories

JOMAR LANOT REUNITED WITH HIS MOTHER in Vancouver in 2002, after years of separation while she worked in Canada as a domestic worker. One year later, he was beaten to death in Vancouver at the age of 17, a victim of youth violence. The theme of invisibility surfaced in mainstream media representations after his death. We were told that, despite the large numbers of Filipinos in Vancouver, "they are less obvious than their neighbours. There is no 'Filipino Town' as such, as there is a Chinatown or Little Italy." To detect a Filipino presence, one must "know where to look." With Jomar Lanot's death, however, Filipinos were said to be "a community that is now coming together in grief."[1]

In the days following his death, the news cameras appeared to be searching for Jomar Lanot's mother (Figures 10 and 11). The camera finally located her two years later, at the trial of one of the three youths charged with her son's murder. In a highly formalized photograph, she was displayed as defeated by her loss. In the caption to the accompanying text, Jomar Lanot was effectively blamed for his victimization (Figure 12).

Media representations of mourning for Jomar Lanot reproduced stereotypes about Filipino emotional and political life and raised troubling questions about the politics of witnessing and how our own research might be received. Media stereotypes of this tragic event tended to emphasize the centrality of the family to the Filipino community and a pervasive tendency among Filipinos toward religious fatalism and passivity.[2] Moreover, the images evoke the same passivity in the viewer. In her posture of defeat, the photograph of Jena Lanot appears to ask nothing of us. Indeed the most active response to this photograph might be a slight anxiety about her living sons' continuing presence in Canada; these sons—two young Filipino men dressed in black—seem to be giving us the cold shoulder, impervious to our gaze and impenetrable to our visual inspection.[3]

I begin this chapter with media representations of the mourning of Jomar Lanot as a way of asking how one might bring into visibility the pain

Figure 10. Mourning Jomar Lanot. Photo by Steve Bosch, courtesy of the Vancouver Sun, *December 6, 2003.*

Figure 11. Mourning Jomar Lanot. Photo by John Lehmann, courtesy of the Globe and Mail, *December 2, 2003.*

associated with the Live-In Caregiver Program (LCP) and circulate representations that work in other ways. Much like the photographers criticized here, we have sought out Filipino mothers, just like Jena Lanot, who
have left their children in the Philippines to work as domestic workers in
Canada, and who have recently reunited with them after years of separation. In the first instance, life narratives have been collected to share within
the Filipino community. But, in the testimonial tradition, these stories
also function as evidence to make claims on a Canadian public and government that have failed to problematize the long-term effects of the LCP.
This is a process that Anne Cubilié describes as speaking oneself back into
"the juridical structures from which one has been 'disappeared.'"[4]

The pressing need to strategize about ways of constructing a wider public attuned to these issues, and the promise and challenge of constructing
such a public through narratives of maternal loss are the focus of this chapter. The scholarly and activist critique of the LCP is well developed; this is

Jena Lanot, mother of Jomar Lanot, speaks with her sons yesterday during a break at the B.C. Supreme Court in Vancouver. Mr. Lanot was beaten to death two years ago.

Boy died because he was slowest runner, court told

Figure 12. A family grieves. Photo by Lyle Stafford, courtesy of the Globe and Mail,
November 1, 2005.

not the problem. We (alongside many other researchers and activists) have demonstrated that the LCP creates deeply exploitative working and living conditions, and leads to the long-term deskilling of the mostly college-educated women who eventually migrate to Canada and often sponsor their families after completing the LCP. But it seems fair to say that this stream of critique over the last fifteen years or so has done little to improve the lived conditions of domestic workers registered in the LCP.[5] If anything, it is the impression of the Philippine Women Centre of BC that the situation of domestic workers has worsened. We have collected stories of family separation, loss, grief, and traumatic returns to trace yet more impacts of this government program, but also with the hopes that these stories will—finally—find an audience and evoke an affective and effective response from policy makers who thus far seem unmoved by critiques of the LCP. We aim as well to circulate these stories to create a wider public concerned about the marginalizing and dehumanizing outcomes of the LCP.

But will the testimony be heard, and what are some barriers to putting these life narratives into circulation? If we are able to circulate the testimony beyond the Filipino Canadian community, what dangers attend our success? We are counting on the affective force of maternal narratives, as have many feminist activists in other contexts.[6] But maternal narratives make for risky politics, and what Lauren Berlant calls "ethicoemotional performance in the political sphere" often preserves rather than disrupts the status quo.[7] Elaborating some of these risks and worries, I experiment with two women's testimonies to strategize about ways to push a wider Canadian public into an engaged witnessing relationship with those who testify.

I note at the outset that this chapter has a complicated voice that moves between the individual "I" of Pratt and the collective "we" of our research collaboration. One of the representational experiments considered in this chapter emerged precisely out of and within the differences collected together through our collaborative relationship. Unprepared for and somewhat overwhelmed by the tearful, emotional reactions to my early presentations on family separation to Filipino community audiences, I felt like a fraudulent ventriloquist of other peoples' troubles, and was compelled to think harder about how I fit within this process of circulating affect. In this chapter, I place myself and my own son firmly in the middle of domestic worker testimony in order to think concretely about the politics of what is shown and not shown, and as a method of implicating Canadian audiences in domestic worker testimony in intimately troubling ways.[8]

On Not Being Heard

In her recent book on the boom in testimony, autobiography, and memoirs emanating from Iran, Iraq, and Afghanistan, Gillian Whitlock considers why it is that some life narratives enter a "transit lane" that allows them to move quickly into and within Western media, while others do not. She argues that refugee life narratives, in particular, "rarely reach the threshold that allows testimony to spill into the public domain," and they remain "trapped" within the immediate community that has suffered the pain.[9] "Sometimes testimony does not summon witnesses," and this "has little to do with the experiences of trauma and dispossession that constitute testimony" and everything to do with "whose lives count, and under what circumstances." To "accrue value and jurisdiction," she argues, "testimony needs fortune, history and national history on its side." To have traction, testimony from marginalized groups must become linked to "civic virtue and the national good," as was the case with the Truth and Reconciliation Commission hearings in South Africa and the Stolen Generations' testimony in Australia.[10]

History would appear not to be on our side. In the U.S. context, Thomas Keenan detects a cultural shift toward shamelessness; Karen Ball perceives a culture of numbness.[11] "The public figuration of trauma," Ball writes, "is a moral missive about suffering that is perpetually returned to its sender because repeated circulation has emptied it of its psychological and rhetorical force."[12] We are saturated with stories of grief and suffering, so much so that Mark Seltzer has coined the term "wound culture" to describe a public life organized around a "fascination with torn and open bodies, and torn and opened persons."[13] If voyeuristic pleasure is one possible reaction to the spectacle of suffering at a distance, so is the production of "low grade angst,"[14] a particularly troubling reaction in relation to recent immigrants. Immigrants and refugees have particular difficulty finding a receptive audience in the post-9/11 era in which national security and belonging have been revalued. They are as likely to be objects of fear and hatred as compassion and concern.[15] In Whitlock's assessment, the testimony of refugees at present is "epistemologically disabled."[16] With multiculturalism in doubt in many national contexts,[17] the same could be said for the testimony of immigrants.

There are other, more specific reasons why Filipino mothers' and children's narratives of loss may fail to find a receptive public. First, a kind of cultural relativism can come into play: mothering long distance may seem "natural" for Filipinas, especially given popular imaginary in Canada of large extended Filipino families that can effortlessly care for children in a mother's absence. Second, along with the ambiguity of the LCP as a temporary work visa rather than immigration program (outlined in chapter 1), it is unclear where and when the ethics of feeling and national responsibility start. The regulations of the LCP create years of family separation, but equally the program offers the opportunity to immigrate to Canada. While conditions under the LCP may be unimaginable and unacceptable to Canadians, many Canadians assume that they compare favorably to life in the Philippines. This recognition short circuits discussions of ethics and civic virtue *within* Canada and renders the rescue of Filipinos from the Philippines as self-evidently virtuous. Further, those registered in the LCP are not yet Canadians: what are our obligations to not-yet-but-likely citizens living within the nation? If Sara Ahmed is undoubtedly right to argue that the circulation of affect creates borders and communities of insiders and outsiders,[18] the opposite is also the case: existing imaginative geographies structure the flow of affect and create borders and chasms across which affective claims and relations simply do not cross.[19] As an index of this kind of affective blockage between Canada and the Philippines and the shamelessness that this creates, one nanny agent interviewed in 1994 happily told me that domestic workers leaving their children in the Philippines make the very best nannies because they miss their children so much that they have no choice but to redirect their affections to Canadian children.[20]

Even so, we cannot wait until history and national milieu are on our side, and our aim is to produce a wider public through the powerful rhetoric of mother–child separation, child trauma and failure, and maternal loss and grief. This chapter assesses the risks of deploying maternal discourse and engendering empathy through the mother–child relation and attempts to construct testimonials that are less vulnerable to these risks.

Risky Stories of Maternal Grief

Theorizing an ethical relation to others, Judith Butler follows Levinas in locating it in the awakening to the precariousness of life itself: "This cannot be an awakeness . . . to my own life, and then an extrapolation of my own precariousness to an understanding of another's precarious life. It has to be an understanding of the precariousness of the Other."[21] Although in

Levinas's philosophy this is understood to be an ontological, presocial rec-ognition,[22] pragmatically, young children, with their biological dependence and vulnerability, readily seem to evoke an ethical awakening to the Other. Focusing on mother–child separation calls up the precariousness and vul-nerability of children, and there is a rich tradition of women's organizing that presses political claims through children's vulnerability and a discourse of maternal loss and grieving. There are, however, reasons why maternal discourse—even if heard by a receptive public—may fail to engender an ethical relation. Here are three reasons.[23]

First, a maternal discourse is both easy and treacherous to mobilize because focusing on maternal loss and absence not only works through conventional, potentially conservative notions of the family,[24] but it can and does quickly turn to blame. Stories of family troubles among Filipino immigrants might provoke anti-immigrant sentiment rather than empa-thy and an analysis of the injustices of the LCP. Women who speak pub-licly about their experiences of leaving their children and the difficulties of reuniting in Vancouver invite their own stigmatization—as bad mothers. Accusations of bad mothering tail domestic workers, both in the Philip-pines, where they are stigmatized for leaving their children, as fathers working overseas are not;[25] and in Vancouver, where problems that arise among reunited youths are in part attributed to their bad mothers. Soon after (and in reference to) Jomar Lanot's death, for instance, a local set-tlement organization reportedly made the astonishing statement that there are no delinquent children without delinquent parents.[26] In an article appear-ing in the mainstream national press in 2007, the executive director of the West Coast Domestic Workers Association—an organization dedicated to supporting the legal rights of domestic workers—is quoted as saying that "they've lost their capacity to mother their own children."[27] Maternal discourse typically operates within a moralistic and polarized ethical frame, and within this framing it is difficult for absent mothers to be seen as good mothers, as capable and caring mothers who deserve empathy.

Second, testimonials of mothers' grief may evoke empathy through an imaginative identification with their loss. Maternal discourse can be so powerful because parental love has a universal quality that speaks across cultures and social groupings: it is an emotion with which many of us can identify. But the politics of such empathy and identification are complex and by no means straightforwardly benign.[28] Empathy in terms of shared identity as a parent or child (along the lines of: "What would this feel like if it happened to me?") can allow a middle-class non-Filipino listener or reader to recuperate domestic workers' stories within their own familiar frames of meaning. Operating within this type of incorporative or self-reflective identification, the listener or reader learns little about the specific experiences of Filipino families who come through the LCP, and thus fails to enter into a relationship with those who give testimony. As Kelly Oliver argues, there is a crucial difference between listening "for what we already know and recognize in . . . testimony and listening for what we don't know, for what is beyond recognition."[29] She argues, along with others,[30] that an ethical relationship arises in response to the singularity of the demand, because this enables the possibility of responding in ways that open up rather than close off the response of those who have testified to their experience.

Moreover, the capacity for a wider public to empathize—including and possibly especially with those we perceive to be different from ourselves—can be self-affirming in ways that stabilize existing social hierarchy. "This sentimental moral psychology [has become] a vehicle for delivering virtue to the privileged, who [get] to feel good about themselves for having the appropriate feelings about a subordinated kind of person or population."[31] Middle-class non-Filipinos can feel good about themselves as liberal persons able to empathize across difference. And "because empathy makes us feel good, it is very easy to bear."[32] This is especially so if testimony is framed so as to ask very little of the reader/listener. Instructive in this regard is a feature article that appeared in the *New York Times Magazine* in 2007 on Filipino families' multigenerational experiences of working abroad as guest workers.[33] The author attempts to balance the economic benefits of remittances to the Philippines against the costs of family separation. This calculation is, however, kept at a safe distance from the American reader. Stories are told of workers who go to Saudi Arabia, Singapore, Japan, Hong Kong, the United Arab Emirates, and Taiwan, but the United States is not implicated in the guest-worker system that leads to family separation. In contrast, the United States is identified as the primary destination for legal, permanent (presumably family-based) migration: "American visas, which are probably the hardest to get, are also the most coveted, both for the prosperity they promise and because the Philippines, a former colony, retains an unrequited fascination with the U.S."[34] The *New York Times* readers may be saddened by the state of the world, but nothing more is demanded of them, and certainly none of the long-term implications of U.S. imperialism in the Philippines are explored. Unrequited indeed. Lauren Berlant has argued that this kind of politics of sentimentality now dominates the U.S. political scene, and that personal identification and empathy with narratives of pain have replaced and dissolved a politics of dissent.[35] Distanced empathy with suffering can provide the illusion of action and political engagement.[36]

Finally, those who testify to loss and suffering can be simplified, de-individualized, and contained within narratives of victimhood.[37] When testimonies of many different people are collated as evidence of a collective experience, "the purposeful repetition of stories [can produce] what might be called an 'ur' narrative of victimization."[38] This extends a familiar tendency to represent Third World women as pure victims, which both robs them of agency and fuels the "rescue fantasies" and sense of empowerment of the First World reader/listener.[39] Colonial stereotypes of Filipinas' propensity to endure hardship through religious fatalism only exaggerate this rendering of a subjectivity saturated in victimhood.[40]

Recognizing these three risks—calling up the stigmatization of the bad mother, inviting a violently sentimental appropriation of experience, and congealing subjectivity in a simplifying narrative of victimization—how might we work with these potentials to avert them, to invite more complex readings and ethical engagements? Drawing on Anne Cubilié's (*Women Witnessing Terror*) distinction, how might we shift readers from being spectators to ethical witnesses? I turn to two testimonials to offer some tentative responses to these questions. These are testimonials that beckon me, and I have found myself presenting—inhabiting—long extracts from them in conference presentations and other formats. What follows is an attempt to understand why and how these testimonials make ethical claims, and to think of ways of crafting them to maximize this potential.

Understanding how testimonials make ethical claims requires close attention to the peculiarity of the textual form that emerges from the act of witnessing, an act that many see as paradoxical if not impossible. Cubilié argues that there is no single paradox, no single obstacle to witnessing. So, for instance, the difficulties of using language to testify to the extreme bodily pain of torture differ from the obstacles to testifying to the horrors of Holocaust concentration camps, and most definitely to the challenges to testifying to leaving one's child to do domestic work in Canada. But a common thread is that both the power and paradox of testimony come from the inability to testify from within an event: "What makes testimony powerful is its dramatization of the impossibility to testifying to the event."[41] Testimony is of necessity an aestheticized production, marked by the limits to language, trauma, and the work of memory. It is in the fissures of testimony that Cubilié finds its ethical force. Testimonial texts are themselves witnesses to the struggle to witness; they invite the reader—through their fragmented form—to witness this struggle and to engage with experiences that are incommensurate to their own. Fragmentation and incompleteness are "integral to the act of testimony, as [this] refutes the possibility of building complete narratives and solid truths through which readers can integrate such traumatic experiences into their own historical narratives."[42]

If testimonials are always produced outside the event that is being testified about, so much more so for the *translations* that we circulate. In this project, we are involved in several acts of translation: from oral testimony to written document, from Tagalog to English, from testimony delivered by a domestic worker to one edited and offered by activists and academics, from an audience consisting of those who have shared elements of the experiences described, to those who know little of the LCP except, possibly, as employers or friends of employers. But rather than seeing these layers of translation as creating distance from first-person authenticity in problematical ways, we might recast them in a more positive light. Recognizing the constructed nature of all testimonials reframes translation as an opportunity and draws attention to our responsibility for our own textual productions. An important aspect of our responsibility in these textual productions is to open what Oliver would call the infinite "response-ability" of the testimonies given to us.[43] That is, we have a responsibility to present oral testimony in ways that encourage responses that affirm the testifiers' capacity to respond and hence their agency and subjectivity. I tackle some of these challenges through the testimony of Marlena and Liberty. A careful reader will note that Liberty already has been introduced in chapter 1, and some aspects of these two women's testimony bear similarities to those presented in chapter 2. This repetition is important in itself to underline the nagging commonality of domestic workers' migration experiences under the LCP. But Marlena's and Liberty's narratives are developed at some length here, and reading *within* rather than across individual life narratives (as was the case in previous chapters) runs against a tendency to collapse individual lives into common experiences. It is an important means of affirming the individuality and agency—the response-ability—of those who testify and is integral to the strategy of producing an ethical

witness across sociocultural differences. With Marlena's testimony, I consider (in a somewhat idiosyncratic way) the possibilities of implicating
(some) readers in Marlena's narrative in destabilizing ways. With Liberty's
testimony, I turn more explicitly to the possibilities of framing her narrative so as to exhaust the categories of good and bad mother, and to force
the listener/reader to listen/read more closely, beyond the expected story
line or cultural cliché.

A More Difficult Contract

I begin by presenting a segment of Marlena's testimony in the manner in
which I have presented it orally on several occasions:[44] that is, to illustrate
it with pictures of my own son. At first blush, this strategy is highly problematic because it seems to exemplify a crude form of empathetic identification: literally putting one's self in another's place. When the Australian
Labor opposition leader criticized Prime Minister John Howard for failing
to apologize to the Stolen Generations of Aboriginal children removed
from their families, he was moved to tears and "made reference to his own
children to figure the historical injustices wrought upon Aboriginal children"; this public episode is taken by Jennifer Biddle to be an instance of
identification rooted in racism.[45] I may be guilty of the same charge. However, I want to stay with this problematic performance to explore its unsettling potentials.

Marlena

"I am Marlena . . . from Laguna in southern Luzon. Before I came to Canada,
I have worked in Singapore. That was in 1984. I was working in the Philippines, but I had to leave because our income was not enough for our financial needs. [Marlena is 9 credits short of a degree in economics]. I had one
son who was 1 year old when I left. . . . It went quick with my application
[to work in Singapore] because it was direct hiring. It took only about a
month to process my papers, so I found that very exciting. But when the
plane left the Philippines, I felt very sad at the same time because I did not
know what would happen to me. I was lucky that my employer turned out
to be very good. The man was a doctor and they had only one child. . . . On
my first day I could not sleep. I was thinking of my son who was only 1 year
and 5 months, I think. [Figure 13] So that night before I went to bed, I was

Figure 13. Leaving.
Photo by the author, with
permission of her son.

looking outside and thought that maybe I did a big mistake of leaving my
son under the care of my mother and sister and sometimes, my husband.

"I was very homesick. Everyday I was crying, especially when I thought
of my son. When I called up my mother, she told me not to think very
much of my son because he is also affected. He could not sleep. I would
feel it when he was not well. I think that is the connection between mother
and child. I would not sleep when he was sick and I would just be thinking
about him. When he was starting to talk, I called up and my mother gave
him the phone and I heard his voice. I just started to cry, I could not speak.
It was very difficult. I think I stayed away too long. (Crying.)

"I stayed in Singapore six years, more than six years. And I never went
home because I was building the house. . . . I remember one time, my son
was already 4 years old, so I wanted to talk to him. When he said 'Hello'

(sorry, every time I think of that time, I cry . . .) my tears started to fall down. I said, 'Hello, do you know me?' and he said, 'Yes, they tell me you are my Mom.' So he did not really know me. It is only because *they tell him* that I am his Mom. And I felt so bad about that. I was calling up almost every week and telling him that someday we will be together because I love him so much. So my sister who was already in Canada told me to come here because here I can be an immigrant and then I can take my son with me after a few years.

"In 1990, I went home to the Philippines. It was in December, I was on my way to Canada. I stayed there for a month and a half. But six years was the longest separation I had with my husband and when I was there I felt that something was already wrong.

"I came here in Canada in December 1990 . . . I felt so lonely because, you know, you are caring for this family with the kids. I remember when I went home to the Philippines after six years in Singapore. [Figure 14] On the first evening I asked my son, who never knew me, to sleep with me on my bed. You know that in the Philippines the children usually sleep with

Figure 14. Visiting. Photo by the author, with permission of her son.

their parents. So he did, but it was already almost eleven o'clock and he could not fall asleep. I think his heart was not yet with me. Finally I asked him if he wanted to go back to his grandmother and he did. After about three days, I was surprised that he asked me if I could hug him and take him up in my arms. He was already 7 years old, but he was behaving like a 2-year-old. But I liked that. That means that he was already feeling at ease with me. And my mother's heart was so touched. Then when I was about to leave, I told him that I did not want him to cry when we are at the airport because he will make me cry, too. In the morning before I left, he asked if he could miss school so he could be with me. But I told him that he should go at least in the morning. I did not want him to miss his classes because he was always the first in his class. I told him he could come home early so we could still be together. Then he asked again, 'Mom, can I cry?' I said, 'No, because that will break my heart.' But at the airport we were both crying all the time. It's very hard. You have a dream, but you have to sacrifice something. You cannot get it at the same time. (Crying.) So I kept going until it was time for me to get my open visa. Meanwhile I kept communicating with him [by phone.]

"[After three years, I began processing my papers.] The Immigration told me that when I get my landed immigrant status, my son and husband can also get theirs. But while their papers were being processed, I suddenly got the bad news that my husband had another kid [with another woman]. So that hurt me. Their visa was almost ready, so I talked to the Immigration officer, I was calling them up every day, and I told them that I changed my mind about sponsoring my husband because we have a family problem and I did not like to take him here and have our personal problem here. So they finally approved my son's application alone." (Her son arrived in Canada in 1995 at the age of 12; Figure 15.)

Inserting my son's photograph into Marlena's story is an invitation to one type of viewer who is not a domestic worker (or child of a domestic worker)[46] to imagine leaving one's child for nine years in order to earn enough for her family's survival. Rather than the nine hours that a Canadian mother might leave her child for full-time employment outside the home, I am asking: imagine leaving for nine years. The invitation to empathize with Marlena's loss also works formally. By Barthes's reading, the affective dimension of every photograph is loss: "*This will be* and *this has been;* I observe with horror an anterior future of which death is the stake . . . Whether or not the subject is already dead, in every photograph

Figure 15. Reuniting.
Photo by the author, with
permission of her son.

is this catastrophe."[47] The photos quite literally chronicle the aging of my
son and the loss of his childhood. It is for this reason that Heather Nunn
draws the direct parallel between the photographic wound and the experience of trauma.[48] But are not this invitation to empathize and the sutur-
ing of different kinds of losses deeply problematic, in part because they
mask the recognition of fundamental differences between Marlena's and
my experiences—of the specificity of the precariousness of Marlena's life—
in which Butler (and so many others) locate the ethical relation?

But perhaps the photographs do something else: to create a more compromised relationship between Marlena and listeners/readers, what Whitlock terms a "more difficult contract."[49] Inserting my son's photograph
instead of displaying photographs of Marlena's son can be seen as a ges-
ture of disrupting the ethnographic gaze and communicating that you (the
reader) cannot fully know Marlena's experience.[50] It fragments identification and performs the incompleteness, the impossibility of fully witnessing.
Further, I juxtapose the stillness and stasis of my son's images with Marlena's moving narrative, possibly reversing conventions about who owns
interiority and who is subject to the visual gaze. And even more significant,
if we imagine that my son's image works in a doubled way in Marlena's

testimonial, standing in both for her son *and* the child that she cared for in Vancouver, this situates me (and *possibly* you)[51] as Marlena's potential employer. The story told is no longer simply about Marlena's loss but is an encounter between Marlena and me (and possibly you). I am inscribed in the text, not only in the anticipated role of research collaborator, but in a more directly compromised way: as a middle-class white mother with the need and resources to employ Marlena.

It is in this kind of encounter that Whitlock locates the difficulty of what she calls the "interracial autobiographical contract": "the second person, who is the witness [to the autobiographical testimony], . . . is called upon to witness her own complicity and implications to the loss and suffering which is finally being spoken."[52] This complex ethical and political space brings us closer to the ethical relation theorized by Butler, among others, that arises—not simply from the recognition of alterity but from a struggle between the impulses to preserve or benefit oneself and anxiety about hurting the Other,[53] grounded in an assessment of material interdependencies.

For the purposes of our political project, this ethical relation can be constructed for a privileged reader, not just through the artifice of inserting my son's photographs (to create a mobile, partial, and troubled identification with both Marlena and the privileged researcher), but also through a careful rereading of Marlena's testimony for all the encounters that she narrates. As Marlena describes her son's troubles at school, which led to his eventual arrest after being falsely accused of assaulting another student with a knife on the school grounds, she outlines a full cast of characters, with whom she interacts and judges, and with whom the Canadian witness must also establish a relation.

Marlena

"One day my son was playing with another guy. They were wrestling on the playground, as they used to do in the Philippines, and this other boy had a nosebleed. When the principal talked to them, they told him that it was nothing serious, they were just playing. But the principal sent me a note telling me to call him. I tried to call him several times from 8:00 until 10:00 A.M., but I couldn't reach him. Then I got a call from my son. He told me that he was sent home because I didn't call. He told me that if I don't show up there, he would be suspended. So I left my work, told my employer that I had to go." Interviewer: Did you leave a message in the voice machine of the principal? "No, I just gave my name and said this is Marlena [last name]. I rushed from my work in West Van and went to Van Tech [her son's high school]. I talked to the principal and told him that my son is still in the period of adjustment. That those newly arrived youths still carry some of their ways in the Philippines, and it is really hard for you to understand that sometimes when they are playing, you think that they are already fighting. They are not fighting. So I thought that was already cleared. I told him to give a warning to my son, that that is not tolerated here, so he would know better next time, so he would not be suspended. But after one week my son was suspended for that same case. That was not an isolated case in Van Tech. It happened several times that they picked on the Filipinos because these boys when they are together and joking and teasing one another, the school staff and principal already interpret that as fighting. Even the Filipina liaison in the school, when she talked to the kids, she blamed them for their actions and told them that she was ashamed of them, instead to trying to understand that they were still adjusting to a new culture . . .

"[When my son was arrested], he was only 16. So I went to the police detention center on Hornby [Street], where they said they had my son. When I arrived there, it was already closed and nobody was around. Then I went to the police station on Main. They told me they had no one with the name of my son. So I called up everywhere. Always I was told that they did not have my son. It was only when I asked the help of my employer, who is a lawyer, and he made the call that he was informed that they had my son at the Main police station but that I could see him only the next day. At about 3:00 A.M., they transferred my son to the Burnaby police station. I was told that I could see him at 9:30, but when I arrived there they told me to come back at 2:00 P.M. But I refused to leave because they might take him away again and I would not find him. So I waited outside the station. It was very cold. It was snowing. When I finally saw him at 2:00, I pitied him very much because the first thing he asked was if I brought food. He was so hungry. They did not give him food since the day before. And he was so cold because they made him sleep only in his underwear without any blanket. I was also shocked to find out that he was already forced to sign all the documents and to admit to his guilt, without me around or a lawyer."

Marlena testifies not just to her own and her son's suffering, but to a Canadian society in which a school principal and multicultural worker infer Filipino youth violence with insufficient evidence, and a criminal system opens and closes depending on class and race. Marlena makes those who dominate (and assist) her and her son an object of study. She passes judgment and describes her agency in a series of conflicts and the resources she deploys to reach her son. As much as vicariously experiencing her family's trauma, the middle-class witness is required to interrogate their own assumptions and privileges, which have harmed (or could assist) Marlena and her son. When Jennifer Biddle asks, "What would it mean for identification to do its work properly?" she resolves that it requires that anthropologists write intersubjective encounters into their depictions of others.[54] There are many ways of doing this, including uncovering the encounters that already reside in the testimonials that we have collected. Rather than the researcher self-reflexively narrating the terms of the encounter, much as I have done with the insertion of my son's photographs into Marlena's testimony, intersubjective encounters staged within the testimonials are also narrated by Marlena. She stages them from within her world in ways that invite both empathy and an uneasy speculation about all of our relationships to the suffering so described. The grounds for this complicit empathy and some ways that it might circulate further into the world are preoccupations of the following chapters.

Witnessing between the Fragments

I turn to Liberty's transcript to consider a different path away from spectatorship to witnessing.[55] Liberty narrates fragmented subjects, and neither she nor her employers are easy subjects for identification (or disidentification). The complexity of her mapping of mothering and maternal attachments unsettles a binary of good and bad mother, and her rendering of her employers displaces our assessment from the matter of good and bad employers to the conditions of migrant work. Our inability to fully identify, in other words, forces attention to the structural conditions that cause the experiences of fragmentation and the dispersal of Liberty's emotional attachments.

Liberty

"My name is Liberty and I am here to discuss everything that happened to me and my family before and after I came to Canada. I am a mother with four children; two boys and two girls. I have been separated from them for almost ten years. I left the Philippines in 1990. I went first to Hong Kong, to work and try my luck at working abroad. My eldest son at that time was in the first year of high school, 13 years old. It was with a heavy heart that I had to do this.

"I worked in Hong Kong because I wanted a good future for my kids. Anyway, all parents want this for their children. I have no riches or property that they can inherit; only a good education is what I can afford to give them. Not just education but a good one, which I was able to do by sending them to university.

"I had only one employer in Hong Kong. The first time [that I left my children] was really painful because you are away from your kids, and you take care of other people's kids. I entrusted my kids to other people—to my parents and other siblings. But it is still different, for parents really take care of their own kids. But I could not do anything. From 1990 to 1997, I was a babysitter for a rich Chinese family in Hong Kong. They liked me; that is why I had only one employer during that time. I stayed seven years with them . . . I did not want to go out on Sundays; that is why I did not have too many friends in Hong Kong. They were paying me on Sunday if I worked for them. They would ask me to go with them on Sundays to take care of their children and they would pay me 150 Hong Kong dollars for this extra day of work. So in a period of one month, I would take only one day off. . . . We would go out on Sundays, out to lunch, watch movies and visit, eat nice food in plush hotels and restaurants. So it was a nice experience for me. They had two kids and I took care more of the youngest because he was only 8 months at the time. . . .

"Before the Hong Kong turnover to Mainland China, my employers were already planning to move to Canada. At that time they would just visit Hong Kong while living in Vancouver.[56] The three helpers (the driver, my sister, and me) were all left in Hong Kong. When the handover was coming close, they finally decided who they wanted to bring with them to Vancouver. It was me because I had been with them the longest and I had taken care of the kids. I was very lucky that they brought me here from Hong Kong.

"When I arrived here in 1997, they met me at the airport. They even gave me a bouquet at the airport. They really welcomed me and we ate in a restaurant. My employers even arranged flowers in my room. . . . After a few months, my employers left us for Hong Kong. At that time [their] kids were around 7 and 13. So, as a 'mom' to them (they were almost like my kids to me), I had a good chemistry with the kids, and even with my employers. In 2000, they returned to Hong Kong. They gave up their residency here because they observed that they could not make a good business here. They also wanted to bring me back. This time, I told them that I was thankful for them for bringing me here to Canada, but I was also looking for opportunities for my kids. I told them to give me more time to bring my children to come to Canada, and then maybe I would have time for myself and would return to work for them. They understood even if they were sad to let me go. We were crying when we separated."

Liberty's narrative is one of dispersed mothering, contradictory emotions, displaced attachments, fragmented subjectivity, and momentary distances from self. It invites analysis beyond identification and assessment beyond the binary of good and bad. Liberty constructs a portrait of herself as a dutiful and loving mother. She expresses deep sadness ("a heavy heart") about leaving her children, parsed against her luck and joy about her opportunities to migrate. Dispelling clichés about the adequacy of leaving children with extended family members, she draws a distinction between the care provided by a parent as opposed to grandparents and aunts: it is parents "who really take care of their own kids." She cannot live this model: "But I could not do anything," either in relation to her own children or those of her employer, insofar as she herself substitutes as mom to her employers' children, one of whom she cared for since its infancy. In fact, there was a period when she cared for these children on her own in Vancouver because the parents had returned to Hong Kong. The moments in the first interview when Liberty expressed feelings of being fully valued came in relation to her employers. When the employers from Hong Kong left Vancouver, Liberty stayed behind in order to sponsor her children, but she expressed the possibility of returning to these employers when her time is her own. At the time of the first interview, she had just reunited with her children and there were significant challenges: "They are not happy to be with me. That's how I interpret things with us. . . . I told them: 'You know, guys, instead of appreciating what I do for you, of trying to get you here—look what I get! All complaints.' Nothing that I do is valuable to them but complaints. And so they stopped complaining." In a later interview, she revealed that the Hong Kong employers had retained their home in Vancouver "because the children said that when they are old, there is always Auntie Liberty to take care of them."

Liberty tells a story of mothering that moves us beyond the unified subject and the binary of good and bad mother. She is a loving mother, a sacrificing mother, who simultaneously defends the primacy of the maternal bond and recognizes her inability to practice this ideal in a conventional way. Liberty's narrative about her own experiences of mothering stops us from making a quick assessment. She is hard to judge: she unsettles gender conventions and opens the meaning of good mothering to include the role of an economic provider who buys a good future for her kids. But she simultaneously naturalizes mothering and throws her own good mothering in doubt through her understanding that only parents "really take care of their kids." Her relationship with her employers is equally arresting, and we feel the extremity of Liberty's constraints *because* of her affection for them. The employers are neither entirely good nor bad; they are good employers who always hold the power to terminate her. "The first night [that I arrived in Hong Kong]," Liberty recalled, "I was crying and my aunt [whom she was replacing] said, 'This is a Chinese family and they are very superstitious. If they see you are unhappy, they will terminate you.' So I'm scared . . . I have to smile and try my best to be funny."

Neither Liberty's nor Marlena's narratives are accessible within a polarized moral frame, and this is key to their disruptive potential. Berlant diagnoses the stultifying political effects of emotional transparency as it is relayed into a simplified moral clarity. "The idea that feelings are transparent to subjects becomes ideologically continuous with the moral claim for the clarities of a certain brand of patriotism. . . . This is why anyone who says otherwise, who asks for 'nuance' or seeks to measure degrees of magnitude, is to be revealed as a dangerous thinker."[57] Emotional complexity and moral nuance can build critical, subtle, nonhegemonic thinkers who are threatening to the status quo. The complexity of Liberty's narrative about her emotional attachments and her distanced, fragmented subjectivity demand a nuanced reaction, one that draws us toward rather than away from the political and economic conditions that structure her seemingly contradictory attachments and choices. Her narrative forces us to ask: What kind of social conditions create the circumstances where Liberty would want to return to her employers, with whom she must perform only happiness, to work in paid employment every single day of the month, less one? The same could be claimed of Marlena's testimony, which also performs a welter of open-ended, contradictory emotions. Marlena is excited to go to Singapore but also "very sad at the same time." She is "lucky" to have such a good employer but "did a big mistake" to leave her family. Like Liberty's testimony, this chaos of emotions communicates Marlena's complex subjectivity and her entrapment within the contradictions of her situation. Her narrative of mixed and missed emotions invokes an inquiry into the impossible lived conditions that produce them.

Mention of a second interview with Liberty raises the fact that her narrative is fragmented in another important sense; she was interviewed twice, first soon after her children had joined her in Vancouver and again two years later. At the first interview, the family was in crisis and Liberty literally bore bruises from some of this conflict. Two years on, circumstances were very different and Liberty was experiencing great pleasure from her relationships with her children, especially her 12-year-old son, whom she had never lived with before. Our scholarly narratives need to build in the passing of time, a temporality that allows us to witness and convey the agency of those we study: how they work with and sometimes work away from some of the sadness of their life's experiences. At the end of the second interview, Liberty said: "Well, for now, we are already fine. We have adjusted and I'm always looking for where everything is always good, fine with us." Gerry: "It's good to see it's so much better." "Yes. But we're all trying." Liberty describes herself as a survivor:

And I am just very thankful because my mom told me from when I was young until I grew up to be independent. And I think that is one of the qualities that gives me the spirit, the spirit to be courageous. Like look, I've been through a lot in life, and still I face it squarely. Like my husband is not sending us money. I'm not scared to be poor. And I went abroad. I leave my children behind. I told myself I have to win all the battles. I have to fight them squarely and face every problem eye-to-eye . . . I'm a survivor. We separated. I'm still a survivor. Because I have this attitude of putting negative things into a positive way.

Paired as testimonials, Marlena and Liberty do not tell the same story. Both narratives are of courageous and tenacious women who struggle against their structural circumstances. Marlena tells a more singular story about her love of her son: her terrible loneliness when separated from him, and her fierce attempts to protect and defend him in Vancouver. Liberty testifies to her grief over years of separation from her children in a more fragmented, oblique way, in part by describing her affection for her Chinese employers. Her narrative is different in tone, and focuses as well on a second loss, that of the family of her Chinese employer.

Our project is not to tell about the similarity of experiences of those we have interviewed, but about the conditions that they share: namely, origins in a country where a university education did not buy either a living wage, and participation in a Canadian temporary work visa program that contributed to their immiseration and separated them from their children for many, many years. We have no interest in bringing a Filipino community together *in* grief. We tell these stories to bring the Filipino community together to organize to end the conditions that create this grief. And we hope to tell stories *about* grief in such a way that a wider witnessing public cannot keep its distance, and is neither numb to nor able to gaze voyeuristically upon the spectacle of suffering and shame in ways that further objectify and dehumanize. These witnesses must come in closer, listen more carefully. We hope that the narratives that we present produce contradictory and ambivalent emotions—emotions that provoke analysis and critique, rather than replace it.

Coda

When Jomar Lanot was killed, the media immediately pursued the murder as an instance of racial conflict between Filipino and South Asian youths (the accused were from the latter grouping). To dispel this interpretation Ugnayan BC (the Filipino-Canadian Youth Alliance) immediately united with the South Asian Youth Alliance on the grounds that "it could happen to any marginalized community, and it has in the past, especially to the South Asian community." With research, Ugnayan BC found that the parents of the accused worked in entry-level jobs: "so we can also really relate to their situation as well."[58] This is empathy—and analysis, and a form of identification that shatters identity as the grounds for political judgment.

This chapter is a more modest effort to restage identification beyond identity by speculating about and pushing the potential of testimonial to produce responsible witnesses. Inserting my son's photographs into Marlena's testimony creates an obvious rupture in her narrative, and I have argued that this has the potential to create an uneasy, mobile, partial identification between the privileged reader/listener, Marlena, and me. Rereading

Marlena's narrative for her own descriptions of her conflictual encounters with dominant Canadians engages a wider range of emotions, and is another way of engaging a privileged reader in a complicating way. Reading slowly across long passages of Liberty's account of her migrant experiences allows the opportunity (and privilege) of apprehending her conflicted and fragmented subjectivity, as well as her varied relations of love and belonging. Forced to make impossible choices, Liberty is a subject who is impossible to swallow whole as a singular subject or identity, and one who resists assimilation into simplifying moral schemas. Our hope is to push our readers to take the risks of subtle critical analysis, and to become the dangerous thinkers evidenced by Ugnayan's political alliances beyond identity.

Addendum: Another Kind of Opening

At an interview with an adolescent boy, separated at the age of 7 from his mother for five years, we heard the following:

INTERVIEWER: How did you feel about that? Like initially when your mother left and you found out that she wasn't coming back. What was your initial reaction?

BOBBY: She said she was going to Canada, and I thought she was coming back so I wasn't crying. So I wasn't crying. Then when I didn't see her, I thought she was just, like, she was just shopping. And so I was looking for her and my dad's like, "No, she's in Canada. We'll go to Canada soon." So I was, like, "Okay." . . . [And] I wasn't really sad cuz she keeps yelling at me. And she forces me to sleep, at like noon.

INTERVIEWER: So it was a little better, I guess? So what about when you found out that she was in Canada or that she was away for a long time? Then what did you feel?

BOBBY: I wanted to go to Canada. I wanted to see what it looks like. She kept sending us like cards. And seeing what it looks like, I was like "Oh, it looks fun."

INTERVIEWER: What did she write in the cards?

BOBBY: She says that she loves me. Then she asks me, "What do I want?" And she'll send it to us.

INTERVIEWER: Oh really? Cool. What did you ask for?

BOBBY: She has like a catalogue and it's like "Oh, Rice Krispies!" I didn't know what it tasted like, so I was like "That looks tasty." And so I asked for that and a toy.

[...]

INTERVIEWER: When your mom left the Philippines, what was it like? Describe the day, I guess.

BOBBY: It was fun. Cuz all I did was yell all day. And then she let me go out. It was like "Go out, it's not for kids. Like the television was: 'Please tell your kids to get out cuz the materials on the television is not for kids.'"

INTERVIEWER: What materials?

BOBBY: Dead bodies and stuff. Like violence.

Reading for one type of violence: the violence of family separation, Bobby speaks of other violences, and of some unexpected pleasures as well. His family is clearly a complex site of meaning, a space of discipline and punishment as well as love and care. Bobby does not strip away or simplify the emotional complexity of his reactions to his mother's migration. Liberation from his mother's discipline, access to new commodities, and the possibilities of a country that looked like fun: there is a jumble of emotions and reactions, only some of which involved missing his mother. He tells us of his deep sadness at leaving his extended family in the Philippines: "I forgot to hug my grandfather [when I left the Philippines]. And then when I got here, I was crying. I regretted that day. Oh, I wish I could go back. And then I saw [remembered] my grandfather and he was crying. So I felt bad." These memories stand exactly next to those of pleasure and wonderment: "We got here and it was snowing. It's cool, I saw, like when I breathed, it's like there's smoke."

There is a spate of recent feminist writing locating political options for overseas domestic workers in notions of suffering, yearning, and grief, and a vulnerable human body embedded in familial relations. Aihwa Ong, for instance, argues that NGOs in Asia are finding in suffering ways other than citizenship to revalue the politically excluded.[59] The impetus for this comes from the fact that few migrant domestic workers are interested in gaining citizenship in the country in which they labor. What they want more is moral legitimacy. The at-risk body of the female mother, life-giver, and life-nurturer can be used, Ong argues, more effectively than a language of abstract legal rights to appeal to employers' Asian family values, and to elicit their sympathy for domestic workers' bodily needs: their need for a day of rest, reduced overtime hours, and adequate health care. Neferti Tadiar also searches for something beyond citizenship, rights, and resistance predicated on territorial identity through notions of suffering.[60] And although she recognizes that a discourse of suffering and familial sacrifice often contributes to the reproduction of Filipinas as a "transnational race-class," she works through this language to attempt to articulate what it might mean to live life beyond territorial identity. She understands labor migrancy as a form of suffering, suffering not as a property of the subject, but as a passage of practice that connects Filipina migrants to others who have gone ahead (and who will come after). The political possibilities emerge from social connectedness, not only among migrant domestic workers and their families or to Filipinos more generally but to many others "suffering under the violence of a dominant modernity." Tadiar posits (divine) sorrow as "a placeholder—a prayer perhaps—for forms of political agency and notions of community beyond what our prevailing notions of politics . . . might allow us to recognize."[61]

What Bobby's interview suggests is that we need not narrow the emotional tonalities of our accounts to tell this narrative of social suffering. We receive the shock of social dislocation through and not despite his casual and even gleeful attitude toward his mother leaving, filtered through his misapprehension that she has merely gone shopping. His grief and guilt about his grandfather is remembered through and not despite his pleasures in migration—the phantasm of breath as smoke. Those who suffer need not be reduced to human vectors of sadness to solicit our identification. We might multiply points of identification beyond identity by loosening our directorial control over the emotional scripting of social suffering to tell stories of the more fully human lives of those who experience it.

CHAPTER 4

Creating New Spaces of Politics:
Nanay: A Testimonial Play

A<small>T AN EVENT ORGANIZED IN</small> 2004 to bring together Filipino families who had participated in our research on family separation, an older participant turned to me and said: "I would like to ask you. After doing this research, what are you going to do with it?" He and his wife earlier had spoken at length and with great honesty about their marital conflict after twelve years of separation while she worked as a domestic worker in Vancouver and he cared for their children in the Philippines. I said we would use our research to write academic papers and to lobby government for changes to Canada's Live-In Caregiver Program (LCP). He pressed: "It won't be put on the shelf to gather dust? I mean, there must be some action." Within the year, he died of a stroke; the finality of his death made my promise both more pressing and less believable. After all, our previous twelve years of research and critique had produced no discernable changes in policy or public opinion. And so, when Caleb Johnston and Alex Ferguson, two Vancouver theater artists, approached us in 2006 to use our research transcripts to create a testimonial play,[1] we leapt at the chance to work in an entirely new way with interviews carried out over the previous twelve years with domestic workers, their families, nanny agents, and Canadian employers. Testimonial or documentary theater offered an opportunity to bring our research not just to policy makers but to a wider public, to create a broader debate around the Live-In Caregiver Program and the challenges of care in Canadian society. It was an opportunity to turn our testimonial archive of feeling into repertoire, to create a distinctive theatrical time-place in which to circulate our scholarly knowledge in embodied, performative, and challenging ways.[2]

The Philippine Women Centre of BC, Caleb, Alex, and I began by identifying transcripts that seemed rich enough to sustain a monologue, because the interview was detailed, a person emerged off the page, or their experiences brought an important perspective to the issue. In February 2007, we worked for a week with three professional actors at Vancouver's

Playwright Centre editing the most promising interview material into monologues, experimenting with staging and the possibility of creating dialogues
or scenes out of a composite of interviews.[3] Very little of this material was
used in the end, but documentation of the four or five scenes worked up
during this workshop convinced the PuSh International Performance Festival in Vancouver to include our play in their 2009 program. Our work
began again in the spring of 2008 when Caleb and I and a member of the
PWC (now designated as writers) began to work with a dramaturge, Martin Kinch. Alex (now the director) took us (along with five professional
actors, a stage manager, a scenographer, an additional set designer, lighting and costume designers, and three Filipino youth apprentices) through
a two-week development workshop in July of that year, from which emerged
Nanay: A Testimonial Play.

Pitching the play on a local radio station before it opened in February
2009, Alex and I were asked: "It's the middle of winter. It's going to be
cold. It's going to be wet. It's going to be dreary. Don't people want to go
to the theater to have a good time? Why should people see this production?"[4] We reassured listeners about the intensity of emotional engagement they would experience while attending our play (using phrases such
as "compelling," "engaging," "stories that draw you in," "heartbreaking").
We evidently were successful in achieving the desired effect because at
the end of the PuSh festival the Children's Choice Awards, determined by
twelve children from a Vancouver-area elementary school, declared our
play the "Saddest" of the seventeen plays presented at the festival that year.[5]

Through *Nanay*, we aim to pull audiences to the issue—including Canadians who have been oblivious to it—and to affect them through speech,
bodily sensation, objects, movement, and touching details from individuals' lives. As Kathleen Stewart writes of "these intimate impacts of [affective]
forces in circulation": "They're not exactly 'personal' but they sure can
pull the subject into places it didn't exactly 'intend' to go." They can produce "hard lines of connection and disconnection and lighter, momentary
affinities and difference. Little worlds proliferate around everything and
anything at all."[6]

Even so, as Lauren Berlant cautions, the "affective turn emerges within
the long neoliberal moment of the attrition of the social," and deep emotional responses, affective transformations, and momentary connections can
be a replacement for rather than a step toward sustained social engagement.[7]
As one cranky audience member put it on a *Nanay* feedback questionnaire:

"The pretentiousness of the people [presumably us] who are going 'Oh no, the poor third world women are having their human rights violated.' The sentiments are wonderful but give them something to act on." There is, as well, nothing particularly radical about conceiving theater as an intensified site of circulating affect, intersubjective encounter, and ethical communication. Quite the opposite: theater as a heightened space of emotionality potentially maintains the hegemonic (and gendered) distinction between emotionally laden leisure time and artistic practice, and the rationalities of economic and political life.[8] In short, our success at producing "the saddest" play need not be a step toward critical thought and political action.

But *Nanay* received honors for more than extreme emotionality; the Children's Choice judges also considered it to be the "Most Realistic" and the "Most Interesting" play in the PuSh festival. And I take it as more than chance that the Most Interesting trophy dwarfed the other two that we received: in its height and exorbitance of feathers, pompoms, and beads (Figure 16). I hold these three awards in tension: saddest (affect), most realistic (realism), and most interesting (thought), to approach the politics and possibilities of *Nanay*. I begin with a tour of the play—offering the odd glimpse behind the scenes—to tell you how we attempted to construct complex emotional and ethical relationships to the issue, and to weigh the evidence of our success. But yearning to do more than inhabit the long

Figure 16. Children's Choice Awards for Nanay: A Testimonial Play. *Photo courtesy of Caleb Johnston.*

neoliberal drift toward sentimentality and feeling, I then linger in public talkback sessions that end every performance of the play, in order to speculate about whether and how *Nanay* animates politics, within and beyond the space of the theater.

Dusting off our research, taking it off the shelf, and putting it into the public eye is challenging business; in the form of a play, it risks alarmingly visible failure. *Nanay* involved a complex three-way collaboration between academics, political activists, and theater artists who came to the project with compatible, overlapping, but somewhat different objectives and traditions of collaboration. We at times fought bitterly over decisions taken about script and staging. But we continue to collaborate and develop *Nanay.* I offer this assessment of the Vancouver production to those who believe that "there must be some action" and that the time is ripe for experimenting with academic scholarship to build publics and proliferate worlds of affinity, solidarity, and connection.

A Tour of *Nanay*: Melancholic Realism, Dis-identification, and Strangeness to Oneself

Nanay is a site-specific play, developed and first performed in Vancouver's Downtown Eastside at Chapel Arts, located across from Oppenheimer Park, a place that reverberates with memories and historical incident. In the park, a community-carved totem pole commemorates the many aboriginals who have lived and died violent deaths in the neighborhood.[9] An ill-maintained baseball diamond was—many years ago—home field for the Asaki Tigers, a famed Japanese Canadian baseball team that was permanently disbanded during World War II, when members (and the entire Japanese Canadian community) were displaced from Vancouver and interned in camps. The Kalayaan Centre, where the Philippine Women Centre of BC was located until 2010, lies on the other side of the park, a convenience that allowed for steady traffic between the theater and the PWC during the development workshop in July 2008, and through periods of rehearsal and performance in January and February 2009.[10]

Reopened in 2007 as a performance space, Chapel Arts was formerly a chapel and funeral home. We created the nine scenes of the play in relation to the building's ambience and architectural form.[11] The audience experienced the play in small groups, guided from room to room to hear Canadian employers and Filipino domestic workers speak about their lives;

Canadian employers in the public areas upstairs, domestic workers in the unheated, dank spaces below. At a PWC community assessment after the event, one activist spoke of *"feel[ing]* the contrast—you know, the damp, the dark atmosphere downstairs, the cold and no [theatrical] lighting. So when you go up: the luxurious, you know, the well-appointed rooms. So it was really the best portrayal of the two solitudes: of the slavelike conditions, and the richness of the society that exploits these women."

Memories and sense of loss run through the testimonial stories and the place. Audiences saw domestic workers' monologues in one of two sequences; one sequence began in the former embalming room, still fragrant with the scent of its previous function.[12] And while the Filipino Canadian actor Hazel Venzon told in her monologue—as she scrubbed and cleaned this place—of her great optimism, gratitude, and joy leaving the Philippines to do domestic work, her departure is grounded in loss (Figure 17). She testifies to being abandoned by her husband when he left to do overseas contract work in the Middle East, which created the necessity of leaving her children, her mother, her father, and her siblings in order to try her luck as a migrant worker, first in Hong Kong and then in Vancouver.[13] With a grueling schedule of sixteen performances on one of the performance days,[14] Hazel told us afterward that she maintained her own stamina as an actor by silently dedicating each performance to a different female family member: this is for my mother, this is for my aunt, . . .

Figure 17. Ligaya tells of leaving her children. Photo courtesy of Caleb Johnston.

The audience was then guided into an adjacent garagelike room where the mechanism for raising coffins and corpses through the ceiling for public viewing upstairs is still evident. It was so cold that the actor was, of necessity, dressed in an overcoat. The actor, Lisa Neptuno, delivered the testimony of Joanne in a compressed space, wedged between a small mounted cage and a calendar-grid drawn on the wall behind, upon which she charted her progress through the Live-In Caregiver Program (Figures 18 and 19). Joanne's angry monologue is about her treatment under the LCP, and it too is punctuated by loss, absence, and defeat: of her husband and two children left in the Philippines, of being dismissed by her first employer, of the death of another elderly employer, which again left her temporarily unemployed, and of the revelation by the guide,[15] after her monologue is finished, that she failed, because of the succession of employers, to complete the program within the required thirty-six months and was obliged to return to the Philippines. She is absent. She is gone. We cannot help her, even if we wish.

The audience was then moved to a narrow darkened hallway to sit and listen to an eight-minute audio recording of mothers' and children's recollections of separation.[16] This is the only testimony delivered directly by domestic workers and their children (and not by professional actors). We hear only voices, symptomatic of their disembodied experiences of connection. The tearful voice of a domestic worker describing leaving her

Figure 18. Joanne counts off time during the Live-In Caregiver Program. Photo courtesy of Caleb Johnston.

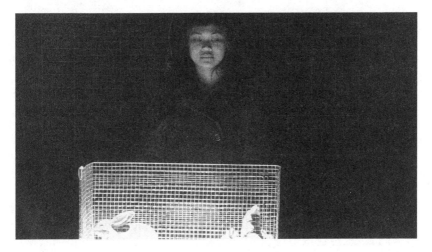

Figure 19. Joanne testifies to her mistreatment during the Live-In Caregiver Program. Photo courtesy of Caleb Johnston.

children is interrupted and overlain with the less impassioned voices of children recalling their memories of their mother coming and going, leaving and returning, and simply staying away for years at a time. At one moment, for instance, a mother speaks: "Four years and eight months. I never went home in-between these years. It's so I could have a better life in the future . . ." This is interrupted by a young woman's voice: "My mom would take care of me in ways that . . . she would send money and letters. But it's hard to connect when you're just sending letters right? It takes a month before it gets to the Philippines." The mother's voice resurfaces: "I did receive letters. Like if I sent them letters. I'd receive . . . up to two months, I'd receive an answer. And then I can answer that back after six months again. That's the only comfort I have there. You just cry every time you will miss your family . . . It took me awhile, like six months, before I stopped crying when I get there. It was very hard." A young man, again in a more matter-of-fact tone, begins to speak over her voice: "She was writing letters, but we just get to see the letter. We don't really get to read it. We just see, 'Okay, she wrote letters.' But to us it's just like: 'Okay, yeah.' We were like . . . we want to know how she is, but we didn't know how to show it kind of thing."

The final scene in this sequence of domestic worker monologues was a space we called "the object room." Domestic workers from the PWC took charge creating this room: it was a model bedroom assembled from memories of their rooms (Figure 20). An exact replica of a domestic worker's daily journal lay on the bedside table, inspirational and devotional religious passages interspersed with an unrelenting schedule of domestic duties. Christian iconography—images of Pope John Paul and a rosary draped on a small figurine of Christ—were carefully arranged in the small space. A small, ancient black-and-white television was turned on, positioned on a dresser at the end of her bed. (Oblivious of trespass, when a hockey game was on during one performance, audience members perched on the end of the bed to watch it.) Around the edges of the room were framed handwritten and drawn descriptions of different domestic workers' Canadian bedrooms (Figure 21), as well as actual letters, cards, and photographs sent between family members in the Philippines and Canada.

As a tangible container of memory, the bedroom was richly evocative for many who attended the play. Glecy, whose description of her Canadian bedroom informed the piece, said that even though "I shared some of my experience there, I am still wounded [when I saw it] and I could still. . . . It's a flashback in my memory when I hear [audio recording of] the water splashing down [through pipes in the wall]. Oh, it reminds me of how noisy my room was." From Coretta, who was not part of the construction of the room: "like the bed . . . I really can't control my tears. Because at the

Figure 20. Model of a domestic worker's bedroom in Vancouver. Photo courtesy of Caleb Johnston.

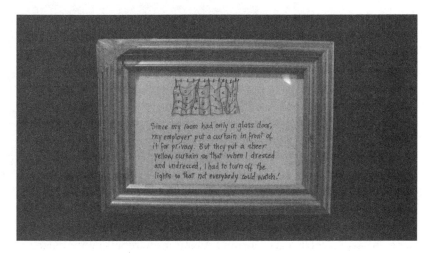

Figure 21. A framed description of a domestic worker's bedroom hanging in the model bedroom. Photo courtesy of Caleb Johnston.

moment I can really feel the environment, the temperature, the smell of the room, as well as the materials around the room." Even those who had no direct memory of such a room felt moved by it. Leah spoke of its impact on her son: "But my son said that for him the one that impacted him the most was going into that bedroom because he felt it was so heavy. Like you couldn't breathe [because it felt so claustrophobic and the air was very stale], and it was quiet but not at the same time because of all the noise [of simulated water running through pipes in the wall] and the air. And the darkness. So it made a lot of the stories we hear tangible and sort of . . . you are stepping into their space." Non-Filipino audience members wrote on an audience feedback survey of "a dreaded sense of hopelessness looking through the nanny's room," and that "the little bedroom with all the photos, letters and the like really affected me." "The replica bedroom was the most touching," wrote another; "the little room montage [of letters, pictures, and postcards] was so very sad."

Before proceeding upstairs to hear testimony from Canadian employers, I want to pause to consider what kinds of ethical situations we sought to generate with these domestic worker monologues and take some measure of how they were received. I want to suggest that these spaces of relics and embodied monologue set in motion what Ian Baucom has identified as a distinctive "knowledge grammar" for apprehending the world.[17] Baucom draws a distinction between what he calls speculative and melancholic realism, arguing that each operates in a distinctive epistemological register to create different kinds of observers. In what is undoubtedly a rough caricature of social science, Baucom argues that scientific facts are constructed in relation to the population or aggregate, and through a process of abstraction: by being emptied of local significance and networked into a system of thought. Melancholic realism operates differently, mimicking the process of melancholy. Within psychoanalytic theory, melancholy is understood as a process of refusing to mourn and relinquish what has been lost or to substitute it with other attachments. What has been lost is swallowed and preserved, and the subject constructs a "cryptic vault" of memory.[18] A melancholic insistence on the nonexchangeable singularity of what has been lost has implications for how it can be expressed. In particular, because any representation is a form of substitution, representation itself is suspect, and melancholic realism thus operates through a "mode of reference that aims to pass itself off not as a representation of the lost thing but as that lost thing itself."[19]

The theatrical experience that we created is arguably working within the terms of melancholic realism, and while the testimonial texts considered in the last chapter can be used to the same effect, the embodied, performative spaces of theater are particularly powerful vehicles for it. The ghostly remains of Joanne, long ago deported, are brought back to life: the organizer at the PWC who did this interview spoke of the visceral impact of "seeing it alive again."[20] The darkened model bedroom embalms objects—an actual diary, the very letters and cards sent between mothers and children—in a tomb of memory. The domestic workers' and children's testimonies, each performed by a different Filipino actor in a distinctive setting, are constructed to incline the audience to the melancholic fact, to attach themselves and bear witness to the distinctiveness of migrant workers' experiences. Each domestic worker's look, tone, sensibility, manner of moving and speaking, mode of storytelling, and engaging the audience is distinct, not easily compressed into a representation of typicality. Encountering domestic workers' testimonies in a small group of twelve, in intimate spaces where the domestic worker addresses you directly, for instance, asking you—that is you—to move in order that she can carry on her work as she tells you her story,[21] forces you—that is you—to engage her as a person, as a sensible and singular human being (Figure 22). To witness injury, Baucom argues, is precisely to attach to the singular, the historically particular,

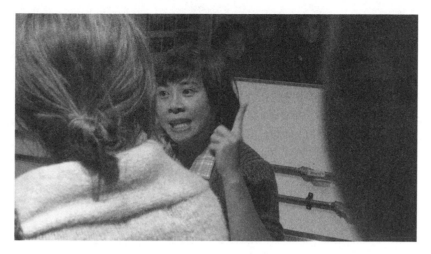

Figure 22. Ligaya tells her story close up. Photo courtesy of Caleb Johnston.

the unverifiable. It is, he argues, an entirely different mode of observation than is produced by speculative realism, which he takes to be the language of social science. The latter, he argues, encourages disinterested spectatorship of the universal, the exemplary, or the theoretical fact. He argues that different politics take shape around these two observers: on the one hand, an interested, romantic, melancholic politics of witnessing, which involves a tenacious, committed holding to an event; on the other, an impartial, disinterested, liberal universalizing politics of abstract human rights. In Baucom's terms: the former is "cosmopolitan interestedness," the latter "liberal cosmopolitanism."[22]

We pose a choice between the two epistemological registers in the final scene of the play, for which all fifty members of the audience are reassembled. In the one constructed, nonverbatim monologue in the entire play, a representative of Citizenship and Immigration Canada enumerates the costs and benefits of the LCP, harnessing a barrage of statistics to establish the balance in favor of the program. He ends his monologue by introducing Michelle, a child of a mother who came through the LCP (whom you may have already met in chapter 2). Michelle (performed by Melissa Dionisio) is positioned at some distance from him, at the other end of a twenty-foot table. Her testimony is often flat in emotion, and we are made to understand that this tone originates in her migration experience: the loss of her friends and future in the Philippines and an absence of feeling for her mother in Vancouver. Giving the last word to Michelle, we declare ourselves attached to her melancholic testimony of loss.

There are familiar risks that attend this attachment: risks of entombing Filipina women in their victimhood and—as discussed in chapter 3—of binding Canadian spectators too closely to Filipinas' injury and loss, thus instantiating the liberal subject of compassionate sentimentality. Martin Kinch, our dramaturge, was dogged in his advice to counter these tendencies by introducing more positive testimony from Filipina domestic workers. In response, we worked with Ligaya's (Liberty's) testimony to emphasize her agency, mining her interview transcripts for lines such as these:

> But I have a fighting spirit, something like that. I'm the eldest.
> I'm the rebellious one. And I think that is one of the qualities that
> gives me the spirit, the spirit to be courageous. Like look, I've
> been through a lot in life, and still I face it squarely. I'm not scared
> to be, you know, for being poor. And I went abroad. I left my
> children behind. I told myself I have to win all the battles. I have
> to fight them squarely and face every problem eye-to-eye. And
> yeah, I'm very thankful that my mom taught me this. With all
> these challenges, I'm a survivor.

But the scene of the most positive testimony that Caleb and I could find (that of Tita in chapter 2) was cut.

Nonetheless, there are three features of *Nanay* that disrupt the tendency to sentimentality, the first tied to the verbatim or documentary genre. The hybrid nature of documentary theater encouraged audience members to wrestle actively and productively within the two epistemological registers that Baucom identifies. Documentary theater, Ben-Zvi argues, is a "special kind of double agent," deploying claims of truthfulness—in this case actual social scientific truthfulness—while simultaneously using the aesthetic devices and embodied presence of theatrical performance. We can hear one audience member explicitly weighing melancholic and speculative facts in a talkback session:

> I found the stories of Ligaya [in the kitchen] and Joanne at the
> beginning [of the play] exceedingly powerful. It seemed to me that
> they dominated the whole play. My question is: how representative
> are they? It's hard for me to imagine how things could be much

worse than they were for Joanne, up there in Whistler with three kids, working around the clock. But maybe it can get even worse than that. On the other hand, I would have thought it could get a good deal better, too: that there would be cases where families really do love their caregivers and where things are working out well. So these are two enormously powerful introductory stories. My question is about their representativeness.

This question—unsolicited—was repeated in almost every talkback and in a good proportion of the audience surveys.[23] But rather than dismissing this type of speculative realism as Baucom does, as the mind-set of the actuarial accountant, we might consider what each type of realism brings to the other. Arguably, one brings us close in order to experience the exposure and vulnerability of domestic workers; the other provides some distance necessary for political judgment.[24]

A productive oscillation between distance and proximity, judgment and its suspension, comes from another source as well: the intercultural nature of *Nanay*, which forced the Canadian spectators in particular to recognize their inability to fully apprehend the play. We introduced the question of intercultural translation in the first instance through the naming of the play. A Tagalog word for mother, *nanay* is almost intelligible to the English speaker as the word "nanny." It thus signals to English speakers that they both know and do not know the content of the play, or that they may not know what they think they know. It certainly shifts the ground of linguistic competence.[25] But beyond the name, the play was an intercultural *event*, and this fact fundamentally altered its meaning and reception. An audience survey taken at the Vancouver performances revealed the mixed nature of the crowd: 119 audience members identified themselves as domestic workers or family members, even more (184) had been employers or knew employers of domestic workers, and 255 had no relationship with anyone who had direct experience with the LCP (they were there for the theatrical experience). The PWC ensured that at least five domestic workers or family members attended each performance, and the presence of so many Filipino domestic workers and family members as fellow travelers both drew Canadian audience members close to domestic workers' stories and kept them at a productive distance. One audience member commented: "I found it really moving to see the show, as someone without direct experience of the program, being able to see it with people who had had direct experience with the program. I found it extremely moving."[26] But equally, another wrote in the audience survey about the significance of gaps in cultural understanding: "[What resonated?] Seeing women in the audience crying at fragments of conversation in the [sound room of audio recordings of mother and children describing their periods of separation]—that I couldn't entirely follow/get. Seeing philli audience nod during Canadian gov't testimony."

There is a peculiar scopic economy in the performing arts as compared to a written archive or other visual arts that heightens this attentiveness to intercultural reception. This is especially so in a performance such as *Nanay*, with the absence of theatrical lighting in the domestic worker scenes, and an intimate proximity between actors and audience, and among audience members themselves. Filipino domestic workers read Canadian audience members for their reactions. Ate Letty recounted: "I'm pretty sure some Canadians really don't know what is happening. Really don't know the reality of the live-in caregivers. I know that some of them reacted at the play because I was there, too." From Glecy:

I have these feelings [at the play]: maybe they [non-Filipino Canadians] will get upset or how can they accept the message or the contents of the show? But my observation of other audience [members] . . . when we go first into the sound room I could feel that the majority of my group is really amazed. They were saying: how could they get the person to share their story? How do you ask individuals to speak out? I could hear their whispering, like "Oh, this is not an easy job." For me, I can say this is not an easy job: it's hard to overcome the deskilling or your self-esteem being lost.

A third break from liberal sentimentality comes not from the staging of the domestic worker scenes but through the employer scenes upstairs. And so let us climb the elegant stairway in Chapel Arts to encounter these scenes. For these parts of the play, a larger audience of twenty-six was reassembled and placed in more conventional theatrical seating, to view from a stable vantage point three employer scenes.

Staging the employer scenes was the source of the greatest conflict among those who created the play. The director, Alex Ferguson, found it challenging to find the complexity of many employers' characters or to empathize with their circumstances. A short excerpt from one employer scene may convey a sense of the challenge:

RICHARD: When Stephen was six months old, we chose a Filipino nanny because we heard that they were very caring for the very young ones. So we basically only interviewed Filipino nannies.

STEPHANIE: We found out about Marlena from a friend of ours. How we worked it out was like this: we had two bedrooms upstairs and one room that we used as an office. So we sacrificed that. In that information booklet, it told what a live-in caregiver is entitled to have. And it was a room with sleeping arrangements, and a lock on the door. Although no one's ever locked the door.

RICHARD: And then we also gave her separate bathroom facilities. And she didn't need a separate phone, but we gave her one. We gave her a TV, a desk, an answering machine. It's different than working in Singapore or Hong Kong. Marlena told us stories of where the nannies were sleeping. It wasn't a pretty scene.

STEPHANIE: They're treated like second-class citizens in other countries!

RICHARD: At first she wanted to call us "Madam" and "Sir"! But we said, "Wooahhh, wait a minute." I think she was kind of taken aback by that! And we said to her, "That's not the Canadian way."

STEPHANIE: More than anything, we've become friends.

RICHARD: Yeah, we wanted to break the ice.

This exchange accommodates a comedic parody, an opportunity that the director took up through his choice of set (a bedroom overlooking a picturesque scene of gentrified downtown Vancouver), selection of costumes (plush bathrobes followed by a quick change into formal evening wear), emphasis of particular words, tone, gestures, and gloating glances between husband and wife (Figure 23). And yet, as Judith Butler observes, the risk in parodying employers is that "condemnation, denunciation, excoriation works as quick ways to posit an ontological difference between judge and judged" and can have the effect of foreclosing a fuller knowledge of oneself.[27]

For the other two scenes, we sought the most sympathetic employer stories that we could find in the existing archive of research material, in order to force the audience into a relationship with Canadian employers. Caleb and I conducted more interviews with friends and acquaintances in our search for less easily demonized employers. In one of the two scenes we eventually included, two white middle-class women sit across from each other in a kitchen, elaborating their futile efforts to find child care in Canada (Figure 24). Taken from two separate research transcripts, it is

Figure 23. A Canadian couple speaking about their nanny. Photo courtesy of Caleb Johnston.

Figure 24. Two Canadian women talk about their child-care problems. Photo courtesy of Caleb Johnston.

staged as two concurrent monologues that thread into each other, with the women repeating, repeating, repeating the same experience of Canadian caregivers coming and going, being hired and fired, or just failing to show up. Each extremely stressed by the unreliability of Canadian home-based caregivers, they come to different ways to alleviate their stress: one hires a Filipino nanny through the LCP, the other quits her job.

It is the third employer scene that comes closest to the testimonial genre of the domestic worker monologues and encourages the audience to engage with the complexity of her situation. In this scene, a middle-aged academic tells of the pain and difficulty of arranging twenty-four-hour care for her mother, who has had a stroke and is coping with Parkinson's disease but wants to stay in her home: "When she came home from three months in the rehab hospital [after the stroke], I woke up one morning and she was on the floor and she couldn't get up. She said she'd been there for five hours and she's freezing cold because the air conditioning was on and she didn't have a blanket on her. I just started to cry. It was awful. And after that happened she finally resigned herself to the fact that she did need someone all of the time."

The woman who testifies to her experience has critical resources: "My mother doesn't understand why . . . she doesn't really see it as a job, taking her to the bathroom. She just thinks of it as like something you would do for anybody. If you just happened to live there, you would do it. She doesn't see it as wage-gaining work. It's like it doesn't compute to her that people have lives and they have other things to do. That this is actually labor." Knowing at some level that the relationship is exploitative, that she pays her Filipino domestic worker who has come to Canada under the LCP a fraction of what she pays the Portuguese Canadian housekeeper who has cared for her mother during the day for years, she wrestles with the ethics of the situation and her economic constraints, worrying and rationalizing, weighing and balancing her political commitments against her love of and uncompromised allegiance to her mother. The testimony anticipates her loss, her mother's death, and documents her efforts to make her mother as comfortable as possible as her body deteriorates toward this end. It is difficult not to sympathize with this loss and the trade-offs that she makes.[28] And yet to witness—truly witness—her testimony is to enter into a complicit relationship with the LCP and to entertain the possibility that you too could become a domestic worker's employer.

These employer scenes proliferated attachments to people positioned

differently to the issue. In a community forum after the Vancouver performances, a Filipino Canadian activist, father of two young children, spoke
of being "surprise[d] to like parts that I didn't think I would like. In particular, the two women in the kitchen. I don't know why it resonated so
much, but I think it was really seeing the Canadian issues collide with the
[Filipino] community's issues as two mothers, I guess they are single moms,
I'm not sure, but just talking about their difficulty finding child care as a
family. [My reaction] was really surprising to me." Attaching to the stories
of *both* domestic workers and Canadian employers takes the play beyond
the sentimental: absorbing multiple and divergent stories of loss forces
critical thought and some hard political work. As one audience member
put it: "They all sound real AND they also seem to contradict each others'
stories. I felt compassion for these overstressed women/employers AND
for the equally exploited overstressed workers."

Knowing oneself as a potential employer is possibly to know something new and unwanted about oneself. Butler has argued that it is relationality, and not the (autonomous) moral subject, that grounds ethics.
Foreignness to one's self—a rupture in self-mastery and a sense of being
acted upon by relations that one has not chosen—are key, in her assessment, to this ethical connection with another. By this schema, it is not
one's moral superiority to Canadian employers who hire domestic workers that grounds ethics. It is being acted upon by relations that make the
LCP a viable option for oneself that establishes the grounds for ethical
responsibility toward Filipina domestic workers *and* Canadians who need
to care for their parents and children. Being caught between compassion
for Canadian employers and Filipina domestic workers also refocuses attention, we hope, away from the issue of bad or immoral employers to a larger
story of global inequity, the scandal of undervalued care work in Canada
and the export of maternal labor from the Philippines. How all of this might
shape up as politics is the question I turn to next by entering the last scene
of the play.

A Performative Space of Politics

At the end of one of the Vancouver performances of *Nanay* a friend of
Caleb's (a "theater person") came up to him in a state of bemusement. He
said something like this: "I don't know what the fuck just happened in there.
First this one woman starts asking the actor questions from the audience.

And then a second woman asks her a question . . . " He was referring to the final scene of the play, when the child of the LCP speaks her monologue. In an effort to make transparent the constructed nature of the monologues, the director staged this particular scene closer to its original form as an interview. Seated among the audience, in my role as researcher, I prompted the young woman's monologue through a series of short questions. This evidently destabilized the boundary between performers and audience quite effectively because on this occasion an audience member filled a brief pause in the actor's monologue with the sincere question: "How do you get along with your mother now?" In an instance of astonishing good fortune, the next line answered the question.

The current attraction of documentary or verbatim theater, some argue, is that it fills an important gap in the political landscape by feeding a public appetite for a more diverse set of stories and opinions than are delivered by conventional media, so as to stimulate more complex analysis and debate. [29] In short, it is an antidote to infotainment. While this may be, it is more than the content or information conveyed that is significant. Its potential lies, as well, in being a performative rather than didactic space. In this we follow Jacques Rancière's argument that the emancipatory potential of theater rests not so much in the genre or subject matter of the work presented, but in the relationship of the audience to the material performed, the actors, the space, and to one another.[30] Theater's political potential rests in the opportunity it provides to blur the opposition between those who look and those who act (between passivity and the capacity to take action), and between those who are locked within their functions, roles, and social identities and those who exist beyond them. The potential lies in being and not just professing an egalitarian space.[31] Theater can be a distinctive public space where it is possible to *perform* (and not simply preach) equality.

Nanay can be seen as an egalitarian space in the first instance because it allows migrant domestic workers, in their precarious and slippery status as noncitizen residents, to command the attention of a mainstream audience on an equal footing with Canadian employers and a representative of the Canadian government. But opportunities for democratic participation go far beyond this.

The equalizing potential began with the location of the play, where many in the audience felt somewhat out of place. When we first selected the location of Chapel Arts, some of us had concerns that its marginal and

highly stigmatized location in Vancouver's Downtown Eastside would dis-
courage a middle-class audience from attending.[32] And although the venue
was so close to the Kalayaan Centre, comments made by Filipino activist
collaborators suggest that they too saw it as a foreign place: "Seeing the
play in a completely mainstream setting—it gave us an idea of how much
we have to do to continue the debate in the public arena"; "you attract a
different . . . not too many people can go to elite venues. So bringing *Nanay*
into [Chapel Arts], we are also reaching out to people who would not otherwise go to the Kalayaan Centre."

The structure of the play and the audience's mobility through it also
disrupted a sense of authoritative control over interpretation and participation. Filipinos and non-Filipinos, those with and without connections to
the LCP, employers and domestic workers, theater patrons and activists—
these audience members were arbitrarily assigned at the beginning of the
play to one of three groups that were informally guided though the mono-
logue/scenes in different orders. Their mobility and informal sociability
contrast to what Rancière characterizes as the policing of audiences through
a system of reserve seating, the audience positioned "like so many temporary owners of property."[33] The structure of the play is itself episodic and
fragmented, with a multiplicity of entry points. Some encountered the
employers before the domestic workers; others saw the show in reverse
order. Domestic worker scenes were experienced in different sequences.
There is no single narrative arc, suggesting, we hope, an open encounter
and interpretation. At least some audience members noticed: "I enjoyed
how piecemeal it was—to step in/out of different stories/perspectives
added physical/material complexity to an already complex issue."

And although we used professional actors, neither actors nor audience
members were locked into their roles. There was much speculation among
audience members about the blurring of the boundaries, as well as active
transgression of them. We chose to use professional actors because our
community collaborators were interested in developing skills and networks
made possible by working with theater professionals, and because those
whose testimony was used could not appear in the play. The domestic
worker who testified to her life under the LCP had long since been forced
to leave Canada; the domestic worker delivering her monologue in the
kitchen did not have the luxury of time or money to leave her children and
employment for rehearsal and performance; and issues of privacy and consent were complicated in the case of the child of the domestic worker who

revealed details about her father's girlfriends. In any case, the politics of "real" people performing their authenticity are as fraught as the danger of appropriation; in neither situation do power relations go away.[34] Further, actors open an interesting possibility for democratic politics precisely because they have no sanctioned authority to speak the words they speak, or at least none grounded in an identity, mirroring (or literally performing) the contingency of the democratic authority to speak.[35]

Audience members actively searched across the blurred line of acting and identity, fiction and fact, genuinely troubled by the indistinction. In audience surveys, they made comments such as: "What is real? What isn't?"; "Are actors people who went thru LCP?/hired nannies?"; "The way they portray their roles were really really real"; "Do the actors or any of them have any reaction about the true stories of the women? How would they feel if they were in that story?"; "When looking at 'the' nanny's diary in the bedroom, I felt uncomfortable not knowing if it was a fictionalized diary or a real one." Especially for the Filipino actors, audience members tried to fix the actor in their character: "The philipina actresses were extremely powerful, genuine, and convincing—I believe the stories resonated more with them (family backgrounds) than it did for the Caucasian actors, who probably had no connection to this issue." And though we might read this as a tendency to naturalize migrant care work in the body of the Filipina, the effect may have been the opposite. As one audience member put it: "The 'Philipina' part was overall more effective in troubling issues of representation—it wasn't clear if these women were actors or testifying at times (which catches the viewer in a lot of assumptions)."

Audience members themselves were destabilized in their role,[36] to the point that one young woman at one performance asked for clarification of the norms as they had developed within this particular production: "I have a question to ask everyone who watched the show. I didn't clap at all during any of the show. I wanted to clap. But—I don't know if it was the tone or mood—I didn't know how to express how grateful I was for them doing the show. I was wondering... did anyone clap in any of the sessions?... Is it okay if we clap?"

Because of the ambiguity of the distance between reality and fiction and the intimacy of actors and spectators, audience members periodically crossed the line from spectator to actor. My 16-year-old son, for instance, became part of the action when, pressed against the wall, he inadvertently turned off all the lights in the cramped kitchen scene. The actor simply

moved him, turned on the lights, and scolded him (as a nanny might), telling him she preferred to work with the lights on.

But more than these periodic improvisational eruptions within the performance, the expectation of active participation was demanded by the fact
that the talkback session flowed directly out of the performance without
break. For all performances, most of the audience stayed for the talkback,
about fifty people arranged to face one another in conversation (Figure 25).
The actors, producer, and director often slipped without comment among
the audience as equals (rather than experts) in a conversation that typically
focused not so much on the play but on the economics, politics, and (in)jus-
tice of the LCP.[37] The talkbacks created the time and space for extraordinary
public conversations between those who most likely would not otherwise
speak or listen to one another: domestic workers spoke directly to employers, activists to government officials, activists to other activists aligned
around different issues. In audience surveys, the talkback was described as "a
very interesting space." "I liked the talkback and the permission it gives to
the audience to ask questions and to hear more directly from the community"; "[What resonated?] The talkback with the real women speaking";
"Appreciated the personal accounts in the talkback session especially"; "I
loved the talkback between the employers and caregivers and their families. Destabilized the notion of audience. Moving, compelling."

Figure 25. Talkback sessions followed every performance. Photo courtesy of
Caleb Johnston.

Performance theorist Jill Dolan writes about the potential of performance to "inspire moments in which audiences feel themselves allied with each other, and with a broader, more capacious sense of the public, in which social discourse articulates the possible rather than the insurmountable obstacles of human potential."[38] She calls these moments of affective intensity among audience members "utopian performatives." They are moments of feeling or experience—not something received didactically as information—in which we get an inkling of "how powerful might be a world in which our commonalities would hail us over our differences." They "resurrect a belief or faith in the possibility of social change."[39] Such moments were palpable in some of the talkback sessions, and we seemed to witness personal transformation, right there, on the spot.

In one talkback, for instance, a white middle-class woman introduced herself as an employer: "We have a live-in nanny and she's wonderful." She recognized that her nanny was working beyond her contracted hours and posed the problem to the group: "My 7-year-old's job is to jump up from the dinner table and drag her from the kitchen. . . . I wonder if there is some way, like some culturally appropriate way, that I can say that it's really okay to stop working at six. Because I want to be a good employer. Like the guilt associated with this show tonight: *oh my god* [laughing]." A member of the Filipino-Canadian Youth Alliance responded to this personal inquiry with a generalized argument about the deskilling of domestic workers, to which the woman answered acerbically: "It's very evident to me that she is skilled." Another audience member took a more congenial approach, first identifying herself as "half Filipino and half Canadian. My mom came here and of course I'm very Canadian. As my 16-year-old says, 'The only Filipino thing about you is your mother.'" In her view, a "white empowerment model" was inappropriate: "I was raised by a Filipino mother to take pride in my work: whatever your job is, you keep a smile on your face and just motor on. . . . What I mean is, help them to acculturate, help them to understand." An activist from the PWC then shifted the discourse to one of rights and advocacy. This seemed to resonate with the woman who first posed her dilemma because she thanked the PWC activist: "This is helpful. Like I guess I feel a little more comfortable because I asked her what her long-term goal was. I tried to sign her up for courses and pay for her time and that sort of thing."

This employer's concerns about being a good employer were forgotten

when, with great emotion, a domestic worker spoke of her delayed understanding of Canada's family sponsorship regulations, which meant she could
not sponsor her eldest son: "It was only when I finished the twenty-four
months and then I processed the papers, I read there: 'Oh my god, my eldest son cannot. . . . He doesn't qualify.' We will be separated forever unless
I go home [to the Philippines] and see him there. It's the only way." The
Canadian employer once again spoke to the activists in the room: "Did
someone say there are workshops in Tagalog because I would hate for this
to happen to my nanny." From the domestic worker who could not sponsor
her eldest son: "That's true." Another Filipina member added that her friend
had suffered the same experience. The Canadian employer then erupted:
"[When domestic workers] phone back home, do they say 'Canada's better' or do they say 'This really sucks' and tell everyone they know not to
come to Canada because they've been lied to, or exploited, taken advantage of, the structure of the thing sucks, 'I got tricked, my sick kid can't
come when everyone else can.' So like, isn't there some kind of word of
mouth or some kind of awareness? Journalistic coverage? Something?"
Carlo Sayo, one of the talkback facilitators, turned the question to the
domestic workers in the room: "Maybe that is something we can ask to
some of the people who have been through the program. What do you tell
your family back home?" In the space of twenty minutes, after hearing
personal testimony from domestic workers themselves, the middle-class
liberal employer moved from simply wanting to be a good employer to
asserting that the "structure of the thing sucks."

Such moments of common feeling, unhinged from shared social identity, were deeply satisfying. Equally productive were moments of disagreement, when the possibility of translating across experiences was both refused
and openly desired. During one performance, Caleb and I, quietly chat-
ting in the lobby, were surprised by a woman in tears rushing past us. She
had left her group in the "objects room" and was headed to a bathroom for
privacy. In the talkback, she identified herself as Colombian, and explained
what lay behind her reaction:

> I just wanted to know, do you ever have on this show actual
> Filipina workers? Because I felt, I felt really weird. I have been
> in the same kind of situation and I felt that looking at people
> [audience members] sitting on the bed [in the model bedroom],
> it was like an invasion of my privacy. And for me it was awful to

see Canadians like, you know, for me it was a little bit offensive. During the whole play, I was wondering, like I felt like a colored person watching the white people watching the play. . . . Because when I have been in that situation and you're talking about me, that's really different. I felt that they were looking at my room. . . . I just felt that this play is for Canadians. It's not for Filipinos and it's not for immigrants.

Charlene Sayo, a representative from the PWC who had been involved in the play from its inception, explained:

Yes, there were Filipino people that were involved, because the script was taken from interviews from Filipino domestic workers and there was consultation with members of the PWC and SIK-LAB [another Filipino migrant organization]. In particular, in that room we did have domestic workers involved here, with their time and by donating their things and setting it up. . . . In a very hands-on kind of way, they would say, "Don't put that here. This has to go there. This has to go on the calendar. . . . For the women who participated, it was for them very liberating and empowering in the sense that people wanted to hear their stories and this was an opportunity to tell them.

Attempting to reengage the woman's concerns, I added: "But I think absolutely people should go through that room in a very complicated way. I guess what you're saying is that you didn't witness this complicated relationship to this room."

It was almost fifteen minutes, after the Colombian woman had slipped out of the room, that another audience member, this time white, male, in his early thirties, returned to her comments. He began by introducing himself: "I'm [first name]. I'm a theatergoer, theater artist, and landscaper and stuff." He proceeded to analyze the bedroom from this perspective:

I thought it was a very interesting choice to allow us, to invite us openly, to encourage us to go into that bedroom and to look at that bed and to sit on that bed. And how you carpeted the platform [on which the bed is placed]. Very interesting choice and definitely a very complicated interaction. As an audience member

and as a theatergoer I am trained—and I think that is an appropriate term—to engage with a piece. And obviously I engage with it
from my own background. And I think it's fascinating and I think
it's a great choice and I'm really interested in dialoguing with that.

He then returned to the Colombian woman's comments:

> Because personally, the reaction of the woman who's left now—
> and unfortunately I didn't have the courage to speak up earlier,
> but I wish she was still here—is a really interesting perspective for
> me because I had the reaction, "That's wrong [to enter this space],
> but this is a theater piece and therefore I can do it." What I'm
> interested in now is that it evoked such a strong reaction. Because
> she could be speaking to me directly. I'm interested in opening a
> dialogue about that because how do you [know]? I mean, I don't
> know. I mean, I'm only me as a person from Canada. And how do
> you . . . ? So I just want to open a dialogue because I don't know if
> it was a piece for white people. It feels to me like it was piece . . . I
> don't know. So that's a question for you guys. . . . I would like to
> engage with that anger more. Because it's quite rare. And I don't
> mean from a masochistic point of view. Because I think here in
> Canada, certainly here in Vancouver, we exist within a really politi-
> cally correct environment, which is for a very good reason, but it is
> also an environment that stifles conversation and dialogue and the
> ability for people to engage in that way. I don't know if what I'm
> saying is massively offending people. But I'd be really interested to
> hear more of that angle and more of that perspective.

"She could be speaking to me directly." The talkback evidently created a
time and space to take the risk of sounding angry, offensive, or foolish, that
is, to take the risk of encounter beyond identity. It created a time and
space for an immigrant woman to level the accusation that the play is
offensive and exclusionary, and "a theatergoer, theater artist, and landscaper
and stuff" to invite a conversation that would allow him to see the work
differently, to disturb his "trained" eye, to better understand whether and
how his world is constructed "for white people." In short, in Rancière's
phrasing, this talkback created a time and space to redistribute the sensible: reconfigure what can be seen, heard, felt, and thought.

One of the most interesting talkbacks occurred when three representatives of the Philippine embassy attended the play. This talkback was
itself a performance—an actual demonstration—of the discursive work-
ings of state power. As a liminal space, the talkback brought into conversation people who would not usually have or take the opportunity to speak
to one another. Embassy representatives dealt with this situation by using
very effectively two counter-political strategies: privatizing and minimiz-
ing the claims to injury made by migrant domestic workers and, by extension, the play. Rancière claims of state authority that, "rather than solicit a
submissive subjective recognition or response, [those in power] dismantle political stages by telling would-be spectators that there is nothing to
watch. They point out 'the obviousness of what there is, or rather, of what
there isn't: Move along! There is nothing to see here!'"[40] The exchanges
between one of the facilitators, the representative of the PWC, and the
embassy representatives took this form. Let me restage one of them:

PWC REP: In the Philippines we are forced to leave our country because
we don't have a future. There is no job in the Philippines. . . . The
government is targeting one million workers going abroad [for the
remittances]. . . .

EMBASSY PERSON 1: I am [name] from the Philippine embassy. You
could also confirm this by searching for the information online. But
it has never been the policy of the Philippines government to send
domestic workers abroad. In fact it is perhaps a consequence of the
fact that they would like to look for the so-called greener pastures. But
what we have always been trying to do is to keep people home where
they belong. . . . So it's not the policy. I just wanted to clarify that.

PWC REP: It's not a matter of choice. . . . I didn't want to leave the Philippines . . . but I don't have a choice. I need to support my family in
the Philippines. . . . So it is not a matter of choice. We are forced to
leave the country.

EMBASSY PERSON 2: If I may add, it just shows that people are free to
leave if they want to leave. The official migration policy started
roughly in the seventies. . . . It was just a temporary measure at the
time when there was an oil crisis. But somehow it seemed to gain
some roots. But officially now, for the past five years, it has not been
the official policy of the Philippines to send labor abroad because
the social costs far outweigh the remittances if we add them up.

ALEX FERGUSON: Did you say for the last five years it hasn't been a policy? Because I was under the impression that there used to be a policy.
EMBASSY PERSON 2: That was the brainchild of the late foreign affairs
secretary, Blas Ople. Somehow in the Labor Department it became
roughly there. But ever since five years ago or so it became very clear
in the Department of Foreign Affairs, which has been sending reports
to the Home Office to stop this employment abroad, especially in
the Middle East. . . . I mean Canada appears to be good. But the official stance from the Labor Department is to continue sending. So
somehow there is a dichotomy . . . But officially the Philippines does
not promote labor as its export. Never.

In this short exchange, embassy officials use a discourse of individual
choice (discussed in chapter 1) to privatize and individualize the situation.
The statement made by the representative of the PWC about the labor
export policy is refuted ("it has never been the policy"), but with a question from the artistic director, Alex Ferguson, it is localized in space and
time: in the seventies and now in the Department of Labor. The situation
in Canada appears to be good, suggesting that there is not much to look at
here. The PWC representative's expression of her experience of forced
migration is ignored: "If I may add, it just shows that people are free to
leave." She was later further disqualified when the second embassy person
answered a question from the audience about the length of separation of
mothers from their children: "If you take a country like Saudi Arabia. . . . An
accountant can go home three, four times a year. An ordinary nanny could
go home after two years, or three. . . . If you belong to a lower class, you
suffer more." This social order, including a hierarchy of rights to family
life, is taken as a given: it is unremarkable.

This open public forum nonetheless created the opportunity for direct
commentary and confrontation. For instance, activists from a Europe-wide
migrant domestic worker advocacy organization, RESPECT, countered
(one member translating for another from Spanish to English): "For her
[her fellow activist for whom she was translating], she feels that your discourse as a representative of the state is kind of messed up. All the things
that you are doing for them. All the things that you receive from these
workers. We're not sure what help is coming from the state. There's a mixture of discourse." A good number of audience members, beyond those representing migrant domestic workers, challenged the embassy representatives

in a heated talkback conversation that went on for well over an hour.[41] But while the conversation was exhilarating, it also allowed the embassy representatives the opportunity to explicate more fully the official discourse. One of the embassy representatives ended the talkback with a long impassioned speech, delivered first in Spanish and then in English.

> EMBASSY PERSON: And to the gentleman who has been asking that you must see that the social cost is so great. Of course we do. Canada did not need to make this study or this play for us to know the problem that we have. It is everywhere. It is something that is even in the papers and in countless studies before we came today, that the problems and the social costs of migration are stupendous. We end up educating people for a career that they can never practice perhaps because there is no job waiting for them. But these are things that we are already working toward solving. . . . And the lady [PWC representative] said that so many Filipinas approach the Philippine Women [Centre] in Canada. In fact, I'm sure the consulate and embassy in Canada are using you as a partner in reaching out to the Filipinos. There may be cases . . . of some abuse. . . . That is the job of the [Philippine] labor attaché. And if he is not doing his job well, it is also your job to take him to task to answer for that. . . . I can also share with you the experience of a young man: I think he topped either the law or medical board exams back in the Philippines and he was very proud to say that his mother is a domestic worker. There are many stories out there about children who know exactly what their parents give up to give them the kind of future they are enjoying now. There are. It is not always that you have an ungrateful child who has ended up having wayward ways. You also have some happy endings.
> GERALDINE PRATT: Except in that case it came at the cost of family separation.
> EMBASSY PERSON: Oh, yes, of course.

Oh, yes, of course: hardly a decisive victory for either *Nanay* or critics of the LCP. But what we can claim for *Nanay* is that it creates a public space in which it is taken as foundational that all participants have an equal capacity to speak and an equal right to be heard. This is, as Rancière notes, "a reasonable-unreasonable idea."[42] It is a reasonable idea that is unreasonable if one considers the way that societies are actually structured. *Nanay* creates public spaces that not only authorize but perform the rights to and capacity for speech of those with uncertain or low status. Such a perform-ance, Rancière argues, is "always both argument and opening a world where [such] argument can be received and have impact."[43] It is, in other words, a performative argument, one that posits the possibility of a common world of argumentation.

Outside the Theater

Recent criticisms of Rancière's theory of politics trouble an easy celebra-tion of the political possibilities of *Nanay*. Jodie Dean argues that moments of staging equality have little effect beyond producing a sense of pleasure and satisfaction among those who stage them. This is political visibility, in her view, without the risk of politics.[44] Peter Hallward delivers a similar criticism when he argues that Rancière encourages us to do little more than "play at" politics. "Once the stage is struck, little or nothing remains."[45] And while these are criticisms of Rancière's general theory of politics, they raise serious questions about what can be claimed for sporadic moments of egalitarian discussion, improvisation, and contestation in the space of a theater.

Performance theorist Jill Dolan cautions against measuring the success of theatrical performance by its impact on a world outside the theater. "Let it live where it does its work best," she argues, "at the theater or in moments of consciously constructed performance." "The utopian performative, by its very nature, can't translate into a program for social action, because it is most effective as a *feeling*. . . . Perhaps such intensity of *feeling* is politics enough for utopian performatives." Such politics live in the desire "to feel the potential of elsewhere: the 'not yet' and 'not here.'"[46] As embodied, interactive events that take place in concrete spaces in real time, such per-formances are typically concerned, Tom Burvill argues, not so much "with ideological as with affective transformation in the audiences and consti-tut[e] a performance of ethics in themselves; they [are] forms of ethical practice."[47] Theater can create the occasion to model a different, more vul-nerable, egalitarian way of relating to others. Most of our lives, Berlant points out, occur in "modes of lower case drama, as we follow out pulsations of habituated patterning that make possible getting through the day." Upper-case drama potentially creates a little world for a short period of time—a space-time—to "slow things down and to gather things up, to find things out and to wonder and ponder. 'What is going on.'" On occasion it might even constitute "the event of feeling historical in the present."[48]

We have hopes that the space of the theater and the event of feeling historical can bleed into everyday life; certainly audience members at *Nanay* very quickly made all kinds of productive connections between the play and their own lives outside the theater. They created, to use Rancière's phrasing, "their own poems with the poem that [was] performed in front of them."[49] We found these scribbled on audience surveys:

I have known nannies through my work as a landscaper.
We often communicate with the employer through them.
They never let on for a second what is going on with them . . . their situation.

I really would love to have pre-service teachers come to watch this.
I speak with teachers sometimes
and occasionally there is this idea
that parents who are more involved in school somehow care more.

Thinking back
I realize now how little I truly knew of our nannies' isolation
and aloneness.

Although we did our very best to include them in our family life,
they were so far away from home
in such a different place
I doubt they ever truly felt at home.[50]

It is difficult to trace where these feelings and these connections go once the show is over and the stage is struck. We do know that the fusion and confusion of art, testimonial, research, and activism proliferated audiences and multiplied opportunities for publicity. The play was reviewed in popular media as theater, but more often it created opportunities to publicize and more widely disseminate our research; it spawned, for instance, full-length articles on the Live-In Caregiver Program in two widely distributed community newspapers. It offered opportunities for development and learning among our Filipino community collaborators: in the Vancouver production, there were three paid internships for members of the

Philippine Women Centre of BC and the Filipino-Canadian Youth Alliance, as assistant stage manager and assistant directors. After seeing the play, a local government councilor posted a long review on his blog, noting that migrant domestic workers are "paying the price for our failure to create decent care for our children and seniors."[51] The director received the following e-mail soon after the Vancouver performance: "I loved *Nanay* because it was completely not what I was expecting. . . . I also had a great group with me, which certainly made the talkback more intense. Even afterwards, different advocacy group members were shaking hands and planning meetings with one another, and if that's not live theatre . . ."

Advocacy groups and audience members found connections over the need for national child care and health care for seniors. One PWC member spoke of the play as giving her "a space to try to understand how we can bridge those two groups [domestic workers and employers] while appreciating the distinction between the classes, between races, between genders."[52] A less inspiring but fascinating instance of chance connections occurred only days after the play closed in Vancouver, when the co-producers received an e-mail from a nanny agent located across the country accusing us of slandering their business: this agency's Web site was one of many bookmarked on computers set up in the foyer for audience members to peruse while waiting for the performance to begin. Finally, during the run in Vancouver, Caleb received an e-mail from the Hebbel Theater (HAU1) in Berlin, asking for documentation of the play. Organizing a series of performances on the theme of the family, they found his production company and the play through a Google search engine.

Hebbel Theater brought *Nanay* to Berlin in June 2009, where it was performed as part of the "Your Nanny Hates You" festival on the family. Hebbel is a much grander venue than Chapel Arts, and we staged the play to creep around the interstitial and back spaces of the theater. The tone and meaning of the play were very different in this new context, in large measure because the voluble presence of Filipino domestic workers in the audience was lacking. But something else emerged in their place. From Vancouver, we had contacted RESPECT, a migrant domestic worker network that organizes mostly Latino migrant domestic workers in Berlin. Not only was the representative of the PWC, who traveled with the play to Berlin, able to connect with this network, but RESPECT arranged to come to a number of our performances, which they utterly transformed by filling them with the insistent hum of the whispered translation of English into Spanish. In doing so, they put *Nanay* and our research more fully and differently into the world.

In the World

When we began the translation of our interview material into performance, many of us were unaware that we were a small part of an international trend. As Julie Salverson notes: "Theater that engages people's [actual life] stories is very fashionable these days."[53] Burvill documents a profusion of "performance responses" around the theme of migration and refugees in particular, and in a recent issue of *Research in Drama Education* (June 2008), dedicated to the topic of performance and asylum, no fewer than four of the contributors located in different parts of the world were writing book-length projects on performance and international migration.[54] In Canada, two plays on the Live-In Caregiver Program alone were produced and performed in the span of a year: *Nanay* in Vancouver and *Future Folk* in Toronto.[55] The belief is widespread that documentary or verbatim theater in particular works on audiences in persuasive ways. For instance, in a critical review of *Future Folk* (which is not a documentary play), the theater critic ventured that "a well-researched piece of documentary theatre that put the voices of actual Filipino caregivers on stage might have reached a larger audience and made the battle cry louder."[56]

Linda Ben-Zvi identifies three threads connecting the superabundance of documentary performances at present: a desire to reinstate the voices and stories of those who are unheard; the belief that telling these stories offers a meaningful corrective to mediatized versions of reality; and the recognition of the power of performance.[57] This chapter has been an attempt to understand where the power of these performances might lie. I have located it in the ways that documentary or verbatim theater can instantiate performative epistemologies. The intimacy of witnessing operates in a different epistemological register than facts received from a distance. This form of melancholic realism involves encrypting injury in presence. Ian Baucom argues that such witnesses become attached to the world in its historical singularity, not necessarily to a single wrong or injury, but to the historical and geographical specificity of the world's traumas. At the same time, documentary or verbatim theater keeps alive a persistent questioning of the veracity and representativeness of specific claims to injury so as to arrest the problematic shrinkage of the globe that occurs when another's injury is too easily and too sentimentally absorbed: it works to create a spectator who productively oscillates between proximity and distance, what I have described in chapter 3 as a difficult contract of witnessing. Performing (and not just describing) the inevitable limitations of intercultural translation and creating situations for experiencing the self-alienation necessary for relationship work toward the same effect. Dis-identification, that is, becoming unfamiliar with one's self and existing identifications is as significant as empathy and partial identification with another. And finally, theatrical experiences are opportunities to construct an expanded egalitarian public sphere by *being* places of active and equal participation, for spectators no less than actors, noncitizens no less than citizens and government officials. They are times and places where it is possible to redistribute the sensible. If only for the moment.

Whether these moments become linked to other significant moments is an open question. In the case of *Nanay*, it may have gotten stuck. But, again out of the blue, Caleb recently has been asked for documentation from presenters in Austria; I am in informal conversation with theater artists in the Philippines. We cannot predict where our efforts to generate critical public debate might go, but we do have an obligation to dust off our research and send it into the world.

CHAPTER 5

Acting on Attachments: Intimate Witness to State Violence in the Philippines

THE PHILIPPINE WOMEN CENTRE and I have striven to make visible the lived experience of government programs in Canada and the Philippines that regulate Filipina migrant domestic workers' lives. Many Canadians, including government workers, fail to see the violence of these state policies despite often living close to women (and then their families) who are experiencing it. There are two failures of perception: seeing and feeling the extent of family separation, and then seeing and understanding the implications of this separation for children's lives in Vancouver. This chapter addresses a third site of invisibility that lies outside the borders of the Canadian nation. Witnessing and attaching to the violence associated with the Live-In Caregiver Program (LCP) in the melancholic sense explored in chapter 4 opens a radiating set of obligations to witness, not only within Canada but beyond. This position is supported by recent thinking about the relational nature of space, and the ethics and politics of care and responsibility. "If space is a product of practices, trajectories, interrelationships," Doreen Massey writes, "if we make space through interaction at all levels . . . then those spatial identities such as places, regions, nations . . . must be forged in this relational way too, as internally complex, essentially unboundable."[1] Canadian identity—for Filipino and non-Filipino Canadians alike— is created in relation to and not apart from other places, including the Philippines, and this carries with it an obligation to be curious about and attentive to these other places. Iris Young has located relations of justice in social and economic arrangements: whenever interdependencies generate benefits and burdens that are contingent on existing spatial and institutional relations, those living within this network of institutional relations "stand in relations of justice."[2] The benefits that Canadians enjoy because so many Filipinos come to Canada to care for our children and seniors place Canadians in a relation of justice with the Philippines. Critical theorizations of care ethics similarly locate responsibility in mutual dependence.[3] This would include the dependency of Canadians on the care given by Filipino migrant workers: "to benefit from the caring that others provide or have provided to ourselves and our social partners, and yet to refuse to contribute to the caring scheme, violates the most basic principles of fairness and ultimately erodes the basic preconditions of human existence and social reproduction."[4] There is no reason to contain this "caring scheme" within national borders, especially in the case of migrant workers who live between nations.[5]

This chapter is an invitation to witness events in the Philippines from the vantage point of Canadians who have already accepted this responsibility for mutual care. In November 2006, Filipino Canadian activists from the Kalayaan Centre in Vancouver—a number centrally involved in the research on domestic workers and their families described in this book—took seriously their obligations to the Philippines and assembled a team of Canadians to conduct a fact-finding mission there. The focus of the mission was the state-sanctioned murders since 2001 of many human rights workers and members of the political left in the Philippines. Filipino scholars and activists have made the argument that middle classes and elites living in metropolitan Manila are as inattentive to state violence as are middle-class Canadians, in their case to an even more muscular mode of state violence within their national borders.[6] Introducing the film *Dukot* in Vancouver in 2010, a feature-length film based on stories of real-life disappeared persons, the scriptwriter, Bonifacio Ilagan, spoke of the need to show stories "commonly happening but not commonly told" in the Philippines. Another panelist framed the political violence as "a very silent topic" in the Philippines and beyond.[7] In response to this quiescence among Filipino elites and middle classes, international witnesses have been solicited by human rights activists in the Philippines to place pressure on the Philippine government by making visible internationally these gross human rights abuses.

As a response to this call, the mission from Canada can be viewed as an instance of the Filipino diaspora "striking back" at the government corruption they see as one factor forcing their migration to Canada. Although usually not the sole or even the most immediate cause for migration (poverty and employment incommensurate to education and skills are typically foremost), state violence in the Philippines circulates in many domestic workers' migration stories. In the play *Nanay* (discussed in chapter 4), for instance, Ligaya (Liberty) tells of her reasons for migrating from Manila: "I'm going to work abroad. Because at that time the Philippines is really a corrupt country. And it's not only that. The prices are getting high, and there're strikes everywhere. And there's brownouts. Yeah, and every time there's a brownout in the middle of the night, somebody said that it's some of the soldiers are being—what's this word?—delivered by the military for fighting the insurgents in Mindanao." In the sound room, we hear directly from another mother: "Then I heard about Canada. So I said: 'Oh, it's a safe place for my family. I want to bring my kids to a safer place.' Because our place is in trouble all of the time. Especially Mindanao. I said, 'Oh, Canada is better. Canada is heaven.'"

But the obligation to witness this state violence extends to all Canadians, and the fact-finding mission organized by activists at the Kalayaan Centre has much to teach us about how to exercise these responsibilities to care. The solidarity literature is rife with criticisms of the power dynamics that emerge when those from the North/First World enact their relational identities and responsibilities in the South/Third World.[8] Popke is optimistic that in recent years scholars from the North have made "considerable efforts . . . to develop models of ethics and care that reframe our responsibilities to 'distant strangers' and disrupt the power dynamics of North-to-South humanitarianism."[9] For the Canadian activists on the 2006 fact-finding mission to the Philippines, such efforts to theorize long-distance care rest on a deceptive cartography: they do not understand themselves to be so distant from their allies in the Philippines, and their actions are based in mutual solidarity as much as a framework of care and ethical responsibility. As witnesses to state violence, their situations are more complex than that of outsiders coming to the Philippines with offers of international help. Their analysis embeds the (Canadian) witness in a more geographically extensive set of relationships and thus explodes the opportunities and obligations of ethical witnessing by multiplying Canadian reader's complicities in state violences that are distant from and therefore likely invisible to them. It simultaneously expands Canadians' obligations to domestic workers living in Canada by more fully investigating the Canadian state's role in some of the processes that have driven their migration.

The placement of this chapter within this book is significant; situating a discussion of state terror in the Philippines after and alongside an analysis of Canadian state violence dislodges the evident virtuousness of Canadian observers, which is a necessary foundation for building effective alliances. In Butler's phrasing: "Only with such a critique of state violence [in liberal democratic countries such as Canada] do we stand a chance of finding and acknowledging the already existing alliances and sites of contact, however antagonistic, with other minorities in order to consider systematically how coercion seeks to divide us and keep attention deflected from the critique of violence itself."[10] The argument goes beyond claiming that Canadians and Filipinos committed to popular democracy can find common ground in a shared critique of state violence. Interlacing the forced migration of the Filipino labor diaspora to Canada with violence in the Philippines stakes the claim that the banalities of state violence in Canada are intimately interwoven with state violence elsewhere.

We hold the reader to the obligation to witness—and to the commitment of cosmopolitan interestedness in historical and geographical specificity—by tracing some of the complexity of the experiences of those who went on the Canadian mission to the Philippines. What the Canadians observed cannot be understood without fully appreciating the embodied nature of witnessing. If one of the compelling aspects of the theatrical performance discussed in chapter 4 is that it forces a wide public into an embodied relation with those who testify, the embodied nature of witnessing is even clearer for the Canadian observers to human rights abuses in the Philippines. And the stakes are much greater. In both Central Luzon and Southern Tagalog, the Canadians witnessed a military "terror system" in operation. In part because of the way in which such military terrorism works, what they experienced could not be closely scripted or staged.[11] Borders shifted and sometimes collapsed, destabilizing geographies of both identity and place in ways that complicate more abstracted theorizations of witnessing across differences. The status of the Canadians as outsiders nonetheless kept reappearing in productive ways that kept alive assessments of ethics and politics of international solidarity. Irresolvable through the application of abstracted, universal norms, these ethical dilemmas require judgments situated in the specificity of events.[12] In other words, they return geography to considerations of the ethics and politics of witnessing.

The Canadian mission went to bear witness to human rights violations in the Philippines, and the intent of both the mission and this text is to circulate more widely documentation of military violence. The politics of this doubled act of witnessing and circulation are fraught. Taussig writes of the pleasures of terror talk, of the frisson that (liberal Western) observers might feel as they exchange stories of state terror.

What do we do? Carry out more stories of other people's resistance? Surely not. For while it is crucial that the whole world be

informed of injustice when it occurs, and make that injustice
its concern, surely part of that concern should be with the whole
Western project of self-fashioning through constructing the Third
World as an object of study. . . . Who benefits from studies of the
poor, especially from stories of their resistance? The objects of
study or the CIA?[13]

I describe the efforts of the Canadian human rights activists to extract themselves from "the whole Western project of self-fashioning" by reimagining
the linkages between Canada and the Philippines.[14] But the negotiation
with violence by those who went to the Philippines continues within this
text. I have attempted to follow Taussig's advice of turning scholarly attention away from the poor and powerless to focus on military strategies of
civilian control but, equally, to approach such description so as to mini-
mize the potential for what Bernstein has termed the "pornography of
horror." Descriptions of devastation are pornographic in Bernstein's view
when they are framed "for the sake of the moral satisfaction of the liberal
gaze" and this is especially likely to happen when experience is decontextualized and detemporalized so that abstracted pity is the only response.[15]
I stay very close to the experiences of some of those who went on the fact-
finding mission, to bear witness to the complexities of their experiences
and with the hope of avoiding an aestheticization of the terrors that they
witnessed there.[16]

State Violence in the Philippines and Appeals to the International Community

Among international and domestic human rights organizations, there is
broad-based consensus that the Philippine government under the leadership of President Gloria Macapagal-Arroyo was killing at least some of its
political opposition.[17] Since 2001, more than one thousand unarmed civilians—members of legal leftist political parties and other organizations,
human rights activists, church workers, lawyers, judges, and journalists—
have disappeared or been killed,[18] evidence of what Sarah Raymundo describes as "a barbaric will to kill the political."[19] The killings extend far
beyond those involved in the ongoing armed struggle between the government, the Communist Party of the Philippines (CPP), and the New
People's Army (NPA), and critics argue that the distinction between armed

combatants and unarmed civilians, between legal and illegal struggles, has become blurred.[20]

In its efforts to address the issue, the Philippine government has alternately spurned and wooed the international community. When Amnesty International ventured its conclusion that the killings "constitute a pattern of politically targeted extrajudicial executions" for which the Arroyo government has demonstrated "an implicit policy of toleration," the Philippine government rejected the report for what it called "blanket accusations."[21] Just months later, in January 2007, President Macapagal-Arroyo announced that she would invite the European Union, as well as Spain, Sweden, and Finland, to send teams to help investigate the extrajudicial killings.[22] In actual fact, Arroyo was slow to sanction independent international investigations and it was only in February 2007—after several attempts to get Arroyo's permission[23]—that Philip Alston, United Nations Special Rapporteur on extrajudicial killings, was allowed to conduct a ten-day investigation.[24] When Alston's investigation led him to conclude that "there is absolutely no evidence that the recent surge in killings of leftist activists is due to a communist purge [as the military has claimed]. . . . On the contrary, strong and consistent evidence leads to the conclusion that a significant number of these killings are due to the actions of the military," Defense Secretary Hermogenes Ebdane offered the opinion that Alston was "blind, mute, and deaf. We can't do anything about that."[25]

Critics of the Arroyo government welcomed the intervention of international witnesses. In response to Arroyo's invitation to European governments, one journalist ventured that "much of the optimism rests on Filipinos' views of Europeans as being serious about the protection of human rights and as having been, more than most members of the international community, vocal in their outrage and in their demands for the violence to stop."[26] With respect to Alston's visit, Dr. Rogue, a professor of international and constitutional law at the University of the Philippines, stressed that "the U.N. human rights mechanisms must be put into full use to shame the Philippines."[27]

While attention to European values and the practical and moral persuasion of shame are important factors to consider, they also reactivate some familiar, persistent, and problematic imaginative geographies. The Philippines has been represented for over a century, by U.S. state officials and academics alike, as a place of chaos, disorder, and corruption, needy of assistance from outside its national borders.[28] As Campbell notes, such

representation is performative; it does not simply reflect existing geopolitics but "is itself geopolitical, both manifesting and enabling power relations."[29] In other words, positioning Europeans (or Canadians) as saviors
of the political left in the Philippines reactivates at another scale concerns
about the politics of victimhood elaborated in chapter 3; it is a way of
thinking that also legitimates the LCP.[30]

It is therefore important to recognize the existence of extensive human
rights work within the Philippines and that international missions to the
Philippines are in large part a response to a call from within the country
itself. Along with the capacity to circulate stories widely to generate international pressure on the Philippine government, KARAPATAN (Alliance
for the Advancement of People's Rights), a broadly-based human rights
organization in the Philippines,[31] offers another pressing reason for solidarity and assistance from international human rights observers: Filipino
human rights observers are themselves being targeted for elimination. Eight
members of a fact-finding mission investigating the murder of Racqel
Aumentado in Malanay, Quezon, were, for instance, abducted in 2006.[32]
Beatriz Perido, a representative of KARAPATAN in Central Luzon, speaks
of the difficulty of mobilizing observers for fact-finding missions because
so many activists have been killed or gone into hiding: "Before, we could
mobilize more than 50 people to conduct fact finding. Now in this area
there are only four leaders available to do it."[33] The killing of human rights
workers, writes Neferti Tadiar, "should not only be considered an attempt
to cover up evidence of political killings, although it is certainly that. It
should also be viewed as an attempt to destroy any political possibility of
representing the people ... [and the potential for] different forms of [more
democratic] political community."[34]

It was in response to KARAPATAN's call for people-to-people solidarity in April 2006 through its International Solidarity to Stop the Killings in
the Philippines campaign that nine Canadian human rights activists entered
the Philippines in November 2006 on a grassroots fact-finding mission.[35]
The Canadian human rights activists broke into teams that accompanied
KARAPATAN activists to four different areas: Central Manila, the Western Cordillera region, Central Luzon, and Southern Tagalog. The choice
of regions is significant: Southern Tagalog has the second largest number
of recorded deaths since 2001 (168 between January 21, 2001 and March
31, 2009), followed by Central Luzon (139 during the same period);[36] and
since 2004, KARAPATAN had not been able to access the barrio in San

Narciso that was the destination of the Southern Tagalog team and the reputed site of many human rights offenses. It is the missions to the latter two areas that are reported on here (Figure 26).[37]

Entangled Geographies of Solidarity

When she returned from the fact-finding mission to Central Luzon, Merryn Edwards wrote the following:

> This morning I arrived in Vancouver at 2:00 A.M. yesterday in
>   Manila.
> I take a hot bath and try to find my bearings, take deep breaths.
>
> Each breath is a wave, advancing, receding, marking the shore by
> pushing and dragging it. I have just crossed the Pacific, carrying
>   faces
> and stories home with me.
>
> I try to unpack them from where they have lodged in my back, hips,
> calves. In the wince that keeps my left eye squinted against the
>   woman
> who is still telling me about how the military came at dawn. Came in
> uniform and with long arms. Came to burn her house and beat to
>   death
> her husband in front of her and their children and grandchildren.
>
> They must have screamed long after the last shot, casually fired
>   through
> her husband's skull by one who had already turned to leave, pivoting
> as if his gun were a cane or an umbrella that rested there.
>
> She estimates that he was dead already because he was bleeding
>   from
> his eyes. "It's not normal to bleed from the eyes," she says. With the
> coming of the 71st Infantry Batallion, her *barangay* has had occasion
> to study a scale of pain and blood that now needs to be
>   recalibrated to
> account for Mario's bleeding eyes.

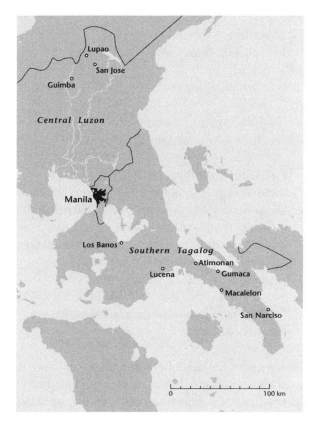

Figure 26. The key sites visited by the fact-finding missions in Central Luzon and Southern Tagalog. Map prepared by Eric Leinberger.

She reenacts the murder for the camera I hold in front of me, but she is looking at my face. I try to arrange my expression to show her I am understanding what she is telling me through a translator.

Sometimes
she moves ahead of me to show how "they dragged him here," "he fell like this," "they lit the fire here." Sometimes when she is not looking at me, I catch the eyes of her grandchildren—two girls,
aged
three and five. I try to smile reassuringly before turning back,
quickly
rearranging my face to try to say, "I'm listening," "I see your fear,
your
pain," "And then what happened?"

She is moving fast, having already told her story once before
consenting to have me and the camera join. During the first telling,
I was sitting across the road, eating lunch with some *kasama*
    on our
team and laughing about the new Tagalog words they are teaching
    me.
Sampaloc, an unripe tamarind that makes my mouth pucker. I suck in
my cheeks and squint my eyes to augment the joke.

I wonder—have they come for her again already? To ask who were
those "nice people," the ones who came with the *Kana* with the video
camera? She told us she was ready to face them. To answer the same
questions they have been asking since before they killed Mario and
kept asking after they killed Mario. It's not information they want,
    but
terror, and that they have already.

I can see her arrange her expression to face the men with guns. She
takes a deep breath.

Merryn Edwards describes an intimacy and complexity of geographical
entanglement that is not adequately captured by the ethical framing of
"normative interventions" as "caring from a distance."[38] Images and stories
are lodged in her bones. The muscles of her left eye hold the squint that
comes from videoing a woman's testimony to her husband's death, their
bodies imaginatively synchronized through deep breaths. She is caught
between reassuring young children and communicating her attention to
Mario's wife's story. At the same time, she recognizes her privilege of distance, her capacity to eat, play, and joke a short distance from this woman's
trauma. She imagines that the military will return after she has flown home
to live her life in Vancouver—one day behind—and speculates that her visit
will be the focus of a further round of intimidation. Rather than caring from
a distance, the geographies that she describes are far more intertwined, and
emotionally and politically messy, suggesting the need to approach witnessing from lived experience and not just abstracted ethical principles (and,
equally, abstracted critiques of liberal humanitarianism) devised in relation
to static, stable geographies of North/South, West/East, First World/Third
World, here/there. We turn to describe some of these complexities.

Struggling to find a place from which to participate in public debate in Argentina, U.S.-based scholar Diana Taylor notes that national identity "is not the only basis for identification and mutual recognition—as the abductions and disappearances of Argentineans by Argentineans make clear."[39] The same obvious but important point can be made of the Philippines. Points of identification and recognition differed for those who went on the mission: more than half were non-Filipino Canadians with links to unions, working-class grassroots organizations, and First Nations struggles, who made connections through other points of identification, most often class politics and their activism in Canada. For Jennifer Efting, this involved singing "The Internationale":

> In between the checkpoints, the [peasants accompanying their mission to Southern Tagalog] would sing revolutionary songs, and then whenever we would get to the checkpoint they would start singing church songs. At one point one of them said, "Do you know how to sing the Internationale?" And I said, "Oh, yeah." So I started singing it. And the look on the peasants' faces was like, "Oh, my god." I don't think that they knew that white people know that song. And they knew it in Tagalog. . . . So that was one way of trying to make that link.

Merryn recounted being asked to position herself in terms of class:

> One woman who I got to know pretty well, she just straight out asked me early on, "So what's your background? Are you rich? Poor? Where are you coming from?" Because she wanted to know why I had come there, what I was doing there. I think if I had said, "Oh wow, everything's so great in Canada and I'm so concerned about the Filipino people," she would have said, "Okay, whatever, but I'm going to work with you anyway and get out of this situation whatever I can." But the fact that we could then have a political conversation [was important]. We talked a lot about First Nations issues here in Canada that she wasn't aware of.

But, as Robinson has argued, against extreme claims about the effects of globalization on identification, for most people national identity remains a strong component of political and social identification: we remain "nationalized." The question, then, is how national identifications are negotiated rather than how they are sidestepped altogether. For the Filipino Canadians involved, their identification as Canadian was interwoven with Philippine nationalism. San Juan has described Filipino Americans as a "bifurcated formation," partially based in a more-than-century-long struggle for national liberation and popular democracy in the Philippines and partially articulated around a history of exploitation and racism in the United States: "These two distinct but syncopated histories, while geographically separate, flow into each other and converge into a single multilayered narrative that needs to be articulated around the principles of national sovereignty, social justice, and equality."[40] In his view, this narrative has not been fully grasped in the scholarly literature: mainstream sociologists distort it through "assimilationist dogma," and a poststructuralist emphasis on hybridity, ambivalence, transmigration, and transnationalism conceals the very specific history of "imperial oppression and the imperative of revolution" that produces a distinctive "dissident sensibility" among Filipino American intellectuals.[41] San Juan's claims for Filipino Americans could be made for Filipino Canadians:[42] among Filipino Canadian activists in Vancouver, campaigns for rights in Canada, including campaigns against the Live-In Caregiver Program, have always gone hand in hand with campaigns for popular democracy in the Philippines, and the Filipino Canadians who went on the fact-finding mission have long histories within this bifurcated formation, including leadership in Filipino Canadian campaigns against the Marcos regime in the 1980s.[43]

But San Juan's distinction between syncopated histories and separate geographies needs to be scrutinized; the borders of nation-states are not so fixed and their geographies also flow into one another. Filipino Canadians associated with the Kalayaan Centre in Vancouver hold the two territories together in their analysis of their lives in Canada.[44] They understand their migration as forced migration: they are in Canada because of the political corruption and economic desperation in the Philippines (itself an outcome of a long history of colonial occupation,[45] and the contemporary discipline of the International Monetary Fund, the World Bank, and other lending agencies); and their experiences of racism and economic exploitation in Canada are intrinsically tied to the circumstances of this forced migration. In effect, the Philippine government furnishes migrants with elements of this same analysis, albeit framed in a more positive way. From 1974, with the institutionalization of the Labor Export Policy, the Philippine government has explicitly linked overseas labor to its nation-building project; as discussed in chapter 1, a succession of presidents has referred to overseas contract workers as the new heroes of the nation. In San Juan's estimation, this "warm body export" is a "scandal of historic proportion ... [that] dwarf[s] the [contemporary] massive human rights violations." He finds some promise in this labor diaspora. Writing while President Arroyo was still in power: "These 'New Heroes' (*mga bagong bayani* to Cory Aquino) are now clamoring for Arroyo's ouster, despite her humorless projection of Filipino 'super-maids' as the solution to the misery and poverty of the vast majority."[46]

The bifurcated formation of Filipino organizations associated with the Kalayaan Centre in Vancouver has not stayed put within the Filipino community; in Merryn's words, it has also altered and "enriched the political landscape of Vancouver." As a non-Filipino Canadian, her identifications with struggles in the Philippines did not evolve simply through other categories of identity such as class or an ethical commitment to help others, but rather from a dense history of engagement with Filipino activists in Canada and visiting activists from the Philippines. She spoke of the ways that these organizations

> have conducted education and mobilization that is really phenomenal. . . . I mean the commitment and patience to not only work so hard for the rights and the welfare of the Filipino community, but to be so generous in their knowledge and experience with other organizations that are willing to learn. . . . Much of my anti-imperialist analysis has been informed by the struggles of the Filipino people. . . . When I first got involved with Grassroots Women,[47] the scale and the scope of the things being discussed sometimes just felt sort of overwhelming. You know, "Give me something winnable and tangible to work on." But as I got more involved, I saw that you have no choice but to take all of these things into consideration. You have to understand the big picture, as well as the smaller manifestations, . . . [which means that you] see how the same forces at work in the Philippines are at work in different ways in Canada.

Merryn's analysis has been sedimented through six years of joint activity and a history of exchange between Canadian and Filipino activists at international conferences. (The personal relationships between Filipino Canadian and Filipino activists have existed for much longer, examples of the type of long-term, face-to-face interactions that Lawson identifies as critical for building deep connections that transform a commitment to abstract principles of rights or justice into a more active politics of social attachment and responsibility.)[48] Merryn is describing how her associations with Filipino activists have shaped the "political landscape" of Vancouver, testimony to Doreen Massey's generalized argument that "each local struggle is already a relational achievement, drawing from both within and beyond 'the local.'"[49] Such solidarities, Featherstone notes, "need to be seen as generative, as actively shaping political identities, rather than merely bringing together different movements around 'common interests.'"[50] Witnessing the vitality of the movement in the Philippines through direct interactions with Filipino activists living in or visiting Vancouver generated an intense desire among the non-Filipino Canadians to go to the Philippines, not as experts but in order to learn from the movement there, thus inverting Western presumptions about where expertise is located and establishing relations of symmetry or mutual benefit.[51] In Jennifer Efting's words, "We don't have a movement here. We have organizations."

Merryn's understanding, shared by others on the mission, that "we're fighting the same battles but from different locations in different conditions," disrupts any fixed notion of where problems and solutions reside and draws lines of connection between her work in Vancouver and the work of activists in the Philippines.[52] This sounds remarkably similar to Cindi Katz's call for counter-topographies that draw the lines of connection across struggles in different places.[53]

Finally, Canadian human rights activists found a place for themselves as witnesses to human rights abuses in the Philippines not only because of Canada's dependency and exploitation of domestic workers coming to Canada through the LCP, but through their analysis of Canada's direct complicities with the military violence in the Philippines. Their mission involved the task not just of bearing witness to human rights violations committed by the Philippines military and paramilitary but of assessing the extent to which Canadian aid to the Philippines inadvertently supports militarization, and whether and how the substantial Canadian mining interests in the Philippines operate within the rubric of "militarized commerce" by benefiting from the current militarization, especially intense in areas of resource extraction.[54] For instance, the Canadian mining company TVI Pacific has employed paramilitary groups (special Civilian Armed Forces Geographical Units [CAFGU] and Armed Auxiliaries, or SCAAs) at its Canatuan Gold Project in Mindanao, and there have been allegations of human rights abuses, such as rape, and the maintenance of checkpoints and blockades to essential commodities and services by the company's security guards and other armed units.[55] As Doel notes, "The world can be (un)folded in countless ways." By charting Canadian culpability for human rights abuses in the Philippines, activists are folding the space of Canadian activity onto the Philippines and unraveling borders that insulate Canadians from their responsibilities there.[56] With this analysis it could be said that they were acting out what Massey (*For Space*) has theorized as a relational nature of space.

Paradoxically, if intimate, entangled geographies linking Canada and the Philippines were essential to how the solidarity mission imagined itself, the notion of international accompaniment and witnessing builds from the understanding (or hope) that states—officially and pragmatically—work with a more stable and conventional cartographic sensibility. Beyond the expectation that international groups will be able to increase international media exposure, as well as widely publicizing their experiences within their political communities at home, accompaniment by international observers plays on the recognition that some lives are more "grievable" than others. The deaths of international human rights observers will likely receive widespread international media attention and cause a furor within international political communities. For both of these reasons, it is anticipated that international observers will have some protection against state violence. Given the popular understanding that the Philippines is a functioning democracy, there is also hope that international observers will be able to call up the privileges of "hospitality" and travel relatively freely within the borders of the Philippine nation, thereby enabling access to militarized zones that are otherwise inaccessible to domestic human rights activists.

Those who went on the fact-finding mission already had some inkling that the Philippine state might work with a more mobile mapping of nation, territory, citizenship, and rights. They knew, for instance, of a history of intimidation of international-solidarity activists by the Philippine state, which has extended well beyond the territorial borders of the Philippines. Choy writes of U.S. antimartial law activists' fears in the 1970s and 1980s that the U.S. government would heed the Philippine government's accusation that they were communists—and deport them.[57] The murders of Silme Domingo and Gene Viernes in Seattle in May 1981 are even starker reminders of the risks of international solidarity, and these deaths and risks continue to haunt the present. (They were mentioned by two of the three Filipino Canadian observers in the 2006 Canadian fact-finding mission who were interviewed.) As union officials of Local 37 of the International Longshore and Warehouse Union (ILWU) in Seattle, as well as members of the Union of Democratic Filipinos, Domingo and Viernes facilitated the passage in 1981 of an ILWU resolution to send a delegation to the Philippines to investigate the conditions that workers faced under the Marcos regime. They were murdered less than a month after the resolution was passed, and the investigating team was never sent; four Filipino Americans, including the president of Local 37, were found guilty of their murders.[58] But significantly, the Philippine government was also implicated: in a civil suit filed in a U.S. federal court, Ferdinand and Imelda Marcos were also found liable for their murders, and they were ordered to pay $15 million to the families of Domingo and Viernes.[59] Along with remembering this history, the Canadian observers have their own personal histories that testify to the leakiness of national borders and the migration of national struggles beyond fixed borders. Teodoro (Ted) Alcuitas, for instance, one of the Canadian observers who went to Central Luzon, was a leader in the August 21 Movement, an anti-Marcos campaign in Winnipeg in the early 1980s. He credits the radicalism of his daughter, Luningning Alcuitas-Imperial, one of the two lawyers who went on the fact-finding mission, to death threats that he received at the time: "In fact, that's why Ningning probably became an activist. Because she was the one who picked up the phone. Someone was asking for me: 'Where is your father? We are going to kill him.' And before they were leaving messages on the machine."

But rather than the reach of the Philippine state beyond its borders, what the Canadian observers experienced on this mission was the disordering of anticipated borders and expected advantages attending their Canadian citizenship rights *within* the Philippines, and the ways that terror systems reorder geographies for all who come into contact with them. The "theatricality" of state terror refers to more than the fact that terror is staged. Terror tactics redefine reality: what is real and unreal, visible and invisible.[60] Writing about the "dirty war" in Argentina, Taylor marks the radical undifferentiation of terror systems: "Anyone associated with or sympathetic to this expanding and amorphous group of subversives might well become the next victim" (150). As international witnesses, the Canadian observers struggled against this process of undifferentiation that marks the grounded techniques of terror. As witnesses, they were fully present and implicated in the processes they observed.[61] "Why," Taylor asks, "is the witness generally depicted as either passive and disinterested or holy and superhuman?" Witnessing is active and embodied, and borders can suddenly shift so that the witness is no longer looking from the outside but rather "inhabits the expanded border zone of the inner."[62]

I turn to describe some of what observers in (two of) the Canadian missions witnessed. In Central Luzon, they witnessed community terror, directly and through their presence there. In Southern Tagalog, the border between citizen and noncitizen was challenged by the military, and the witnessing of terror moved from a third- to first-person account. But in both cases their international status and capacity to leave continued to raise ethical issues that are—in principle—productively irresolvable: they must be worked out specifically, in place, and in solidarity with and through extended conversations with KARAPATAN. For each of the two sites, I consider the unstable geographies and contradictions of international witnessing.

Witnessing Community Terror in Central Luzon

Alston [the United Nations Special Rapporteur on extrajudicial killings] has a good reputation but with all those intelligence agents, people thought it [testifying to Alston] was like volunteering for their own funeral.

—Marie Enriquez, Secretary General KARAPATAN, reported in
Espina-Varonain "Kin, Colleagues Brave Risk to Join in
U.N. Probe into Killings"

Dead people cannot speak.

—Army Major General Jovito Palparan, reported in Manzanilla
"Terror Talks"

When the Canadian fact-finding mission arrived in Central Luzon, it was just two months since General Palparan had retired from his command of military operations in this area. They stayed three nights in Guimba, all thirty-seven members of the mission billeted in the parish hall of a Catholic church, making excursions in a two-jeepney convoy into the surrounding countryside to collect testimony during the day. Some of the thirty-five Filipinos accompanying the Canadian mission were themselves displaced families; others were KARAPATAN organizers from Central Luzon who had the necessary information and contacts to arrange interviews with witnesses as well as the skills to document testimony. But if dead people cannot speak, many witnesses to these deaths in Central Luzon were also reluctant to come forward.[63] As much as collecting testimony, the Canadian observers witnessed the assertion of military over civilian authority through the cultivation of fear, which has led to ineffectual investigations and the "climate of impunity" criticized by Amnesty International (among others). Few people were willing to volunteer for their own funerals.

In some instances, the military actively kept the mission from witnesses. Ted describes going to a village with a well-respected priest to interview a village official:

> [The priest] said that he had already talked to this barrio captain [who arranged] to meet us at a certain time. We traveled to this village, probably an hour or two. When we arrived, the barrio captain said that he would not be able to talk to us. He declined because he had some other commitment. But he would have another barrio official talk to us. So we went there. . . . The guy was sitting outside on a bamboo bench. He would respond but not answer our questions. "We heard there was somebody [killed]." "Oh, no, I don't know about that." "We heard that there were houses that were torched." "I don't know about it." We saw it was useless. And we noticed just beside us some people playing pool. I wondered why they were not curious about us at all. Despite the fact that Merryn had a video camera, they were detached. Later we were told they were military and that they had already instructed the villagers not to talk to us. When we traveled out from the village, there were blackboards attached to trees by the side of the highway saying, "Communists go back home." We saw the person who hurriedly put them up.

A significant amount of time during the four days of the fact-finding mission was dedicated to documenting the death of Mario Florendo.[64] It was the testimony of Mario's wife that Merryn carried home in her back, hips, calves, and wincing left eye. But it was a long process for Canadian investigators to gain Mario's wife's consent to witness her testimony, a process that is itself testimony to a community-wide culture of fear of military reprisal.

It was another relative of Mario who first agreed to be interviewed on the condition that they met in the town of San Jose, about twenty kilometers from Lupao.[65] "She tried to get [Mario's wife] to come, but she didn't want to come."[66] They met her in front of the cathedral plaza, and three or four of their team interviewed her inside a jeepney, while the rest of their team "milled about":

> The [woman] was crying and it wasn't easy to draw out her testimony. She told us that Mario was called by the military to clear his name [of being an NPA supporter], and he was tortured there. He was released, but [several days later] the military, two men, came to his house. They dragged Mario out to the street, clubbed him with a four-by-four, and shot him in the head. She was crying. What hurt her so much, she told us, was that when they went to bury [Mario], the people in the town would not even come out. When you bury the dead in the Philippines, it is common for a one-week wake. But people were so scared. They only came out when the hearse was in the street, because they were so scared. He was buried in another town.[67]

A KARAPATAN organizer terminated the interview when they realized that they had been detected by the military. "We left and two men on motorcycles followed us. [The woman interviewed] was very nervous, like her voice was really showing anxiety." They dropped her on a street corner after they were certain that they had lost the men on motorcycles, and she made her way home on her own: "We don't even know what happened to her." They could not interview her further because she went into hiding.

A day or so later, one of the local activists traveling with them, a United Church minister named Pastor Beatriz Perido, who has herself gone "underground" because she is on the Order of Battle [a military list of "enemies of the state"], was able to reach by cell phone the neighbor living across the road from Mario's house. The neighbor's son—Mario's friend—had hung himself two days after cleaning Mario's brutalized body in preparation for burial; his eighty-year-old mother had agreed to be interviewed about her son's death. Half an hour into the interview, a woman and man rushed in: "Who are you? Why are you talking to my mother? Why have you come here? How come you're taking pictures? And tape recording?"

They were brother and sister-in-law of the man who had hung himself, retrieved from their farm by their young son:

> The son rushed on his bike to tell, "Mom, mamma, there's some people in our house. Gramma's talking to them." They didn't know who we were. So she thought it was the military. So she was scared. In fact, she told her husband, "Stay at the farm. In case they kill me. At least one of us will be alive."
> In the past, her husband also had been called by the military to clear his name. But she said, "What's to clear? My husband is not involved in anything." So they had run away from the province, from the village, and went to Manila to escape.[68] She said they spent 40,000 pesos to rent a house in Manila and for food. Meanwhile their farm was unattended. . . . They ran out of money. That's why they had just come back. And so she was crying, "It's all lost, spent, our savings, and we have to come back to face this again, the possibility of my husband being killed."

The daughter-in-law corrected the old woman's story, in which she had linked her son's suicide to the trauma of Mario's murder: "Don't believe my mother-in-law. My brother-in-law was crazy already." The daughter-in-law refused to be identified by name: "What will happen when you leave? When you leave today, what will happen to us? You're not here anymore." As those on the fact-finding mission later ate their lunch on the road outside this woman's house, a KARAPATAN leader knocked on the door of Mario's house, to ask his wife—once again—whether she would speak with them. "Reluctantly, she agreed."

Fears of testifying, internal displacement caused by fears of being labeled as NPA, the ways that the killings reverberate throughout survivor's lives as psychological trauma—these were all witnessed by the Canadian team of observers in Central Luzon. But it was apparent to the international observers that they were also implicated in, even if tangentially, the production of terror. Merryn described the day of interviewing Mario's wife as "the hardest day," and expressed some of her concerns about being complicit in the production of terror:

> Just the graphicness of the description was . . . At first this man's wife didn't want to . . . She was Catholic and only wanted to meet

with the people on our team who were from church people's organizations. And so she met with them and told her story. And then after talking to them, she agreed for us to come in.[69] So I came, and I had a video camera. And then she basically reenacted the entire night of the murder of her husband . . . And then the woman [across the road] who was really nervous about talking to us. I just kind of felt at the time that I didn't know what to say to her. I was so worried that we were endangering people even more. And that's where the people from KARAPATAN were so great. To be able to remind me that we're not the problem here. We're not endangering the people. It's the military that's doing that. We're here to talk to them if they'll talk to us. And it's part of all of us asserting our right to expose these violations. And if we continue to be fearful, there's not going to be any way to fight it.[70]

Given the widespread campaign of terror in the village, it was clear that not speaking out against violations is no guarantee of safety. And yet Merryn is well aware that the stakes of asserting that right are quite different for her than for the sister-in-law of Mario's friend.

On their last evening in Guimba, when they were thanking the priest who housed them there, he said, "Just a minute," went back to his room and returned with his wallet. He produced a 38-caliber bullet and an accompanying note. "These were put in my collection box just yesterday. A warning and a question: 'Why are you housing these people?'" Ted asked him, "Father, are you not scared to be housing us here?" The priest joked, and replied, "I'm still not on the Order of Battle." In our interview, I asked Ted whether one would know if one was on this list. "That's just it. You wouldn't know. That was his joke."

The Theatrics of Intimidation in Southern Tagalog: Witnessing in the First Person

The day began well enough. The vice governor of Southern Tagalog in Lucena offered his assistance: "Any type of support you need, just call me up"; it was not until Gumaca that they saw any military checkpoints. But these checkpoints were unmanned, the barricades left lying at the side of the road: "So everybody is like, 'Ooooo,' and would give a little cheer. 'We've passed another one! We've passed another one!'"[71] The mission—

three Canadians accompanied by more than thirty KARAPATAN activists, as well as a dentist, nurse, and doctor—reached their destination of San Narciso, Quezon, by four in the afternoon, an hour before it would be dark. Following their established protocol, they attempted to visit the most senior civil authority to inform them of their presence and the purpose of the Canadian mission before proceeding to the billeted accommodation arranged by KARAPATAN. Neither the mayor nor vice mayor could be found, so they visited the chief of police. At this moment the landscape of checkpoints and military presence was reanimated, and claims to Canadian identities and rights to hospitality began to slip:

> We talked to him, trying to explain the purpose of the fact-finding mission, that we were being hosted by KARAPATAN and there's already people waiting for us, everything has been arranged. But you could already sense that the guy was nervous, and he wasn't as diplomatic as [the vice governor]. He knew these people from the local KARAPATAN group had been trying to get into the area before. He kept asking, "Why are you with them [KARAPATAN]? I thought you said this was Canadian." And then he kept going in and out of his office, and we're wondering: "What's going on?"

It became apparent that he was in conversation with the military and the lieutenant in charge of military operations soon arrived. The lieutenant prohibited their entry, on the grounds that there was a military operation in the area and he could not ensure their safety. The harassment then started, which simultaneously questioned their rights to their status as foreigners and ridiculed their naïveté as strangers:

> "Who are you?" "Show us your ID." Because Ning and I are Filipinas, they kept asking us if we're really Canadian." Are you Canadian?" I said, "We just showed you our passports. We are Canadian. What are you talking about?" And Ning and I had already agreed that we're not going to speak to them in Tagalog. . . . They started photographing and videotaping all of us. They said, "Maybe you don't know who these people are, what KARAPATAN is. They're NPA [New People's Army]. You're just being led down the garden path by these people. You should really listen to our side as the military."

Ning, a Canadian lawyer assigned the task of negotiating for the team, was put on the phone with a more senior military officer, a colonel overseeing military operations in the region, who confirmed that the entire *barangay* (village) of 38,000 civilians was under a military operation. He threatened them with arrest: "If you proceed, we are going to charge you. We'll charge you with obstruction of justice." His threats to Ning grew more personal and her objectivity as a Canadian thrown into doubt: "We know who you are. We know you're with the [NPA]." She reasoned that she was vulnerable to this "red-baiting" "because I am a Filipina, and he was talking to me in Tagalog." Doris [Cuario, secretary general of KARAPATAN–Southern Tagalog] contacted a lawyer in Manila, who said, "Of course the charges would be baseless, but there is nothing you can do."

Three hours had passed, negotiations had broken down, and the military and police appeared to be growing angrier; the six negotiators (three Canadians and three KARAPATAN) returned to the others in their party who had been waiting in the dark inside their two jeepneys. They became frightened when roughly thirty armed military—some with faces hidden by balaclavas—formed a line around their jeepneys:

> Doris was really getting angry. She was mad that we were experi-
> encing this harassment. Because [KARAPATAN] had thought
> that they would be more respectful of a Canadian mission. She
> started to yell at them, "Why don't you just let us go? We have
> to sleep. Everyone is hungry. What are you going to do? What are
> you going to do? Are you going to shoot us all?" She started to say
> in Tagalog, "Just kill us all now."

Gathered together in the jeepneys, "all these people yelling," the space was both compressed and expansive. Ning used her cell phone to call the Canadian embassy, but the office in Manila was closed. The number to which she was referred connected her to "somebody in Ottawa, but she was French speaking. She couldn't quite understand what I was saying. I was telling her, "No, we need somebody right now. This is what is happening to us now. You can hear it. Can't you hear it? We need assistance at this moment because we're afraid that we're going to be physically hurt, or killed." They called the vice governor, with whom they had spoken earlier in the day; it was he who arranged for a local town councilor to retrieve them and take them all to his home for the night.

The next morning they started out once again. But they were soon stopped by the lieutenant they had met the previous evening; again he denied them entry into the area without a permit from the vice mayor. It was not until 3:00 in the afternoon that the vice mayor denied their entry, and the fact-finding mission in San Narciso was abandoned. The Canadian embassy advised the mission to leave the area immediately to return to Manila. Too late in the day to travel safely, they returned to the local councilor's house to ask for his help for another night: "But by this time, he is very, very terrified. When we left earlier in the day, the military had intimidated him and his wife. He was still nice but very nervous. [He agreed, but] you could feel the change. So the next morning, there's no more food, they didn't offer us breakfast. But we understood because you could see the military hovering around the compound."

The mission left at 7:00 A.M., but their presence was now well known, and the military had reactivated the checkpoints. After just thirty minutes of traveling, they were stopped at a checkpoint adjacent to a large military camp. One member of KARAPATAN was detained within the camp for three hours, and a peasant rally was organized for the benefit of the others:

> Eventually a big open truck came with people standing on the flat bed. They had placards written in English: "Doris Cuario, why are you lying to the Canadians?" And the military had set up a sound system. They were calling out individuals, telling us who is bad inside the jeep. And then they started saying, "Who's the [Canadian] lawyer here? We don't even believe she's a lawyer."

The Canadians' assessment is that the intervention of the Canadian embassy was necessary for the relatively speedy release of the peasant organizer detained within the camp: "It was the phone call [from the Canadian embassy] that got him released. Because [the peasant organizer] noticed the change right away in the colonel's demeanor." They also felt that it facilitated their passage through the checkpoint.[72]

They were subjected to six further checkpoints, manned by a variety of military and paramilitary units for which the lines of authority and accountability to the Canadian embassy seemed less certain. In this, they encountered the "Philippine model" of counterinsurgency warfare: a heavy reliance on, especially in rural areas, civilian and paramilitary security personnel.[73] Just fifteen minutes from the military camp, they were stopped by three

Scout Rangers,[74] elite counterinsurgency officers: "This checkpoint was the most scary because it was really remote, like there was nothing around. They're not uniformed [like at the previous checkpoint]. No nameplate or anything." Another checkpoint was manned by CAFGU: "In Marcos's time, they were the death squads. . . . They are not uniformed and you lose the chain of command."

There was one last checkpoint after Gumaca. By this time KARAPATAN had obtained the assistance of a labor lawyer, who drove more than two hours to join them there to assist in their safe passage. It was 7:00 or 8:00 at night, and they were stopped by the military stationed near the city hall in Atimonan:

> More than thirty military men. They're hooded. Nobody would talk to us. They were deliberately covering their nameplates. It was more chaotic and scarier than having at least the facade of negotiating. Someone spiked our jeep. [This was the second time that this happened.] And you could see the military were in some of the houses already, on the second floor. So KARAPATAN brought out a megaphone and Doris explained to the onlookers: "This is who we are. This is what we're doing. This is what happened to us, how many hours we have been detained." KARAPATAN was also able to call a congressman from the area: "This is what is happening to these Canadians." Everybody knew about [the mission] because it was in the national media. So he came. He had his staff with him, and he said, "Okay, let's try and figure out what's going on. " And even he couldn't get the military to talk to him. "This is unreasonable. I am still the civilian authority here. So you're under the obligation to tell us who you are." But they wouldn't identify who they were and we never found out who the commanding officer was. But I think we were released because the congressman was there and they knew the media had been alerted.

KARAPATAN would resort to a megaphone one more time, the next day as they entered the city of Los Baños in five o'clock rush-hour traffic, followed by two armed men on motorcycles, their faces covered by helmets.[75] "Doris started educating the people that the two motorcycle men are the death squads of Arroyo," with the hope that calling on bystanders as witnesses would act as the "ultimate protection" against being killed.

The Southern Tagalog team was unable to obtain testimony of human rights offenses. In their assessment afterward, KARAPATAN members said, "We didn't anticipate . . . we thought it would be better. We thought we'd be able to get in because of you guys. Because it's an international mission." But the Canadian team to Southern Tagalog witnessed something else: they witnessed military harassment firsthand, and experienced for themselves the terror of confronting a military seemingly beyond civilian authority, acting beyond the law.

That Canadians were subjected to this treatment warranted attention in a way that daily occurrences for Filipino human rights activists do not. The international press, including the *New York Times,* picked up their story of harassment. The very next morning after their long evening in the San Narciso police station at the start of the mission, the (then) Vice President of the Philippines Noli de Castro dedicated his national radio program to the Southern Tagalog mission. And though he disputed the Canadians' right to be in the country because they were not sponsored by or part of the Canadian government, he found them impossible to ignore. During their first evening back in Manila, they met with Senator Jamby Madrigal, who wanted details of their experiences in order to draft a motion in the Senate that there be a government investigation into the treatment of the Canadians. In Jennifer's assessment: "That's the racist nature of the media.[76] It's more interesting if a Canadian or white person goes through something like this than if a Filipino dies. From that perspective, KARAPATAN was pleased from what happened. The mission was pretty successful from a media perspective, in getting the word out about what was happening."

Making Connections

After days of trying to arrange interviews with Mario's wife, the Central Luzon team drove to her barrio to meet with her neighbor. Ted recalled, "Unfortunately, going to the barrio, we had to pass through the military detachment, two jeep loads." But good fortune was with them: all of the military personnel were inside watching the much-anticipated televised World Super Featherweight boxing match between Filipino Manny Pacquiao and Mexican Erik Morales, and they were able to pass by undetected. Moments before, the Southern Tagalog team had been negotiating their release from the first checkpoint in San Narciso: "A Filipino was fighting in Las Vegas and it happened to be that morning. So we were thinking, he let us go at 10:30 because the match was starting at 11:00, and they all wanted to watch."

The pleasures associated with this story are many. There is the surprise of coincidence and simultaneity as experiences in three places interlace in accidental but consequential ways. The story provides a glimpse of slips in the fabric of existing power relations, in this case when one aggressive, nationalist, masculinity performed in the heart of an imperial power inadvertently disrupted another,[77] so as to create a space for eluding the violence of the state and the power of state violence. There is also the incongruity of a televised boxing match in Las Vegas having these effects in two remote areas of the Philippines. The story's pleasures and interest also come from what it suggests about the liveliness and unpredictability of life, and the joyful potential to create a world otherwise, through stealthful collaboration across places around the globe.

The question is: What should be the nature of these connections, collusions, and collaborations? A critical ethics of care, by Robinson's reckoning, is inseparable from politics and social relations and carries with it an obligation to investigate—to make visible—the production of global patterns of inequality, exclusion, and domination and, in particular, the role that powerful states in the global North play in producing these relations.[78] As beneficiaries of the care of so many Filipinas—in our homes, hospitals, retirement homes, and hotels, to name just a few common workplaces—Canadians have an ethical obligation to understand how they are enmeshed in interdependencies that span the globe, to pay close attention to what is happening in the Philippines, and to investigate their own and the Canadian state's relationship to the structural conditions that force migration, including Canadian militarized commerce and the allocation of Canadian development aid. Certainly military violence in the Philippines is only one site of investigation. (An entire history of colonial domination and development practice needs to be unraveled.) But the Canadian mission to the Philippines provides one means of starting this investigation, and those who went on it are in many ways exemplary guides to the larger project.

The Canadian activists who went to the Philippines on the mission built a model of solidarity as opposed to humanitarian aid through transnational and extranational identifications, linkages between their own activism in Canada and struggles in the Philippines, and by identifying Canadians' direct and indirect responsibility for human rights violations in the Philippines.

Operating within this people-to-people solidarity model, they traveled far beyond Metro Manila and other major cities, where fewer international observers venture. Because of both this and the radical undifferentiating nature of a system of terror that did not allow them to keep their distance, their witnessing was fully embodied, emotionally demanding, and took shape in unanticipated ways. They were caught in a productive contradiction: they could neither fully maintain their distance as outside observers nor ignore the implications of their privilege of distance. The privilege of distance kept reappearing as an ethical and political dilemma. White privilege, Canadian citizenship, and spatial distance were, however, not only problems but also resources. And while it is important to scrutinize the propensity for North/South power relations to creep into well-intentioned international solidarity, it also seems a mistake to harden these distinctions in our own analyses, in the abstract, off the ground, removed from daily life.

Theorizing responsibility to "distant" others, in recent years many theorists have been drawn to Levinas's moral philosophy that locates unconditional responsibility to others as an ontological claim "prior to any significance that might be attached to it by philosophy, culture, politics, or place."[79] But Popke notes the difficulty of moving from the realm of (this particular strand of ethics) to politics. In our view,[80] the urge to locate an unsituated unconditional responsibility prior to dialogue and politics is of questionable value. The Canadian activists who went to the Philippines understand their responsibility to be fully social, firmly rooted in history and politics, and enmeshed in relations of indirect and direct culpability and dependency. This is a materialist, or what Robinson (*Globalizing Care*) identifies as phenomenological, ethics. And rather than relying on presocial ontological claims or abstract principles of rights and responsibilities, the Canadian observers repeatedly turned to dialogues with KARAPATAN to assess the politics of their distance and the justice or injustice of their actions: Merryn was attentive to KARAPATAN's analysis that her (and their) presence are not the source of danger and that silence does nothing to ensure safety from military violence; Jennifer tempered her distaste for the racism that she judges to be at the root of the media attention given to her mission in Southern Tagalog with KARAPATAN's assessment of the significance of this international coverage for their own human rights work.[81]

Their witnessing was embodied, fleshy, lived, emotionally intense; and while their goal is to effect political change both in the Philippines and in

Canada, members of the Canadian mission were also changed through the process of witnessing. They both put their bodies on the line and brought stories back with them in their "backs, hips and calves."[82] Entering into a witnessing relationship involves not only absorbing another person's story, but transforming oneself. Weir argues that making the commitment to bring into visibility the conditions from which women immigrate risks uncomfortable questions such as: Can the wealthy in Canada continue to pass on their care needs to women from poorer countries?[83] Answering in the negative requires a fundamental reordering of how Canadians live and work, and how they imagine and experience themselves as individuals and in relation to others.

Finally, this chapter was written because the women and men who took the risk of witnessing state violence in the Philippines returned to tell their stories, in detail, with passion and political conviction, with the assurance that Canadians and Filipino migrants to Canada needed and wanted to know the details of their experiences. They both assume and inspire listeners, to make connections between violence in the Philippines and the LCP. They both assume and inspire a cosmopolitan interestedness in places that most Canadians have not and most likely never will visit. They both assume and inspire a willingness to listen to their experiences and possibly to reach for a map to trace their journey from, say, San Narciso to Gumaca. Through their storytelling, they pass on the affective intensity of being interested. By recounting their stories in such detail here, we hold ourselves to their witnessing. In Baucom's felicitous phrasing, we "serialize the event" and "elongate its temporality."[84] This is what it is to witness, to attach oneself as an interested historical witness and take the time to learn the details.

Research into Action

THIS BOOK HAS BEEN AN EFFORT TO UNSETTLE COMPLACENCY around temporary labor migration, now commonly framed by policy makers and some academics as a "win-win-win" solution to labor-market shortages in the global North and poverty and debt in the global South. We have argued that a language of migrant choice and freedom obscures processes of forced economic migration and affective tonalities and relations that, quite simply, cannot be assimilated into a matrix of costs and benefits. Although the language of "win-win-win," costs and benefits, and labor migration as a "right" suggests that migrants can be and are brought within the calculations of modern governments in mutually beneficial ways, we have shown that their lives continue to be, through the process of migration, precarious and insecure. The weight of our evidence is that this precariousness haunts the lives of their children in enduring ways.

We have come to this analysis through the lived experiences of domestic workers and their families. The research, a series of collaborative projects conducted over almost two decades, always has been driven by questions and concerns that have arisen within the Filipino Canadian activist community, and the PWC of BC has used it to organize domestic workers and their families and to sharpen their analysis of temporary labor migration. We end by reflecting on the ways that this research not only emerges from within but pushes toward political engagement.

Ethics and Politics

Clearing away a neoliberal discourse of individual choice and calculation only sharpens the ethical impasse created by labor migration. When Linda Bosniak considers what a focus on "alienage," of which temporary labor migration is one instance, brings to an already extensive documentation of social, economic, and political exclusions in liberal-democratic societies, she reasons that it reveals the irresolvable exclusion that lies at the heart of

citizenship. The condition of liberalism is thus inevitably one of ambivalence and ethical conflict: "We liberal national subjects are chronically
divided over the proper location of boundaries—boundaries of responsibility and belonging."[1] As outsiders within a national territory, resident
aliens "pit citizenship against itself" by revealing the exclusions that lie at
the heart of inclusion (in the sense that inclusion always implies a boundary between inside and outside).[2] And in doing so, resident "aliens" force
us to confront the implicit geographies that structure the ethical obligations
of many of us. What Bosniak terms "normative nationalism" and Doreen
Massey terms a "Russian-doll" model of care and responsibility assumes
that ethical obligation is, in the first instance, to fellow nationals.[3] But what
is the basis for this? On what ethical grounds do liberals seemingly devalue
the lives of noncitizens (a process more visible when these noncitizens
reside within their national territory)? How can we justify the practice of
normative nationalism?

   If "alienage" in general troubles liberal values, the treatment of foreign
care workers in particular sharpens the ethical quandary, especially when
these workers must leave their own children to care for more-privileged
children living thousands of miles away from their own. The intimate family holds a tenacious grip on liberal social and psychic life (in ways that
are, as feminists have long argued, also highly problematic).[4] Consider
how Robert Mayer's "liberal egalitarian theory of exploitation" shrivels in
relation to Allison Weir's appeal to the intimate family. For Mayer, the
key question for assessing the ethics of temporary worker programs is
this: with full knowledge of the costs of guest work, would an individual
(under no coercion to migrate because of extreme poverty) still make the
journey? For Weir: "Given the choice, whose children would [a foreign
caregiver] care for?"[5] Appealing to the mother–child relation works in an
entirely different register than individual rational choice, and it renders
absurd both the notion of individual choice completely outside the bounds
of economic coercion and the reduction of the experience of migration to
a rational economic choice. Criticisms of temporary labor programs that
work through appeals to the protection of children also call upon strong
liberal sentiments about the intimate family. Rather than focusing on
migrants' rights, these critics question the morality of excluding their children. This is a maneuver that attaches to a rich vein of ethical thinking
obliging the protection of children.[6] From this perspective, one views the

exclusion associated with migrant work as targeting children rather than, or as well as, migrant workers. Alternatively (or additionally), even without focusing on the families excluded or left behind, the job of care work itself taps into lines of normative argumentation that root ethical obligation and responsibility in mutual vulnerability and interdependency.[7] Intimate care of an other's children or disabled or elderly relations by its very nature draws all those involved into relations of interdependency and mutual obligation. Bounding responsibilities that derive from relations of vulnerability and interdependency, excluding some families from liberal forms of familial intimacy, deeming some children unworthy of protection within our political community—these are all instances of normative nationalism, and they provide ample grounds for ambivalence and dispute.

And this is precisely the point. Ethics is a relational practice that calls forth politics. It is not a personal virtue (as in, "I am an ethical person") or a set of principles that can be applied in the abstract. We have seen, in chapter 1, some of the limits of normative principles in relation to temporary labor migration. Recall that Joseph Carens reasons that temporary work migration programs are acceptable within liberal norms of justice if the period of family separation and impermanency is not too long.[8] But this entirely reasonable principle of time left us empty-handed because, as Carens acknowledges, in the absence of close, specific, empirical investigation, it is unknowable how this principle might work in practice, that is, what length of family separation is too long to withstand liberal principles of universality. We know too little to decide. This study has been an effort to know more in order to sustain a better-informed discussion of family separation and its attendant consequences. It is an effort to make visible what is occluded by state policy and the spatiotemporalities of labor migration, to disrupt a willed complacency about temporary-labor migration, and engender nuanced, wide-ranging debate that embraces the affective and economic: the economics of intimacy and the intimacies that permeate the economic.

The practice of ethics that is embedded in this book takes place as a process in which witnesses and those who testify to their experiences are addressed and remain addressable in sustainable ways. What Kelly Oliver calls "response-ability" is literally to respond so as to enable an other's ability or capacity to respond.[9] It is to respond, in Sara Ahmed's terminology, to *this* other and not *the* other.[10] To respond to this other, in specific embodied, visceral ways is to open one's self to other others, to histories and geographies, material networks and connections, relations of complicity and implication, in unanticipated ways. For those in the global North responding to the address of a Filipino domestic worker, this is an opening to discovering radiating sets of geopolitical relations located at home and far away: from the consequences of the Live-In Caregiver Program (LCP) for domestic workers' families, to histories of U.S. colonialism in the Philippines, to pathways of Canadian development aid, to (possibly) a checkpoint in Gumaca. Responding to *this* other untethers reciprocal obligation from normative nationalism not in a universalizing abstract way but through specific, material histories and geographies of connection and mutual implication. It untethers obligation from the territory of a nation not in principle but because normative nationalism is empirically implausible; it bears scant relation to the ways most of our lives are lived. And lest this sounds too voluntaristic, we read Nancy Fraser's reflections on justice to imply that all those subjected to a governance structure such as the LCP are obliged to enter into these relations of address and response-ability.[11] Throughout the book, I have staged a series of encounters and exchanges with the objective of creating opportunities for address, and of disordering and reordering identifications, alliances, and the boundaries of belonging and responsibility.

Gathering

San Juan argues, with respect to the Filipino diaspora, that migration and transnationalism are category mistakes that mis-specify the processes involved. The situations of Filipinos in the United States (and Canada) are only understandable, he argues, within a fuller analysis of the Philippines as an object of colonization and subjugation to U.S. monopoly capitalism: "It is this foundational process [and not simply the circumstances of settlement *in* the United States] . . . that establishes the limit and potential of the Filipino lifeworld" in the United States. Without understanding this complex process of colonial subjugation, Filipinos will "not be able to define their own specific historical trajectory . . . as a dual or bifurcated formation" based in the continuing struggle both for popular democracy in the Philippines and justice for immigrants in the places to which they migrate.[12] "Ultimately," he argues, "the rebirth of Filipino agency in the era of global capitalism depends *not only* on the vicissitudes of social transformation in the United States [or Canada]." It depends as well "on the fate of the struggle for autonomy and popular-democratic sovereignty in the Philippines where *balikbayans* ("returnees") still practice, though with an increasing trepidation interrupted by fits of amnesia, the speech-acts and durable performances of *pakikibaka* ("common struggle"), *pakikiramay* ("collective sharing"), and *pakikipagkapwa-tao* ("reciprocal self-esteem")."[13] The Philippine Women Centre's insistence on scrapping the LCP is understandable within such a positioning. They reason that care work should be highly valued in Canada, and consequently Filipino caregivers should migrate to Canada with their families as immigrants (and not as temporary workers). But struggle against the LCP is not only against the gross devaluation of care work in Canada (and those who do it); it is simultaneously a refusal of labor export as an economic strategy of the Philippine state, a commitment to work toward altering the conditions in the Philippines that necessitate migration, and a powerful critique of the hierarchical alignment of nation-states globally.

Our position is that this is not a matter of Filipino political agency only. Merryn Edwards spoke, in the last chapter, of the extent to which the PWC has resculpted the political landscape of non-Filipino activists in Vancouver. The concrete materiality of the metaphor is appealing, suggesting as it does a new topography of political organizing that reaches beyond local concerns, existing identities, and national borders. Rather than fighting only local winnable battles, she chose the hard work of broadening the scope of her analysis, which included journeying to the Philippines. And so I have chosen to end the book in the Philippines, to frame the rapid and very troubling marginalization of Filipino youths, whose mothers first come to Vancouver as migrant workers, not as a problem amenable to a narrow technical solution by policy makers in Canada but as enveloped within a more expansive set of political, economic, social, and affective relations. Our analysis should also trouble those who look to amnesty or the extension of citizenship to temporary migrants or undocumented workers as a relatively easy solution to the types of marginalization set in train for their children. What comes before haunts the present, and the long-term effects of temporary migration are not so easily erased. This is why we need to take responsibility for what is here and now, to create the conditions for different presents in the future.

Reflecting on Our Process

In the introduction, I argued that activists and scholars working together can take each other to places neither could reach alone. Literally so. Our collaboration began at a site that academics take for granted, when Cecilia Diocson, then the director of the PWC, was awarded a community-scholar position at the Centre for Research in Women's Studies and Gender Relations at the University of British Columbia. Cecilia, along with a number of others at the PWC and cognate organizations, traces her roots as a community organizer to student activism in the Philippines during the Marcos regime; they are no strangers to universities, intellectuals, and scholarship.

But essential to our collaborative process, we have rarely met at the university since this time; our meetings have almost always been in the times and spaces of the PWC. I came to the collaboration at a moment of being stuck in a research project on domestic workers (so much so that my research grant obtained to study this topic was close to expiring). It seemed possible to interview Canadian families about their child care and nanny agents about their brokering of temporary foreign labor, but interviewing Filipina domestic workers was an uncomfortable prospect given feminist debates of the early 1990s, calling forth the specter of a white middle-class academic appropriating the stories of "third world women" for her own professional advantage. It demanded a different research process. Having met Cecilia and others at the PWC for tentative talks about a research collaboration, I emptied my remaining research funds (with some relief) and placed them in the hands of the PWC. This was an auspicious beginning that, at least momentarily, unsettled a political economy that structures many university–community research collaborations in enduringly hierarchical ways, and which rightly and inevitably builds resentment toward the privilege of the university researcher. We came to the process of defining the research objectives and methods of our first study with domestic workers relatively unencumbered by this concrete manifestation of uneven power relations.

Defining the research together released us from some other protocols of the university as well. Through their work as organizers, women at the PWC had developed another toolkit of methods and they invited domestic workers participating in the research to express their experiences—not just though storytelling but through montage, sculpture, and role-playing. In the end, we did not use the methods of montage and sculpture, but, along with more-conventional modes of testimony and storytelling, domestic workers were invited to improvise the roles of government agents and employers, often to comedic effect. At the time, I had no idea of how to analyze these role-playing transcripts and they lay abandoned, deep at the back of a filing cabinet in my office—carefully translated and transcribed by the PWC. Buried deep in the archive but not entirely forgotten, the transcripts laid the groundwork for a later realization (already taken for granted by the PWC and not so unfamiliar in other disciplines, in particular anthropology) that stories can be told in different, more performative ways and that humor is a telling mode of social criticism. They laid the foundations for the realization that research can do more than document the present; it can be a means of disrupting that present and reimagining and organizing toward a different future.[14] They laid the groundwork for *Nanay*.

It was five years before our next collaborative projects. The slow rate of scholarly production kept us in contact in the interim as we exchanged working drafts of papers and chapters. Our writing methodology has always been one of me (a researcher with the luxury of time) writing drafts and submitting them to the PWC for discussion and feedback. When we began collaborating again in 2002, it was because the PWC and the Filipino-Canadian Youth Alliance had other community issues that they wanted and needed to document and organize around, now the experiences of youths and the circumstances of women after they had left the LCP and settled in Vancouver. We do not stand outside the process of attachment that we write about and hope for in this book. Our projects have proliferated because we have in very different ways with different investments and stakes attached to these issues, to one another, and to the women and families who have come through the LCP, some of whom have participated in almost all of our projects—as domestic workers, as immigrants, as mothers, as sons and daughters, or as youths among peers, that is, in different roles or capacities depending on their circumstances and the focus of research.

Attaching in this way over the long term has been important to the research process. It is difficult to overstate this point. In a session in 2006, when a number of us came together to reflect on our collaboration, Charlene Sayo, then a member of the Filipino-Canadian Youth Alliance spoke of the importance of sheer time together and continuity of commitment. "When we first did the project about Filipino youths [in 2002] . . . it wasn't like you just left and that was it. There was a lot more there that you wanted to explore, which was really important." Charlene saw this as being particularly important for the youths involved: "You know, they have a hard time trusting people. So when they see that their stories and their experiences are being taken seriously, and that they themselves can also develop from it, then, of course, there's really that sense of ownership and also that sense . . . I guess it's a better relationship knowing that their stories aren't being used to further your career." Relations of at least partial trust emerged as well because these youths understood our research to be activist and community-based: "They know they can also do [the research] themselves. That's a big, huge step . . . knowing that there's that benefit of education and that process of development." In other words, the collaboration has persisted as long as it was noncoercive, judged to be non-exploitative, and the PWC could see how it helped them meet their own objectives of community education and organizing.

The PWC has worked with a number of academics over the years and has maintained enduring relationships with several of us. At a community presentation made by one university collaborator many years ago, she distinguished herself from the rest of us by revealing that the director of the PWC had told her that "the others just come and eat our food." Whether or not my memory is accurate or the director said this (and with the meaning implied), I have come to embrace the remark: it captures the deep nourishment that I have received from the PWC within the inevitably shifting personal and power dynamics of organizing work and community/university collaborations.

What the PWC has taken from me is difficult to specify. Some academic framing—social death, trauma, bare life—has resonated and been absorbed into their own engaged theorizing of Filipinos' lives in Canada and elsewhere. Universities also offer practical resources to those currently attached to them, research funding certainly, but—and this is perhaps less obvious to those immersed within a university setting—access to journals and books, data sets and statistics, conferences and policy workshops, and time to write. University-based research carries legitimacy and authority in some contexts, and this key resource can be deployed and shared.

What needs to be shared and deployed is a matter for conversation and will vary with the circumstances. In 1995, there were few Filipino Canadian researchers available to do the research we have done; in 2011, the situation is entirely different, with more than a dozen Filipino Canadian youths enrolled in graduate programs in Canada and interested in researching similar topics. (Notably, none to my knowledge has come through the LCP.) And so the nature of our collaboration will continue to evolve and change.

Next Steps

In the talkback sessions that followed *Nanay,* some audience members were frustrated by our unwillingness to lay out for them a program of action. At one point we acquiesced and brought along a petition for a campaign that the PWC was currently organizing around. The danger, of course, is that signing the petition would function as the final act in the evening's entertainment. Having signed it, audience members would leave the theater satisfied that they had taken the action necessary to complete the emotional "transaction" initiated by the play. More interesting and important to us were those who left their e-mail addresses for further contact with the PWC.

With deep respect for the intensity of recent debate among committed and knowledgeable Filipino Canadian activists over strategy toward the LCP, and for histories of shared organizing and research collaboration among those now split between two organizations, we refuse to finish the conversation. Workshopping the introduction to this book at my university, a colleague asked about the concrete value of a nuanced analysis of the LCP: in practical terms, what comes from this beyond complicating the debate? I hesitated, and turned to activists in the room for help. In the audience were three members of the PWC and one member of Migrante International, Nora Angeles. Nora offered this: it can start a conversation toward finding common ground. In her view, sloganeering has been a factor in the polarization of these two Filipino Canadian activist organizations. She and the members of the PWC then came together in their insistence that the LCP is a Canadian and not a Filipino Canadian issue.

So—here, within this text—we resist the pleasures and closure of sloganeering. We offer no petition to sign. We have diagnosed a problem: the failure of the liberal compromise of deferred inclusion of temporary migrant workers, and the trauma of family separation associated with it, and we have begun to embed these processes within a longer and more geographically expansive history in Canada and the Philippines. We have made clear the PWC position to end the Live-In Caregiver program and to foster opportunities for skilled Filipinos to migrate to Canada through more appropriate permanent migration categories. More than this, we have experimented with ways of circulating these narratives so that you might attach to these issues, question the justice of temporary labor migration, and consider that lawful government policy can be violent in its effects. We have prompted you to reexamine the boundaries of your world. We ask that you might join us; this action is for you to take.

Appendixes

APPENDIX 1: Year of Family Reunification among the 27 Families Interviewed

	Number of Families
1991	1
1992	0
1993	0
1994	1
1995	3
1996	2
1997	0
1998	4
1999	2
2000	3
2001	2
2002	1
2003	1
2004	2
2005	2
2006	2
2007	1

(a) City of Vancouver[c]

	Languages Spoken at Home									
	Tagalog		Punjabi		Vietnamese		English[d]		Chinese	
	GPA	N	GPA	N	GPA	N	GPA	N	GPA	N
Girls	**2.87**	499	**2.80**	702	3.03	747	3.21	9,476	3.32	6,382
Boys	**2.60**	427	**2.49**	684	2.72	609	3.00	9,780	3.09	6,162

(b) Vancouver Suburbs[c]

	Languages Spoken at Home									
	Tagalog		Punjabi		Vietnamese		English[d]		Chinese	
	GPA	N	GPA	N	GPA	N	GPA	N	GPA	N
Girls	3.06	795	**2.94**	3,022	3.12	333	**3.04**	30,514	3.38	6,466
Boys	2.72	829	**2.63**	2,942	2.77	324	**2.77**	29,655	3.14	7,063

Note: The two lowest GPA scores in each row are highlighted in boldface.

[a] GPA averaged over the last 52 credits for foundational courses taken (4 credits usually equivalent to one course).

[b] Includes those who had graduated within six years of entering grade 8. The analyses "track" all students entering grade 8 from 1995 to 2004.

[c] Suburban school districts were selected because of relatively high numbers of Filipino families. They include: Burnaby, Coquitlam, New Westminster, Richmond, and Surrey. They do not include records from North Vancouver and Delta.

[d] Aboriginal English speakers have been removed from this category.

Source: British Columbia Ministry of Education. Statistical analysis by Edudata Canada (Maria Trache).

APPENDIX 3: Rates of Graduation from High School among All Students Who Entered High School in Vancouver, 1995–2004

	Language Spoken at Home									
	Tagalog		Punjabi		Vietnamese		English[a]		Chinese	
	%	N	%	N	%	N	%	N	%	N
(a) City										
Girls	**76**	654	88	799	**74**	1,014	84	11,217	90	7,067
Boys	**64**	672	73	934	**60**	1,021	80	12,192	85	7,266
(b) Suburbs										
Girls	**83**	961	89	3,387	**76**	438	**83**	36,645	87	7,431
Boys	**74**	1,117	80	3,687	**67**	484	76	38,822	85	8,267

Note: The "normal" trajectory would be to complete grades 8–12 in five years. Data include those who had graduated within six years of entering grade 8 and indicate those for whom there is a recorded graduation date. It must be noted that there are real limits to interpretation. Those who do not graduate may have left the British Columbia school system rather than dropped out of high school. As long as students remained within BC, however, they are traced through this analysis, regardless of whether they changed schools within the province. This cohort-based analysis also only tracks the progress of students who were in the school system in grade 8. A child entering the system in grade 9 or later would not be included. The analysis tracks cohorts that began grade 8 in September 1995 through 2004. The two lowest graduation rates in each row are highlighted in boldface.

[a] Aboriginal English speakers excluded

Source: British Columbia Ministry of Education. Statistical analysis by Edudata Canada (Maria Trache).

APPENDIX 4: School Attendance and Educational Attainment for Filipino Youths in Vancouver CMA in 2001, by Immigration Status, Age of Immigration, and Gender

	Male		Female	
	%	N	%	N
Percent age 15–18 not attending school				
Nonimmigrant	16	125	17	115
Immigrated				
Between ages 0–11	19	105	13	65
Between ages 12–16	24	80	24	85
Percent aged 19–22 without high school certificate				
Nonimmigrant	15	125	7	60
Immigrated				
Between ages 0–11	12	30	7	15
Between ages 12–16	24	100	7	35

Source: Statistics Canada, 2001 Census, Special tabulations. Analysis by François Bertrand.

APPENDIX 5: Percentage of Filipino Youths Aged 15–18 Not Attending School in Four Canadian CMAs, by Immigration Status, Age of Immigration, and Gender

	Male		Female	
	%	N	%	N
Vancouver				
Nonimmigrant	16	125	17	115
Immigrated				
Between ages 0–11	19	105	13	65
Between ages 12–16	24	80	24	85
Toronto				
Nonimmigrant	20	280	24	305
Immigrated				
Between ages 0–11	25	345	24	395
Between ages 12–16	17	100	22	160
Montreal				
Nonimmigrant	15	20	6	10
Immigrated				
Between ages 0–11	16	35	17	25
Between ages 12–16	50	30	0	0
Winnipeg				
Nonimmigrant	20	165	23	165
Immigrated				
Between ages 0–11	18	45	25	50
Between ages 12–16	33	30	48	50

Source: Statistics Canada, 2001 Census, Special tabulations. Analysis by François Bertrand.

APPENDIX 6: Educational Attainment of Filipino Youths (19–22) in Four Canadian CMAs in 2001, by Gender, Immigration Status, and Age of Immigration

	Nonimmigrant	Immigrated between Ages		
		0–11	12–16	17–24
	%	%	%	%
(a) Vancouver males				
Without high school certificate	15	12	24	12
High school certificate	22	22	30	25
Other nonuniversity	36	24	20	18
University (with+without degree)	26	43	23	44
(b) Vancouver females				
Without high school certificate	7	7	7	5
High school certificate	20	12	33	15
Other nonuniversity	28	40	25	17
University (with+without degree)	45	35	32	64
(c) Toronto males				
Without high school certificate	10	11	25	19
High school certificate	23	29	33	23
Other nonuniversity	27	25	25	24
University (with+without degree)	38	34	17	31
(d) Toronto females				
Without high school certificate	7	7	15	6
High school certificate	16	24	25	13
Other nonuniversity	21	21	31	32
University (with+without degree)	55	46	26	47
(e) Montreal males				
Without high school certificate	6	14	43	13
High school certificate	19	19	20	33
Other nonuniversity	35	52	16	27
University (with+without degree)	36	14	22	20
(f) Montreal females				
Without high school certificate	9	10	9	13
High school certificate	9	10	52	33
Other nonuniversity	35	40	31	27
University (with+without degree)	50	45	0	20

APPENDIX 6—*continued*

| | Nonimmigrant | Immigrated between Ages | | |
| | | 0–11 | 12–16 | 17–24 |
	%	%	%	%
(g) Winnipeg males				
Without high school certificate	15	18	23	0
High school certificate	23	47	48	27
Other nonuniversity	18	13	16	0
University (with+without degree)	42	20	10	45
(h) Winnipeg females				
Without high school certificate	4	27	18	11
High school certificate	17	18	32	39
Other nonuniversity	17	9	32	11
University (with+without degree)	60	48	17	44

Note: Due to rounding error, columns do not always add to 100. Cases of extreme distortion indicate low numbers.

Source: Statistics Canada, 2001 Census, Special tabulations. Analysis by François Bertrand.

Notes

Introduction

1. For an extended discussion of our collaboration, see Pratt in collaboration with the PWC, "Seeing beyond the State," and Pratt in collaboration with the PWC and FCYA, "Working with Migrant Communities."

2. Kenney, press conference, December 12, 2009.

3. Schmalzbauer, "Searching for Wages and Mothering from Afar," 1320. See also Saunders, "Home Alone," for the case of the migration of Romanian mothers.

4. Global Commission, *Global Migration*, 13–15, 26.

5. Kenney, press conference, December 12, 2009.

6. Ruhs and Martin, "Numbers vs. Rights."

7. Bell and Piper, "Justice for Migrant Workers?" 215. That there may be some truth to this assessment and as an indication of the sensitivity of employer "demand," the Association of Caregiver and Nanny Agents Canada claimed in July 2010 that there was a 70 percent to 90 percent drop in domestic worker placements in the three-month period after the federal government introduced the requirement on April 1, 2010, that Canadian employers pay for the travel costs (including airfare), medical insurance, workers' compensation, and recruitment costs of domestic workers hired through the Live-In Caregiver Program. In a July 5, 2010, press release, this association urged the government "not to treat private families accessing the LCP the same as corporations accessing the Temporary Foreign Worker program. The corporation's main objective is to grow revenue and turn a profit, while the family's objective is to raise healthy children and provide care for future and senior Canadians."www.acnacanada.ca (accessed August 23, 2010).

8. Bell and Piper, "Justice for Migrant Workers?" 213.

9. Fraser, *Scales of Justice*, 398, 395.

10. In some ways, this is in line with the suggestion that Bell and Piper put forward in "Justice for Migrant Workers?" They suggest that unequal rights between citizens and migrants are justifiable only if "this arrangement (a) works to the benefit of migrant workers (*as decided by the migrant workers themselves*), (b) creates opportunities for people in relatively impoverished societies to improve their lives, and (c) there are no feasible alternatives to serve the ends identified in (a) and (b)" (214, emphasis added).

11. We're serious. This is an adaptation by activists of a song by a Filipino popular singer, Gary Granada, who can be heard singing his original 1993 version with the original lyrics at www.garygranada.com (accessed July 21, 2010).

12. For a fuller discussion of this point, see Pratt in collaboration with the PWC, "Seeing beyond the State." It is also important to insist that "transnational" research need not entail physical movement to other places (some of the troubling politics of which are the subject of chapter 5). Indeed this book is an effort to stretch readers through attachment rather than physical mobility. I thank Sarah Zell for this point.

13. Butler, *Frames of War*, 2.

14. The terminology is Kelly Oliver's *(Witnessing)*. I will explore it more fully in chapter 3.

15. Butler, *Frames of War*, 12.

16. San Juan, *Toward Filipino Self-Determination*, 124.

17. Glick Schiller, "Global Perspective." See also Malkki, "National Geographic."

18. Butler, *Giving an Account of Oneself*; Gilroy, *After Empire*; Gunew, "Eur/Asian Vernacular Cosmopolitanisms."

19. Baucom, *Specters of the Atlantic*.

20. Of course, making connections between labor migration and the situation in the Philippines is not relevant only to "comfortable" Canadians. The PWC stresses the need for migrant workers to understand and study these links as well.

21. Buck-Morss, *Dreamworld and Catastrophe*, 18.

22. Ibid., 6. As Buck-Morss puts it: "When democratic sovereignty *confronts* the people with all the violence that it monopolizes as the legitimate embodiment *of* the people, it is in fact attesting to its *non*identity with the people. Thus the attempt to resolve the contradiction between popular sovereignty and state violence with recourse to the conception of the law becomes caught in a vicious circle. And the effect of this circularity is to undermine the very possibility of the legal/illegal distinction" (7, emphasis in original).

23. Critical Filipina and Filipino Studies Collective, *Resisting Homeland Security*. In its 2004 report, the collective records a 67 percent increase in "noncriminal removals" among Filipinos in the United States between 2001 and 2003, the seventh highest among all the countries of origins considered (after Lebanon, Egypt, Jordan, Haiti, Uruguay, and Morocco). Of these, 42 percent involved legal permanent residents with aggregative felony convictions, such as previous drug convictions. Because of divergent state and federal sentencing guidelines, the Department of Homeland Security uses federal guidelines to determine felony convictions, even when individual states do not consider some of these convictions felonies. Filipino permanent residents in the United States who committed petty crimes and were convicted of a misdemeanor thus now face the threat of deportation. Granted, the United States is a different national context, but these events heighten concerns about framing any population as marginal.

24. For discussions of this familial discourse as it pertains to care workers, see Bakan and Stasiulis, *Not One of the Family*; Dodson and Zincavage, "It's Like a Family"; Huang and Li, "Like a Family but Not Quite"; Macklin, "Foreign Domestic Worker."

25. Clough, "Introduction."

26. Thrift, "Intensities of Feeling"; Anderson, "Becoming and Being Hopeful," and "Affect and Biopower."

27. Ngai, *Ugly Feelings*, 94, 95 (emphasis in the original).

28. Baucom, *Specters of the Atlantic*; Berlant, *The Anatomy of National Fantasy*, and "The Epistemology of State Emotion."

29. Berlant, *The Anatomy of National Fantasy*, *The Queen of America Goes to Washington City*, and "The Epistemology of State Emotion."

30. Ahmed, "Affective Economies," and *The Promise of Happiness*.

31. Barnett, "Political Affects in Public Space." The foci of his critique are Connolly's neuropolitics (*Neuropolitics*, "The Media and Think Tank Politics") and Thrift's nonrepresentational theory (*Non-Representational Theory*).

32. Barnett, "Political Affects in Public Space," 189.

33. Rothberg, "Between Auschwitz and Algeria," 184.

34. Mohanty, Russo, and Torres, *Third World Women and the Politics of Feminism*; Spivak, "French Feminism in an International Frame," and "Can the Subaltern Speak?"

35. See Sangtin Writers and Nagar, *Playing with Fire*; Swarr and Nagar, *Critical Transnational Feminist Praxis*.

36. Ahmed, "This Other and Other Others," 569.

37. Ibid., 559 (emphasis in original).

38. Indeed, in *Feminism without Borders*, Mohanty reminds us that her influential critique of Western feminism ("Under Western Eyes," in which she argued that Western feminists tended to construct Third World women as homogeneous, powerless victims, wholly determined by their material circumstances, in ways that solidified Western feminists' agency and superiority) did not lead her toward a position of cultural relativism. It led her to advocate sustained engagements between feminists positioned differently in the international division of labor.

1. Enterprising Women, Failing Children

1. The numbers vary from year to year (and researcher to researcher), but two things are clear: the numbers have been increasing, and they are higher now than they have ever been. One estimate is that from 1992 to 2006 the numbers holding a permit under the LCP on December 1 of each year were: 8,253, 4,628, 3,597, 4,417, 4,942, 5,272, 5,562, 5,724, 5,942, 7,694, 10,148, 12,370, 14,995, 17,697, and 21,489 (Depatie-Pelletier, "Under Legal Practices Similar to Slavery"). In *Home*

Economics, Sharma estimates the numbers from 1982 to 2004 (under the Foreign Domestic Movement Program from 1982 to 1991 and the Live-In Caregiver Program from 1992 to 2004) to be: 11,327, 3,506, 4,562, 5,475, 6,933, 7,889, 8,056, 8,842, 10,734, 8,621, 3,968, 2,098, n/a, 7,781, 7,400, 7,472, 7,685, 7,834, 8,124, 10,531, 13,464, 15,657, and 19,820. See also Kelly, Park, de Leon, and Priest, "Profile of Live-in Caregiver Immigrants to Canada, 1993–2009," for different numbers but the same trend. From 2000 to 2009, *entries* through the LCP grew from 2,684 through 4,372, 4,739, 5,086, 6,708, 7,199, 9,334, 13,775, 12,882 to 9,816 in 2009. Note that the last series of numbers indicate arrivals during the year and not the overall number of registered live-in caregivers.

2. It is not a simple matter to know exactly how many domestic workers leave children in the Philippines. Government statistics do allow us to know that 43 percent of the women coming to Canada through the LCP in 2006 were married, separated, divorced, or widowed (CIC, *Facts and Figures 2006*). Reviewing trends from 1993 to 2009, Kelly, Park, de Leon, and Priest, "Profile of Live-in Caregiver Immigrants to Canada, 1993–2009," report that the proportion of those landing in Canada through the LCP who are married has increased in recent years. In 2009, 37 percent of LCP principal applicants were married and a further 7 percent were divorced, separated, or widowed.

3. Sharma, *Home Economics,* 144 (original emphasis).

4. Balibar, "Outlines of a Topography of Cruelty."

5. Depatie-Pelletier, "Under Legal Practices Similar to Slavery." See also Anderson, *Doing the Dirty Work?,* for an analysis of migrant domestic work as slavery in the European context.

Serfdom status is defined as the condition or status of a tenant who is by law, custom, or agreement bound to live and labor on land belonging to another person and to render some determinate service to such other person, whether for reward or not, and is not free to change his status. The LCP temporary work permit requires that an employee live in her employer's house, perform the service of caregiving, and be tied to a single and particular employer. Those sympathetic to the LCP might argue that the capacity of live-in caregivers to change employers within Canada exempts the program from the unflattering status of serfdom. However, given the requirement to complete twenty-four months of live-in care within a defined period in order to qualify for permanent resident status (from 1992 to 2010, this was thirty-six months; early in 2010, this was extended to forty-eight months) and the long delays in processing work permits with new employers (this can take many months), many domestic workers are reluctant to exercise their "freedom" to change employers.

6. Kelly, Park, de Leon, and Priest, "Profile of Live-in Caregiver Immigrants to Canada, 1993–2009." Not all of Canada's temporary work programs violate the Supplementary Conventions. In Depatie-Pelletier's assessment ("Under Legal

Practices Similar to Slavery"), "only" five of Canada's fifty-nine temporary foreign worker programs violate the U.N. Conventions.

7. Hindess, "The Liberal Government of Unfreedom," 94.

8. Rose, *Powers of Freedom*, 78.

9. Foucault, *Society Must Be Defended*, 254. The basis for this assertion is, however, cryptic at best. As Elden notes, Foucault's assertions about the necessity of state racism are fascinating, "but the course [of his lectures] is nearing an end at this point, and he does not really make good on this claim" ("War of Races," 150).

10. Indeed, one reading of sovereign power is that it is founded in the performative act of determining who is included within or excluded from citizenship and politically qualified life, and who is protected by the law or exposed to violence beyond its protection. Agamben, *Homo Sacer*.

11. Foucault, *Society Must Be Defended*, 256.

12. There are some negative implications for the national population as well, insofar as access to this global supply of cheapened labor buffers the state from national demands for higher wages and better working conditions, a point that Sharma *(Home Economics)* explores.

13. The opportunity to settle permanently places Canada very high in the hierarchy of desirable nations. In her survey of eighty-one Filipina domestic workers in Israel and Palestine in 2007, Liebelt ("On Sentimental Orientalists") found that over half (58 percent) planned to work in a country other than Israel or Palestine, the largest proportion (47 percent) naming Canada as their desired location.

14. Government of Canada, "Regulations."

15. In 1993, fewer than 1 percent of the 3,013 permanent residents immigrating through the LCP were dependents or spouses. By 2006, 48.5 percent of the 6,895 immigrating to Canada through the LCP were spouses or dependents. For annual figures over this time period, see Pratt and the PWC of BC and Ugnayan BC, "Deskilling." See also Kelly, Park, de Leon, and Priest, "Profile of Live-in Caregiver Immigrants to Canada, 1993–2009."

16. Kelly, "Filipinos in Canada," 10; TIEDI (Toronto Immigrant Employment Data Initiative), "Immigrants Coming."

17. McKay and the Philippine Women Centre, "Filipina Identities," 8.

18. In many cases, focusing on two nation-states, the Philippines and Canada, still obscures the geographical complexity. As Liebelt ("On Sentimental Orientalists") argues, many Filipina migrant workers "move on and on" among a hierarchy of desirable destinations, rather than back and forth between a destination country and the Philippines. For a discussion of our transnational approach (and why it took me so long to fully embrace it), see Pratt and the PWC, "Seeing beyond the State."

19. In *Neoliberalism as Exception*, Ong describes the ways in which neoliberalism has led to new degrees of fragmentation and variegation of citizenship and differential rights and entitlements to inclusion. The infiltration of market logics

into politics, Ong argues, "conceptually unsettles the notion of citizenship as a legal status rooted in the nation-state" (6), and we would more accurately conceive of citizenship as an ensemble of elements "that can be delinked and relinked to market rationalities" (10) "in relation to diverse locations and ethical situations" (7). We can expect, in her view, a proliferation of "excludable populations in transit, shuttled in and out of zones of growth," who in most cases have a restricted range of citizenship rights and entitlements (16). Two of the most infamous cases of the Philippine government's failure to protect the legal rights of its overseas migrant citizens occurred in 1995 (the cases of Flor Contemplacion in Singapore and Sara Balabagan in the United Arab Emirates). See Guevarra, "Managing 'Vulnerabilities'"; Rafael, "Your Grief Is Our Gossip"; and Rodriguez, "Migrant Heroes," for discussions of the effects these cases had for transformations in the relations between citizens and the Philippine state. But as Rodriguez argues in relation to the Filipino labor diaspora, migrant claims to extraterritorial rights and protections are also sites of transnational citizenship struggles.

20. San Juan, *Toward Filipino Self-Determination*, 159.

21. Ibid.

22. Rose, *Powers of Freedom*, 50.

23. Legg, *Spaces of Colonialism*. Critiques of overly juridical and binarist framing of sovereign power are now extensive. In relation to Agamben, see Legg, *Spaces of Colonialism*; Ong, *Neoliberalism as Exception*; and Walker, "Conclusion." For the need to articulate sovereign and different forms of liberal power relations, see also Connolly, "The Complexity of Sovereignty."

24. Carens, "Live-in Domestics, Seasonal Workers," 419.

25. Bosniak, "Universal Citizenship and the Problem of Alienage," and *The Citizen and the Alien*.

26. Bosniak, *The Citizen and the Alien*, 125.

27. Bosniak, "Universal Citizenship and the Problem of Alienage," 974.

28. Bosniak, *The Citizen and the Alien*, 124.

29. Ibid., 4.

30. Walzer, *Spheres of Justice*, 58.

31. Carens, "Live-in Domestics, Seasonal Workers."

32. Mayer, "Guestworkers and Exploitation," 12.

33. For example, Carens, "Live-in Domestics, Seasonal Workers"; Walzer, *Spheres of Justice*. For an extended discussion of Walzer's separate-spheres model of citizenship and his critique of guest-worker programs, see Bosniak, "Membership, Equality, and the Difference That Alienage Makes."

34. There is now a vast literature on women's experiences while registered within the LCP, including: Daenzer, *Regulating Class Privilege*; England and Steill, "They Think You're as Stupid as Your English Is"; Kelly, "Filipinos in Canada"; Macklin, "Foreign Domestic Worker"; McKay and the Philippine Women Center,

"Filipina Identities"; Pratt, *Working Feminism;* Stasiulis and Bakan, *Negotiating Citizenship;* Zaman, "Transnational Migration," among many others.

35. As French Algerian sociologist Abdelmalek Sayad has noted, migrant laborers are often viewed with suspicion, as "not like us." They are brought into the nation to do work that citizens will not do. Their fate is "to be and remain . . . a 'labour [migrant]'—and if need be we will ensure that it stays that way to some extent. . . . On the [other] hand, we have an immigration that we judge . . . to be worthy of quickly becoming a 'settler immigration'—and, if need be, we will help it to become that as soon as possible" (*Suffering,* 301). He thus makes the point that guest-worker and immigration programs not only mark a divide between suitable and unsuitable citizens; they also create it.

36. Carens, "Live-in Domestics, Seasonal Workers," 437.

37. Walzer, *Spheres of Justice,* 59.

38. Carens, "Live-in Domestics, Seasonal Workers" 5.

39. There is nothing new about calling attention to the marginalizing effects of guest-worker programs. In her documentation of the differential inclusion of Filipinos in the United States, which she defines as the circumstance of national inclusion only and precisely through a group's subordinated status, Espiritu *(Home Bound)* traces a history of Filipino male guest work in the United States in the early twentieth century tied to U.S.–Philippine colonial relations (see also Fujita-Rony, *American Workers, Colonial Power).* So too, Castles long ago observed that guest-worker programs in Western Europe had led to the development and marginalization of new ethnic minorities: "The cause is not the employment of migrants in itself, but rather, the attempt to treat migrants purely as economic men and women, and to separate between labor power and other human attributes. Because permanent immigration was not expected, and the states concerned refused to take the necessary steps to provide housing and social amenities needed for orderly settlement, migration has exacerbated some of the underlying problems of Western European societies. It is easier now to blame the victims than to come to grips with the causes" ("The Guest-Worker in Western Europe," 776). Writing in the mid-1980s, Castles signaled his assessment that these programs were of historical interest only by titling his paper an obituary. It is now obvious that his declaration of the death of guest-worker programs was premature.

40. See also Cohen, "Mom Is a Stranger."

41. Rose, *Powers of Freedom,* 221.

42. Edkins and Pin-Fat, "Introduction," 14.

43. New hires to Italy increased from 637 to 5,296 (a 731.4 percent increase), while new hires to Canada increased by 167.3 percent, from 3,222 to 8,612 (POEA, *Overseas Employment Statistics).*

44. Philippines National Statistics Office, "One in Three"; Tyner, *The Philippines.* The majority of newly hired and rehired contracts of Overseas Filipino

Workers (OFWs) are still for jobs in the Middle East and Asia: in 2009, 61.2 percent were located in the Middle East, 23.9 percent in Asia, 4.3 percent in Europe, 2.8 percent in the Americas, and 1.7 percent in Africa. Of all contracts in the Americas, 55.7 percent were for jobs in Canada (POEA, *Overseas Employment Statistics*). In 2004 (and note that this is before the increases noted above, and the numbers refer to all OFWs and not only newly and rehired workers), the Philippine government recorded 17,000 OFWs working in Canada and 71,000 in the United States, indicating a much larger number of OFWs in Canada on a per capita basis, undoubtedly due to the existence of the LCP. The demographics of OFWs in the two countries also indicate that the circumstances of the OFWs in Canada and the United States are very different: in 2004, 63 percent going to the United States were male, whereas the opposite was the case in Canada, where 65 percent of OFWs were female (Philippines National Statistics Office, "Number of Overseas Filipino Workers").

45. Kelly, *Landscapes of Globalization*, 17. See also San Juan, *Toward Filipino Self-Determination;* Tyner, *The Philippines.*

46. Guevarra, "Managing 'Vulnerabilities,'" and *Marketing Dreams, Manufacturing Heroes;* Rodriguez, "Migrant Heroe," and *Migrants for Export;* Tyner, *The Philippines.*

47. Philippines National Statistics Office, "One in Three."

48. See Choy, *Empire of Care.*

49. POEA, *Overseas Employment Statistics.*

50. Kelly, "Filipinos in Canada." And the numbers keep increasing: by 2007, remittances from migrant workers had increased to U.S. $14.4 billion, approximately 10 percent of the Philippines GDP (Guevarra, *Marketing Dreams, Manufacturing Heroes,* 8).

51. POEA, *Overseas Employment Statistics.*

52. Parreñas, *Servants of Globalization;* Mohanty, "Women Workers." See also Hochschild, "Love and Gold"; Guevarra, *Marketing Dreams, Manufacturing Heroes.*

53. Kelly, Park, de Leon, and Priest, "Profile of Live-in Caregiver Immigrants to Canada, 1993–2009."

54. Tadiar, *Things Fall Away,* 137.

55. Kelly et al., "Explaining the Deprofessionalized Filipino," 21. Only Jamaica, Mexico, and the United States have lower proportions of wealth held by the poorest 20 percent of the population.

56. Kelly, *Landscapes of Globalization,* 1.

57. In arguing that the Philippine state has been governmentalized, Guevarra is marking a key characteristic of neoliberal as compared to liberal thought. This is the understanding that the economic rational individual is behavioristically malleable. Neoliberalism is thus distinguished by an expansion of direct and indirect techniques for leading and controlling individuals (Lemke, "The Birth of Biopolitics"; see also Rodriguez, *Migrants for Export*).

58. Guevarra, *Marketing Dreams, Manufacturing Heroes,* 527.

59. Commission on Filipinos Overseas, *Handbook,* quoted in Rodriguez, "Migrant Heroes," 348.

60. Guevarra, *Marketing Dreams, Manufacturing Heroes.*

61. Ibid., 527.

62. Interviews were conducted between 2004 and 2008. The methodology was a mixture of individual and group interviews. The original plan was to interview families (adults and children) together, followed by interviews with individual family members. Few families agreed to do this, and the scheduling of interviews accommodated individuals' willingness to be interviewed, as well as scheduling difficulties. Altogether, twenty-seven households were interviewed. Ten youth were interviewed without their parents, alone, or with a friend or sibling (that is, their parents were not interviewed). For eight youths, there was a repeat interview. For four families, children and mother were interviewed together (and in the case of three families, children were interviewed independently after the joint interview). In three additional families, children and adults were only interviewed separately. For six families, the husband was interviewed along with his wife. For seven families, the mother told the family story without the participation of her children, either because the children were too young or did not want to participate. Four families participated in a dinner/focus group in which the PWC and I reported back on initial impressions from the interviews, and they shared their stories among themselves. The Filipino-Canadian Youth Alliance invited youth participants to an evening of feedback and discussion at the Kalayaan Centre with the same objective. Various members of the PWC and Ugnayan BC participated as interviewers, and I attended as many of the interviews as possible. Youth tended to interview youth; adults interviewed adults. The interviews were usually several hours long. In some cases, a preliminary visit to the home of the person to be interviewed was necessary to establish trust and rapport. Contacts came from existing networks of the Kalayaan Centre, from personal networks, and from referrals by an immigrant settlement worker (she asked families about their willingness to participate and passed along names of those who were). Although the sample is by no means representative, we made an effort to diversify the sample by making contacts through different networks. Almost all the interviews involving adults were conducted in either Tagalog or Ilocano. For youth, there was a mixture of English and Tagalog. Interviews were then translated and transcribed. A further set of focus groups was conducted with twelve youth by Ugnayan, and I have drawn on some of this material here.

63. The problems that arose from this arrangement are discussed in chapter 2.

64. Although unable to survive on these wages, they underline the middle-class standing of many of the women who come through the LCP. Half of the population of the Philippines lives on less than U.S. $2 a day (Tyner, *The Philippines*).

65. The inflation rate for the country as a whole was highly variable during this time, for instance, 46 percent in 1984, but closer to 9 percent through the 1990s. If Rosita's salary had merely kept up with the rate of inflation, it would have been only 3,000 pesos at the end of seventeen years. But one would expect her salary to do more than keep up with inflation, and given the privatization of many services, and in particular her desire to send her three children to private school, her salary was insufficient.

66. For an analysis of the use and meaning of remittances sent by Filipino domestic workers, see Fresnoza-Flot, "Migration Status and Transnational Mothering"; McKay, "Sending Dollars Shows Feelings"; Parreñas, *Children of Global Migration*; Scalabrini Migration Center, *Hearts Apart*. Schmalzbauer ("Searching for Wages") describes in rich ethnographic detail the use and meaning of remittances sent by Honduran migrants living and working in the United States.

67. There is a landing fee of $975 and a $500 processing fee for each person sponsored. Fees in the Philippines for processing papers likely amount to roughly the same. What Maria's family found even more difficult was the "show" money to demonstrate resources to sustain dependents: "I told them that they should try to find money there and not spend it. Just use it as show money so they can come. I suggested that they use the land titles of our properties there as guarantee so that they can secure that show money."

68. Pratt in collaboration with the PWC, "From Migrant to Immigrant"; Kelly et al., "Explaining the Deprofessionalized Filipino." In their survey of Filipinos in Toronto, of the forty-four women who had come through the LCP and worked in both the Philippines and Canada, Kelly et al. found that 66 percent had experienced downward mobility, 23 percent had a different job (for which most had retrained), and only 11 percent had perfectly matched jobs in Canada and the Philippines (and all had undergone some retraining in Canada).

69. Rose, *Powers of Freedom*, 74.

70. For a discussion of the "ethnic succession" argument, see Ong, *Buddha Is Hiding*, 3.

71. Rose, "Death of the Social?" 340.

72. Rose, *Powers of Freedom*.

73. For more details, see Pratt, *Working Feminism*. In 1989, women came through a program called the Foreign Domestic Movement program. This was revamped in 1992 as the LCP. See Cohen ("Mom Is a Stranger") and Daenzer (*Regulating Class Privilege*) for histories of these programs and those that preceded them. Daenzer argues that the restrictions to permanent migration under these various programs increased as the origins of women coming through them shifted from Europe to the Caribbean and Asia.

74. See note 15 above.

75. Cohen's estimate is seven to ten ("Mom Is a Stranger"). This is based on

an estimate made by a representative of INTERCEDE, a domestic workers' organization in Toronto.

76. Interview by author, Vancouver, July 31, 2006.

77. Liberty first went to Hong Kong for seven years and then completed her LCP qualifications in Canada in three. It took a further five years for her to sponsor her children.

78. Working in fast-food restaurants is a common destiny for many Filipino youth. Michelle, who was sent to private schools in both the Philippines and Vancouver (when she immigrated at 17), did graduate from high school. But she was depressed and struggling during her first year in grade 12 in Canada and felt alienated from her Canadian classmates. When she got a part-time job at McDonald's, her Filipino coworkers "were the nearest people that I could actually blend in with. . . . Because most of the Filipinos here—if you see—they work in the fast-food area." After finishing high school, she worked in a fast-food restaurant for two years before taking a six-month course to become a medical lab assistant. She spoke of her desire to motivate other Filipino youth to aspire for more than working in a fast-food restaurant: "'Cause I basically don't want to see another Filipino dying in a restaurant kind-of-thing. We already have that mind-set . . . no, no, no, not really a mind-set—but you look at a Filipino right now, and it's either they think of a caregiver, or a maintenance person, or a waitress in McDonald's."

79. Four years since our last interview, this son is taking courses in adult education, while his older brother, who was studying computer science at a university in the Philippines, has not returned to complete his postsecondary education.

80. Interview by author, Vancouver, June 6, 2005.

81. School districts were selected because of the high numbers of Filipino families in them. These include most but not all districts in the Vancouver lower mainland. Included districts are: Vancouver, Surrey, Richmond, New Westminster, Burnaby, and Coquitlam. The analyses do not include records from North Vancouver and Delta.

82. Children who have been separated from parents through the LCP cannot be identified in the BC Ministry of Education data sets. The best "proxy" that we have to identify Filipino children of the LCP is the language spoken at home. Although Tagalog is unlikely to be spoken in the homes of second-generation children, children identified as speaking Tagalog at home will include Filipino immigrants beyond those who have been separated through the LCP.

83. It is worth bearing in mind that studies in the Philippines, while mixed, tend to show that younger children of migrant parents perform well at school, better than children of nonmigrants, and they are more likely to take part in extracurricular activities. As Albert, one of the youth interviewed for this study (who did not complete high school), put it: "I was smart in the Philippines." There is some evidence, however, that children of migrant mothers are slightly less likely

to be on the honor roll as compared to children whose fathers work overseas and children of nonmigrant parents (Scalabrini Migration Center, *Hearts Apart*).

84. May Farrales is currently completing a Master's thesis in the Department of Geography at the University of British Columbia, further investigating educational outcomes for Filipino youths. It is telling that a survey she conducted in the fall of 2010 of forty-five Filipino students attending postsecondary education institutions in Vancouver revealed that none of the respondents had a parent who had migrated under the LCP. Again, this points to the different experiences of Canadian-born and immigrant Filipino youths, and of Filipino youths whose families have migrated through different migration programs.

85. The reasoning is this: because most family reunification has occurred since 1995, the children aged 15–22 who had immigrated before the age of 12 would— at the time of the 2001 census—have been unlikely to be children of the LCP (that is, they would have immigrated before Filipinas began to arrive in large numbers through the LCP). By contrast, few children of the LCP who immigrated at a younger age would have been 15 by 2001 or be expected to have graduated from high school. We recognize that adjusting to a new school system is an entirely different matter for a younger versus an older child and that this factor confounds this quasi-control group among immigrants. But since so many LCP children come at a later age, the finding that children immigrating after the age of 11 have a more difficult time in school is troubling in and of itself.

86. This number is considerably lower than the dropout rate calculated from the BC Ministry of Education data set for boys speaking Tagalog at home. There are several possible reasons for this. First, the analysis of the data was restricted to school districts that had a sizable Filipino population. When the census data are analyzed only for census districts where there is a high concentration of Filipinos (a score of 2 on a measure of residential segregation, such that twice the number of Filipinos live in the census tract than one would expect if the population were evenly distributed), the percentage of 15–18-year-old males who immigrated between the ages of 12 and 16 who were not attending school in 2001 increases to 27 percent—over one in four. We also know that 56 percent of Filipino families reported in the 2001 census that they speak English at home, so the school data are selecting a subset of Filipino students, likely more recent immigrants (Lindsay, "The Filipino Community in Canada"). It is also the case that census data rely on parents' reportage of their children's activities and this may not coincide with the facts as reported by schools. In any case, we see the same phenomenon with the Vietnamese community in Vancouver. High school completion rates of those who identified as Vietnamese in the 2001 census were very low (28 percent of 19–22-year-olds have not completed), but not as low as reported in the Ministry of Education data sets.

87. Another factor that makes this pattern so astonishing and disturbing is that it is at odds with the norm within the Filipino community in Canada: in 2001, only 25 percent of all Filipinos in Canada had educational attainment of high school or less, and twice as many Filipinos (31 percent) had university degrees compared to all Canadians (Lindsay, "The Filipino Community in Canada"). A study by Abada, Hou, and Ram ("Ethnic Differences in Educational Attainment") of educational attainment of Canadian-born children of immigrants and children of immigrants who themselves immigrated to Canada by the age of 12 found a similar tendency for Filipino children to defy the norm of upward educational mobility relative to their parents. Filipinos and blacks were the only two groups for whom children did not attain a higher proportion of university degrees than their fathers. In the case of Filipinos, this is in part an artifact of the high level of university attainment among immigrant fathers (and mothers).

88. Interview by author, Vancouver, June 6, 2005.

89. Interviews were conducted in May and June 2006 with either the principal or a guidance counselor in five Vancouver public schools (including four of the six high schools with the highest number of Filipino students; the principals in the other two schools would not agree to an interview), as well as in two private Catholic schools with significant numbers of Filipino students.

90. Rose, *Powers of Freedom*, 199.

91. Two were never married; nine were widowed or separated before their migration; four separated during family separation associated with the LCP; another four separated, became widowed, or divorced soon after reunion in Vancouver; and eight remain married in Vancouver.

92. In 2009, the number of dependents under 21 years of age sponsored through the LCP rose to 3,533 (Kelly, Park, de Leon, and Priest, "Profile of Live-in Caregivers to Canada, 1993–2009"). These researchers report that 1,063 dependents under 21 were sponsored through the LCP in 2005, a much higher number than the 151 children that we report for this same year. Our data were provided by CIC, with dependents classified by relationship to sponsor (son, daughter, sibling, spouse, older relative, or other). Regardless of this discrepancy, the analysis by Kelly et al. indicates a large increase in sponsored youths from 2005 to 2009.

93. Rose, *Powers of Freedom*, 200, 214.

94. Berlant, "Slow Death," 761.

95. Cheng, *The Melancholy of Race*, 14.

96. Foucault, "Subject and Power," 781.

97. Edkins and Pin-Fat, "Introduction," 18.

98. Parreñas, *Children of Global Migration*.

99. A 2003–4 study by the Scalabrini Migration Center *(Hearts Apart)* interviewed a large, representative sample of 10–12-year-old children in the Philippines, of both migrant and nonmigrant parents. The study found that the children

of overseas migrant workers were more likely to place their families in the middle (between poor and not poor, literally "on the line" between the two) than children of families without a parent working overseas. (Only 12 percent of children of migrant workers as compared to 31 percent of children without a parent working overseas classified their family as poor.) Migrant worker families are more likely to own their homes and own more major household appliances. The study also found that a much higher percentage of children of migrant workers attend private school compared to children of nonmigrants (40.9 percent compared to 14.9 percent, respectively).

100. Saunders, "Why Our Thinking about Immigration Remains Borderline."

101. Edkins and Pin-Fat, "Introduction," 17.

102. As a further way of thinking about this catastrophe, in its 2004 report the Critical Filipina and Filipino Studies Collective (*Resisting Homeland Security*) records a 67 percent increase in "noncriminal removals" among Filipinos in the United States between 2001 and 2003, the seventh highest among all the countries of origin considered (after Lebanon, Egypt, Jordan, Haiti, Uruguay, and Morocco). Of these, 42 percent involved legal permanent residents with aggregative felony convictions, such as previous drug convictions. Because of divergent state and federal sentencing guidelines, the Department of Homeland Security uses federal guidelines to determine felony convictions, even when individual states do not consider some of these convictions felonies. Filipino permanent residents who committed petty crimes and were convicted of a misdemeanor thus now face the threat of deportation. Granted, the United States is a different national context, but these events there heighten concerns about some of the consequences of difficult periods of adjustment among Filipino youths in Canada.

103. Chen, "The Child-Citizen."

104. Rose, *Powers of Freedom*, 97.

105. Miller and Rose, "Governing Economic Life," 10–11; see also Li, *The Will to Improve*.

106. Brown, "Neoliberalism and the End of Liberal Democracy."

2. Waiting and the Trauma of Separation

1. Diaz's short film was one of twenty films made by leading Filipino indie filmmakers, compiled as the film *Imagine Nation*, released in 2007.

2. Rothberg, "Between Auschwitz and Algeria," 170.

3. Edkins, *Trauma and the Memory of Politics*, 100.

4. There is a vast literature critiquing the LCP. See, for example, Macklin, "Foreign Domestic Worker"; Pratt, *Working Feminism*; Stasiulis and Bakan, "Negotiating the Citizenship Divide," and *Negotiating Citizenship*.

5. As another way of reading the "thin" youth interviews, I have considered

them as expressions of a different kind of agency, what Berlant terms "lateral agency" (in "Slow Death"). See Pratt, "Listening for Spaces."

6. Parreñas, "Mothering from a Distance," and *Children of Global Migration.* See also Hondagneu-Sotelo and Avila ("I'm Here, but I'm There") for an analysis of Latina transnational mothering.

7. See Battistella and Gastardo Conaco, "The Impact of Labour Migration on the Children Left Behind."

8. Parreñas, *Children of Global Migration,* 127, 125.

9. Colen, "Like a Mother."

10. Cvetkovich, *An Archive of Feelings,* 37.

11. McKay, "Sending Dollars Shows Feelings."

12. Ibid.; Hochschild, "Global Care Chains."

13. McKay, "Sending Dollars Shows Feelings," 188. See also Levitt ("Social Remittances") for a discussion of remittance flows other than financial.

14. Eng and Kazanjian, *Loss;* see also Cvetkovich, *An Archive of Feelings.*

15. Butler, "Afterword," 472.

16. This text calls upon interviews with the following people, identified by pseudonym (only one person per household is named and others are identified by relation to the person so that family relationships are evident): Albert (interviewed twice in August 2004); Jhimmy (interviewed twice in August 2004); Raphael (March 2005); Raphael's father (interviewed twice with wife, who is identified as Maria in chapter 1, both times separate from son: July and November 2004); Jeanette (interviewed with husband in September 2004); Judy (August 2004); Coretta (interviewed twice, once in the company of her son: December 2005, August 2007); Coretta's son (identified as Carlos in chapter 1 also participated in focus group with other youth: July 2006); Jack and James (interviewed together twice: August 2004, December 2007); Eduardo (November 2007); Rosita (interviewed twice, once alone and once in the company of two children: December 2006, November 2007); Rosita's daughter (interviewed November 2007 on her own and in the company of her mother); Rosita's son (interviewed November 2007 in the company of his brother and once with mother and sister); Tita (interviewed January 2008 with husband); Leonard (interviewed with wife in December 2004); Violet (August 2004); Marie (August 2004); Lisa and husband (September 2004); Susan (December 2004); Liberty (interviewed twice with children: June 2005, August 2007); Joy (February 2005); Michelle (interviewed December 2007).

17. For a discussion of these limits in the case of Salvadoran families, see Miyares et al. ("Interrupted Circle"). In an ethnographic account of communication within transnational Filipino families, Madianou and Miller ("Crafting Love," and "Mobile Phone Parenting") compare the ways that letters, cassette tapes, telephone calls, and text messaging work differently to establish different kinds

and intensities of intimacies. They note a marked discrepancy in the ways that Filipino children and their migrant mothers spoke about letters, mobile phones, and text messaging, with children more ambivalent about their capacity to maintain relations with their mothers through these media.

18. Valentine, "Globalizing Intimacy," 369, 375, 376. For discussions of the use of the Internet and other communications technologies by the Filipino diaspora in particular, see Ignacio, *Building Diaspora*; Paragas, "Migrant Mobiles"; Pertierra, *Transforming Technologies*.

19. Rafael, "Cell Phone."

20. "Philippines," *Internet World Stats*.

21. Fresnoza-Flot ("Migration Status and Transnational Mothering") also found the telephone—and not the Internet—to be the most frequent mode of communication among the Filipino women migrants she interviewed in Paris in 2006. Text messaging and mobile phones are now especially widely used. Dubbed the text capital of the world, there were approximately 42.8 million mobile phone subscribers in the Philippines in 2006, out of a population of 88.5 (Madianou and Miller, "Mobile Phone Parenting"; Pertierra, "Technologies of Transformation").

22. For example, Butler, *Precarious Life*; Saldanha, *Psychedelic White*.

23. Writing against a tendency in cultural theory to focus on vision as an objectifying, alienating modality, Kelly Oliver writes about the sensuality of face-to-face seeing. Vision, she argues, "operates with more seemingly proximal senses and is coordinated with the vesticular and motor systems." The space between the one who looks and the subject of the gaze is, she argues, "not an empty void." Recognizing that it is "full of air, light, and circulation of various forms of electrical, thermal, mechanical, chemical energies can," she argues, "reformulate vision and what it means to see" (*Witnessing*, 12). Although one could, in principle, make a similar argument about the energies that connect one ear to another via a telephone line, the connection seems more tenuous. The criticism that Eva Illouz makes of the Internet as a way of knowing another person seems equally relevant to the telephone: "The internet provides the kind of knowledge which, because it is disembedded and disconnected from a contextual and practical knowledge of the other person, cannot be used to make sense of the person as a whole." ... "Internet imagination is not opposed to reality; it is opposed to the kind of imagination that is based on the body and intuitive thought" (*Cold Intimacies*, 104, 106).

24. This also serves the pragmatic purpose of allowing mothers to purchase correctly sized shoes for their children in the Philippines.

25. This piece bridged art and activism: it included the two posters and a petition to be signed by those who viewed the posters.

26. Although we emphasize the limits to these visits, several researchers (Aranda, "Global Care Work"; Schmalzbauer, "Searching for Wages and Mothering from Afar"; Fresnoza-Flot, "Migration Status and Transnational Mothering") remind

us that undocumented migrant mothers do not have this privilege of return. Schmalzbauer, however, also describes the difficulties of parents' visits home among Honduran transnational families, including the burden these visits place on mothers or "other-mothers" caring for children in the home countries.

27. This is compatible with the findings of a large 2003 study conducted in the Philippines, which involved interviewing 1,443 children 10–12 years old. Roughly half the children of migrant parents said that their family had discussed why the parent had gone abroad (and this was more common when two parents had migrated): "A substantial number of children thus appear to have been left out in the decision making" concerning their parents' migration (Scalabrini Migration Center, Hearts Apart, 18).

28. Three key features of Post-Traumatic Stress Disorder are: intrusion and hyperarousal (or heightened sensitivity), numbing, and repetition. See Herman, Trauma and Recovery.

29. Edkins, Trauma and the Memory of Politics, 37–38.

30. Caruth, Unclaimed Experience, 62 (emphasis in original).

31. Parreñas, Children of Global Migration.

32. This joke turns on the fact that NPA usually refers to the outlawed New People's Army.

33. In a small study of five migrant mothers who returned to the Philippines after working in Asian countries, Asis ("From the Life Stories of Filipino Women") notes a similar distance between mothers and children.

34. For example, Berlant, The Queen of America Goes to Washington City; Brown, States of Injury.

35. For example, Cvetkovich, Archive of Feelings; Edkins, Trauma and the Memory of Politics.

36. Edkins, Trauma and the Memory of Politics, 230, 58, 58.

37. Sharma, Home Economics.

38. Sharma details the classed and racialized nature of temporary migration programs in Canada, arguing that the majority of temporary migrants work in service, farming, fabricating, assembling, and repair occupations. She argues that even those admitted under the professional category (such as physicians) often experience serious restrictions (e.g., their employment is tied to working in undesirable areas), such that "most of these workers are not the high-flyers touted as the future 'global worker' by some business pundits" (Home Economics, 125). A high proportion come from what Sharma classifies as Less Economically Developed Countries in the global South.

39. Edkins, Trauma and the Memory of Politics, 59.

40. Ong, Buddha Is Hiding.

41. Much of this work was shown again at the Vancouver Museum in March 2010 at an exhibit aptly titled "Shattering Our (in)visibility."

42. Joyce, "Caregiver Plan Indirectly Linked to Son's Death."

43. The e-mail continued: "But I have your name now and this will likely come up again soon. Thanks again."

3. Listening to Mothers' Stories

1. Read, "A Community Comes Together in Grief."

2. San Juan describes the controversies around the translation of the term *bahala na*, a cultural style said to be central to Filipino psychology. It commonly has been translated as "let the circumstances take care of themselves" or "Let God take care of it." San Juan argues that a formulaic invocation of psychological clichés has been used by American scholars and others to unlock "a whole people's history of underdevelopment" ("Toward a Decolonizing Indigenous Psychology in the Philippines," 50) and direct attention away from the role of U.S. imperialism in creating these economic and political conditions. An intellectual movement, Sikolohiyang Pilipino, has developed since the 1970s aimed at reconceptualizing Filipino psychology outside a U.S. colonial episteme. *Bahala na* has been reinterpreted as communicating not fatalism but determination and risk-taking, as a boost to morale to enable taking responsibility for action.

3. Indeed, the older of the two sons pictured here—too old to be sponsored as a dependent under the family reunification program—has not been allowed to stay in Canada, despite an appeal on humanitarian grounds after Jomar's death.

4. Cubilié, *Women Witnessing Terror*, 21.

5. The federal government made three changes to the regulations on the LCP in February 2010. First, a second medical examination is no longer required when applying for permanent resident status (the exam conducted when applying for the temporary work permit under the LCP will be sufficient). This is significant for anyone who contracts a serious chronic illness during the LCP, which in the past would have jeopardized their chances for permanent resident status. Second, domestic workers under the LCP can now calculate the twenty-four months required under the program on an hourly basis. They must complete 3,900 hours within a minimum of twenty-two months and can count up to 10 percent of overtime hours toward these hours. This stipulation appears to create the opportunity to complete the LCP more quickly, but consider the following: in practice, many employers do not pay overtime wages, and only 10 percent can be applied to the 3,900-hour requirement. To complete the 3,900 hours in twenty-two months, applying only 10 percent of overtime, a domestic worker would need to be working almost twelve hours a day, seven days a week, for twenty-two months in a row—without a break. Third, an LCP registrant now has forty-eight months to complete the 3,900 hours or twenty-four months of live-in care work. It should be noted that increasing the numbers of years allowed to complete the required time

as a live-in caregiver (from three to four) potentially prolongs the length of separation in ways that may exacerbate the problems detailed in chapter 1.

6. For example, Bejarano, "Super Madres de Latino America"; Bosco, "Human Rights Politics," and "The Madres de Plaza de Mayo"; Wright, "Urban Geography Plenary Lecture."

7. Berlant, "The Epistemology of State Emotion," 62.

8. The experiments with long testimonial narratives developed in this chapter opened additional possibilities; in particular, they allowed us to see the potential for constructing character-monologues and a testimonial play, the focus of chapter 4.

9. Whitlock, *Soft Weapons*, 18.

10. Ibid., 74, 79, 78. The Truth and Reconciliation Commission hearings took place in South Africa from 1996 to 1998 after apartheid was abolished. The commission heard public testimony from both victims and perpetrators of apartheid violence. In Australia, the term "Stolen Generations" refers to the removal of Aboriginal and Torres Strait Islander children from their families by government agencies and church missions. A national inquiry was held from 1995 through 1996, during which submissions were made by indigenous individuals and groups, as well as representatives of church and government organizations.

11. Keenan, "Mobilizing Shame"; Ball, "Trauma and Its Institutional Destinies."

12. Ball, "Trauma and Its Institutional Destinies," 16.

13. Seltzer, "Wound Culture," 3.

14. Ball, "Trauma and Its Institutional Destinies."

15. Ahmed, "Affective Economies."

16. Whitlock, *Soft Weapons*, 80.

17. For example, Brubaker, "The Return of Assimilation?"; Mitchell, "Geographies of Identity."

18. Ahmed, "Affective Economies."

19. Butler, *Precarious Life*; Gregory, *The Colonial Present.*

20. Pratt, "Stereotypes and Ambivalence."

21. Butler, *Precarious Life*, 134.

22. Popke, "Poststructural Ethics."

23. There is a fourth important risk: that mothers separated from their children will be considered as a special case under the LCP, with the effect of displacing attention from the conditions of the LCP shared by all women registered in the program, whether they have dependents or not. The implication might be that single women are more suited to the program because they make fewer claims against it. In relation to organizing against violence against women in northern Mexico, violence that has led to the deaths of hundreds of women in Ciudad Juárez, Wright ("Urban Geography Plenary Lecture") describes the disruptive effects of an essentializing maternal discourse, which has privileged the testimony

of mothers whose daughters have been murdered over a broader coalition of women activists. This type of fragmentation among critics of the LCP seems unlikely, although the issue of displacing attention from other aspects of the program is a potential problem.

A further risk is that the experiences of men in the LCP are marginalized within a maternal discourse. Men make up a minuscule proportion of those registered in the LCP, but they are among the most exploited insofar as they are more likely hired to do elder care (especially if it involves heavy lifting due to the restricted mobility of the person requiring care), which can be an around-the-clock job with virtually no relief. After all, parents typically come home at the end of their workday.

24. Registering the stigmatization in the Philippines of mothers (but not of fathers) who work overseas, Rhacel Parreñas has called for a feminist revisioning of gender relations within the family (such that a mother working overseas would invite no more criticism than a father who does so). This is an important strategy, but given the propensity for Canadians to imagine long-distance mothering as normal for Filipinas, there are important political reasons for stressing the centrality of the nuclear family and maternal bond in the Canadian context. Also, this is not a particularly conservative notion of mothering being advocated, given that Filipinas' continued labor market participation in Canada is unquestioned and so many mothers are lone parents.

25. Parreñas, *Children of Global Migration*.

26. As a further example, in a public event on Filipino youth and violence organized in November 2005 by the Vancouver School Board in collaboration with the Vancouver police, a social worker on the panel (introduced as a parent support person) framed parenting challenges for Filipino families within what she identified as an "ecological model." Challenges included: "communication breakdown," parents who are "too hard, even abusive by Canadian standards," the fact of children and parents belonging to two different cultures, family reunification, and a "cultural tendency" for Filipino parents to be slow to access services due to embarrassment. While these challenges no doubt exist, an adequate analysis would identify a wider ecology, and especially the effects of deskilling through the LCP, which forces many mothers to work in two or three jobs in order to cobble together subsistence wages.

27. Howard, "Steep Price."

28. Cubilié, *Women Witnessing Terror*; Oliver, *Witnessing*; Schaffer and Smith, *Human Rights and Narrated Lives*; Whitlock, *Soft Weapons*; Young, *Intersecting Voices*.

29. Oliver, *Witnessing*, 8.

30. This is central, as well, to Anne Cubilié's *(Women Witnessing Terror)* notion of ethical witnessing (as opposed to spectatorship). She draws on Derrida's argument that an ethical demand arises in response to the singular demands of others.

For Derrida, "The act of justice must always concern singularity, individuals, irreplaceable groups and lives" ("Force of Law," 17); justice thus operates in relation to but exceeds the law, rules, calculation.

31. Berlant, "The Epistemology of State Emotion," 52.

32. Whitlock, *Soft Weapons*, 156.

33. DeParle, "Good Provider."

34. Ibid., 53.

35. Berlant, "The Subject of True Feeling," and "The Epistemology of State Emotion."

36. Berlant, "Trauma and Ineloquence"; Cubilié, *Women Witnessing Terror*, 202.

37. Berlant, "Trauma and Ineloquence"; Schaffer and Smith, *Human Rights and Narrated Lives*.

38. Schaffer and Smith, *Human Rights and Narrated Lives*, 45.

39. Mohanty, *Feminism without Borders*.

40. See note 2 above.

41. Oliver, *Witnessing*, 86.

42. Cubilié, *Women Witnessing Terror*, 205. For the same reason but writing of representation more generally (that is, not of testimony in particular), Butler *(Precarious Life)* has argued that "the other" is humanized through representations that both fail and reveal their failure to fully represent. Such representations disrupt our capacity to absorb another into our identity and keep the process of active identification alive.

43. Oliver, *Witnessing*.

44. These presentations took place (with the exception of the last) among academic, typically non-Filipino audiences: at the Decolonising Affect conference at the University of British Columbia in June 2006, at National Taiwan University in fall 2007, at the University of Arizona in winter 2008, at the meeting of the Association of American Geographers (AAG) in spring 2008, and at the Vancouver Art Gallery in fall 2008.

45. Biddle, "Anthropology as Eulogy," 54. In 1992, Paul Keating, prime minister of Australia, in his Redfern speech, asked Australians to try to imagine the Aboriginal view. Langton writes that "Australians recognise these lines from that speech: 'We took the children from their mothers—it was our ignorance and our prejudice. And our failure to imagine these things being done to us. With some noble exceptions, we failed to make the most basic human response and enter into their hearts and minds. We failed to ask—how would I feel if this were done to me?'" ("Even the Hard Men Know, It Must Be Said"). Critical of this identification, Biddle is drawing upon psychoanalysis to theorize a melancholic model of identification as it operates within systems of racial differentiation and racism. Melancholic identification arises when the refusal to grieve a death leads to the active and repetitive incorporation of loss. Biddle reads white guilt as a way of

continuing a disavowed attachment to a lost object (the racial Other or [in the case of Cheng, *The Melancholy of Race*] the democratic ideal).

46. Of course not all viewers/listeners—even in a discipline as white as geography—were or will be non-Filipino or white, and inserting my son's photographs into domestic worker testimony works differently for differently positioned readers or listeners. At the presentation at the AAG meeting, a Filipino Canadian in the audience was troubled by the disruption that my son's photographs posed for his capacity to identify with Marlena's story and claim it as his own. And a reader of the published article on which this chapter is based e-mailed the following: "I would like to point out that the inclusion of the photos on the assumption that readers would [then] more easily identify with Marlena's story seems to indicate that you believe most or all of the readers of your paper will be white. Your presentation of Marlena's story already moved me and allowed me to empathize with her. The photos merely jolted me out of the feeling of empathy. Though I am Chinese and not Filipina, I think I can safely assume that Marlena's children look more like me than your son does." This is an important point and I thank the sender for it. But it is worth considering that it is equally important for Filipinos and other nonwhite readers to be jolted out of their identificatory practices, to question their relationship to the testimonials offered, and to inhabit the distance that inevitably exists between their experience and Marlena's. Placing a white child's pictures into her testimony is only one strategy toward such an end, one that led me back into Marlena's testimony to see how she already staged within it complicated encounters with privileged Canadians—something that I did not fully recognize or appreciate the significance of until the experiment with my child's photographs. The text has been performative, then, in a number of senses, and in different ways at different moments.

47. Barthes, *Camera Lucida*, 96.

48. Nunn, "Emotional Death."

49. Whitlock, *Soft Weapons*. There is more that can be said about the uneven topography of emotional proximities and distances created by the inserted photographs. One could examine, for instance, the complexity of emotional distances encapsulated in my family photographs by considering the work that such photographs have done to stabilize my emotions in relation to my own child and mothering. Gillian Rose analyzes how white middle-class mothers use photographs of their children to actively mediate and negotiate their emotional relationship with their small children—both to gain some distance and to get close. "I would like to suggest," she writes, "that perhaps one of the reasons hateful feelings towards children are not acted out . . . is because photographs can work to steady the ambivalent feelings of love and hate that most mothers have towards their children" ("Everyone's Cuddled Up and It Just Looks Really Nice," 561). This fragment of analysis

gestures toward a rich field of emotional proximities and distances, unsettling the integrity of the viewer and disrupting what Cathy Caruth has characterized as "our facile empathy and our rush to comprehension" (*Unclaimed Experience,* 52).

50. In this respect, an e-mail from Marlena, responding to an inquiry about the appropriateness of her pseudonym and confirming that she was comfortable with the omission of her son's photographs (which I had in my possession) is telling: "I don't mind about the name, just only my son's photo [which she did not want included]. He doesn't want to recall what happened that time because [people continue to] accuse my son."

51. Or possibly not, depending on your own racial and class identifications. Rather than assuming a white, middle-class audience, I am attempting to explore the possibilities of unsettling identification in differently productive ways.

52. Whitlock, "In the Second Person," 209.

53. Butler is drawing upon Levinas's analysis of the face: "The nonviolence that Levinas promotes does not come from a peaceful place but rather from a constant tension between the fear of undergoing violence and fear of inflicting violence" (*Precarious Life,* 137).

54. Biddle, "Anthropology as Eulogy," 55.

55. For a more extended presentation of Liberty's life narrative, see Lee and Pratt, "Migrant Worker: Migrant Stories."

56. Her employers likely immigrated to Canada under one of the Business Immigration Programs, at the other end of the class (and gender) spectrum from the LCP. See Ley, *Millionaire Migrants.*

57. Berlant, "The Epistemology of State Emotion," 60–61.

58. Interview by author with Filipino-Canadian Youth Alliance, Vancouver, May 10, 2004.

59. Ong, *Neoliberalism as Exception.*

60. Tadiar, *Things Fall Away.*

61. Ibid., 138, 378.

4. Creating New Spaces of Politics

1. For a brief introduction to testimonial or documentary theater, see Anderson and Wilkinson, "A Resurgence of Verbatim Theater."

2. The distinction between the archive and repertoire is Diana Taylor's (*Archive and the Repertoire*).

3. We thank Martin Kinch, of Vancouver's Playwright Theatre Centre, for his incredibly useful and unfailing help as dramaturge and for the invaluable resources of the Playwright Theatre Centre. Thanks also to Norman Armour, executive director of the PuSh Festival for his faith in our production and the material support of the festival.

4. Ironically, the radio program, aired on Vancouver Cooperative Radio, is called Arts Rational.

5. For this, we received a women's rugby trophy dipped in chocolate, decorated with gold and blue stars. The Children's Choice Awards was itself a performance conceived and executed by the Mammalian Diving Reflex, a Toronto-based "research-art atelier." Twelve children from the municipality of Surrey's Bridgeview Elementary School were driven from event to event, and an award ceremony was held on the last afternoon of the festival. The children were given the option to present awards from more than fifty categories, only some of which touched on affective categories such as most emotional, most joyful, most annoying, most horrific. Other categories included: longest tongue, biggest eyes, best costumes, best music. The children awarded in twenty-five categories overall: best beginning, best hair, most educational for parents, funniest voice, best use of technology, most "I don't care" (we're happy not to have received that), best solo, most sad, most funny, most loud and clear, best use of adjectives, the longest, best teamwork, best use of props, creepiest, most interesting, most international languages, most weird, most realistic, most cheering applause, best driver, best overall. (See http://pushfestival.ca and www.childrenschoiceawards.blogspot.com.)

6. Stewart, *Ordinary Affects*, 40, 42.

7. Berlant, "Thinking about Feeling Historical," 6.

8. See also Berlant, "Critical Inquiry, Affirmative Culture." For an early attempt by geographers to resist this geography of emotionality and rationality and to theorize the emotionality of political and economic life, see Anderson and Smith, "Editorial: Emotional Geographies."

9. Burk, *Speaking for a Long Time*.

10. In her resistance to it, one member of the Filipino-Canadian Youth Alliance nonetheless described the steady traffic between the Kalayaan Centre and the theater as we developed and rehearsed the play: "I see people going back and forth to the Chapel Arts, but I really never stopped by because I wanted to be surprised a bit. You know, 'Come, come, its only a block across from the Centre.' And I say, 'Ah, I'll just wait so I don't ruin it for myself.'"

11. When the play was restaged at the Hebbel Theater in Berlin, the same setup was approximated: the Canadian employers were in a relatively richly appointed public area of the theater, the domestic worker scenes in behind-the-scenes working regions of the theater. The only scene in which the actual theater was used was a monologue by a nanny agent, not included in the Vancouver production. The CIC agent and youth scene and talkback were on the stage, literally behind the curtain.

12. There were actually three ways through the play: the audience of fifty was separated into three groups: twenty-five first went upstairs to experience the

employer monologues, and the remainder split into smaller groups of roughly twelve to go through the domestic worker scenes in one of two orders. Those who saw the domestic-worker scenes were then collapsed into a larger group to see the testimonial scenes upstairs, and the larger group upstairs was divided into two smaller groups to witness the domestic-worker scenes.

13. The monologue is developed from the interviews with Liberty, discussed in chapters 1, 2, and 3. Liberty is the pseudonym chosen by the "interviewee," but the character is renamed Ligaya in the play. The entire monologue developed for the play is published in Johnston and Pratt, "Nanay [Mother]."

14. The two actors playing Filipina domestic workers had to perform their monologues four times in each performance because the audience was divided into such small sub-audiences for their monologues in particular. With four performances on the Saturday, this made for sixteen performances altogether.

15. In the Vancouver production, the guides were Filipino Canadian activists who had been involved in the research as interviewers and focus group participants: Michelle Co, Charlene Sayo, and Carlo Sayo.

16. For access to this audio recording, see Johnston and Pratt, "Nanay [Mother]."

17. Baucom (Specters of the Atlantic) provides an extraordinary account of the Zong massacre, the landmark court case, and the political and cultural struggles that followed. A calculation of profit and risk led the captain of the Zong in 1781 to throw 132 slaves overboard, with the prospect of realizing through an insurance claim their value as "jettisoned cargo." "To the extent the case of the Zong was to help define the struggle between slave traders and abolitionists in the late eighteenth century, the way in which that struggle was waged suggests that it was not only a struggle between competing theories of right (the slave's right to human dignity and the slavers' right to trade), but one between competing theories of knowledge, a struggle between an empirical and a contractual, an evidentiary and a credible epistemology" (16).

18. Abraham and Torok, The Shell and the Kernel.

19. Baucom, Specters of the Atlantic, 132.

20. In a community assessment organized by the PWC after the Vancouver production, one activist spoke of the force of seeing this interview, which she had done as a community organizer, transformed into a theatrical performance: "I've been involved [for many years] with doing community-based research, which involves documenting and interviewing women or nurses who come through the Centre to share their migration experience. So Sheila and I conducted one of the interviews [used to create Joanne's monologue]. And we didn't expect it to be part of the play. And I guess it was done four or five years ago. [Crying.] And it was just seeing it alive again. You know, they were done and it's part of our daily organizing and documenting our history as a community. But seeing it presented live in that cultural way, it just struck in a completely different way that I didn't expect."

21. Sarah Zell describes her experience as an audience member: "In our viewing, she actually poured a full bucket of water (for her mop) into the drain in the center of the room, and it splashed up onto the trouser hems of a few audience members, and licked the shoes of everyone in the room."

22. Baucom, *Specters of the Atlantic*, 230.

23. In almost one-third of the questionnaires that were returned with comments, there was a question about the representativeness of the testimony. Some audience members were simply disgruntled because they felt that our play did not represent their experience: they had themselves been a good employer, had as a child loved their own nanny intensely, or simply imagined that some experiences were good. They could not imagine an epistemological framing in which we were not speaking about all Canadian employers, all domestic workers, or some average or typical experience. Our dramaturge anticipated the audience desire for typicality and balance and urged us to include a testimonial from a domestic worker who had had a positive experience. (This we did, but the director cut this testimony because of the difficulty of accommodating it within the time constraints.) Some audience members asked for a positive example from the same desire to help us strengthen the persuasiveness of our case against the LCP by demonstrating our balanced perspective: "Obviously the point of the show is to highlight the horrendous experiences of the LCP participants, but by not sharing any positive stories, you put the question 'What about those who aren't treated this way?' in the minds of the audience, which is distracting from the central message. Better to address it than leave even a friendly elephant in the room." From another: "It would be good to hear about those who the program worked for/had okay employers who can also complicate their experiences. Not a romantic rosy view but a positive critical view. Otherwise I fear some could dismiss the very real experiences as hyperbole."

24. Boltanski (*Distant Suffering*) analyzes the necessity of this paradoxical slippage between singularity and the exemplary for politics.

25. Using the word *nanay* also captures the slipperiness of domestic workers' own passage between mother and servant. It should be noted, however, that the process of naming the play was by no means straightforward and was resolved through an uneasy and deadline-imposed compromise among collaborators. PWC board members and the members of SIKLAB felt that *Nanay* was too "benign" and preferred the title *Atsay* (which they translated from Tagalog as "maid, slave, servant"). Their reading of *nanay* as benign in part reflected their linguistic competence, which led them to interpret the word within its stable meaning in Tagalog, and not for its mercurial slippage between English and Tagalog. A Tagalog word perhaps, but one that works more effectively in the context of an English audience, a sobering example of the politics and limits of intercultural translation. The name of the play met with some resistance from English speakers as well. For

a long time the working title for the play was *Homekeeper*. When the suggestion was made to use a Tagalog word, some worried that this would turn away English-speaking audiences.

26. Another jotted on a questionnaire as he or she went through the show: "I am glad that there are members of the Filipino community in the audience. I'd like to hear their reactions."

27. Butler, *Giving an Account of Oneself*, 46.

28. The potential to empathize with a real living person was heightened in the Berlin production (more below), where the actor delivered the monologue dressed in her own clothes, beside projected images, both of herself as a child in the company of her own mother and of her actual mother aging over the course of time.

29. For example, Anderson and Wilkinson, "A Resurgence of Verbatim Theatre."

30. Rancière is a natural ally for theorizing *Nanay* because theatrical metaphor runs through his theorizing of equality and emancipation, so much so that Peter Hallward (Staging Equality") applies to it the Platonic term "theatrocracy." But even more important, Rancière is alert to theater, not just as metaphor but as a concrete space and practice, and as a privileged site of politics.

31. This is central to Rancière's notion of egalitarian and democratic politics. Politics exist, he argues, when people who do not count or have a fixed place within the social order demand to be included in the public sphere, to be seen and heard on an equal footing. Politics is not the business-as-usual of contestation between already existing interest groups; it is a fundamental disruption of the existing "distribution of the sensible." With this phrase, the distribution of the sensible, Rancière is referring to the limits of what it is possible to see, hear, and say within existing social arrangements. What he calls "politics" arises at the meeting of two logics: "egalitarian" and "police." He does not intend the latter term to be understood pejoratively, and it does not refer, in the first instance, to the legitimate violence or disciplinary practices of a state apparatus. The term "police" refers to social classification, the distribution of private and public space, occupational hierarchy, and normative patterns of inclusion and exclusion. A social scientist investigating the settlement and integration of immigrants or a nongovernmental organization implementing multicultural policy are equally part of this police process of naming and sorting bodies into properties, tasks, functions, occupations, and places. As Rancière notes, some police are better than others and police have the capacity to "procure all sorts of goods" (*Disagreement*, 31).

Although political subjectification is not, by Rancière's reckoning, anchored in specific identities or properties (indeed, the aim of politics is the disruption of classification schemas in the existing order), the structural conditions of migrant domestic workers make them likely prospects for politics because they are neither quite inside nor outside the nation. Migrants' articulation of their exclusion from and within an existing sociopolitical order is a performative contradiction: it performs their equality as speaking human beings with political capabilities at the same time as it speaks of their exclusion from the sociopolitical order. This articulation of political rights is different from claiming victim status; it is in itself an assertion of political capability and a demonstration of equality. For Rancière, equality is not an ontological principle that politics "presses into service" (33); it is discerned only in the practices that make it manifest. That is, it is a universal presupposition in need of constant verification.

32. The concern was unfounded. Almost all performances were at capacity. Over the thirteen performances in Vancouver, 577 people saw the play. There were six performances in Berlin.

33. Hallward, "Staging Equality," 119.

34. Jestrovic ("Performing Like an Asylum Seeker") discusses two fascinating performance events that trade on the cache of using actual refugees, asylum seekers, and immigrants: a fashion show in Barcelona featuring illegal immigrants from West Africa as models, and Christoph Schlingensief's public art project "Foreigners Out!" Although at first blush both performances seem highly exploitative, Jestrovic makes the case for a more complicated ethical and political assessment.

35. I am referencing Rancière's definition of democracy: for him, the term designates neither a form of society nor government but the utter contingency— that is, equality—of those who govern and those who are governed. In other words, in democracy, government elites have no natural claim to their authority. The democratic public sphere is a sphere of encounter in which the logics of politics and police come into contest, in which the contingency of social relations is enacted. He argues that there is a tendency for any particular government to shrink the public sphere, "making it its own private affair," privatizing and removing from common debate and consideration many of the concerns of ordinary citizens (Hatred of Democracy, 55). Democracy, in Rancière's view, is the struggle to enlarge the public sphere, to redistribute public and private, both by publicly performing the equality of those subjected to government, and by establishing the public character of spaces, relations, and institutions (such as the family) that have been relegated to the private sphere. "Democracy really means, in this sense, . . . the challenging of governments' claims to embody the sole principle of public life and in doing so to be able to circumscribe the understanding and extension of public life" (62).

36. In another talkback session, this feeling of being destabilized was expressed in this way: "As a theatergoer, to be led through the different rooms it felt like I was on a tour of a famous old house and there were actors playing the characters in the house, except it wasn't a famous old house, it was a house here in Canada and the actors were playing real people who were working in that house. So it was very . . . it's clear to me that it was a very clinical process of going through these different rooms and looking through materials and sort of being an observer and

sitting and watching as the theatergoer and patron. And then at the same time . . . it's very personal and immediate to people. So it's an experience where you're wearing two hats. It's obviously something that's going to affect someone you know or someone you've met or perhaps you or someone in your family. But the process of seeing it as a performance is detached. . . . It's interesting to try to understand how to read it as an audience member."

37. I facilitated the talkback (I was already in the play as interlocutor of the child of the LCP) with a member of the Filipino activist community. In Vancouver, Carlo Sayo, chair of the Filipino-Canadian Youth Alliance and Charlene Sayo co-facilitated talkbacks. In Berlin, Dinah Estigoy, then of the PWC, performed this function.

38. Dolan, *Utopia in Performance,* 2.

39. Ibid., 8, 21.

40. Hallward, "Staging Equality," 117. The embedded quotation is to Rancière, "Dix theses sur la politique," 242.

41. I do want to thank everyone involved, including Philippine embassy representatives—who could have felt under attack and easily removed themselves from the discussion—for their willingness to engage in such a vigorous public discussion in the talkback, which lasted until 11:00 P.M. (and into the bar afterward)

42. Rancière, *Disagreement,* 55.

43. Ibid., 56.

44. Dean's argument (in "Politics without Politics") is actually two-pronged. She argues that Rancière's political theory is both sociologically naive and politically misguided (the latter for the reason already mentioned). It is sociologically naive in her view because it assumes some level of mutual understanding that is "rather far-fetched." She argues that "our present political-medialogical setting is one of dissensus, incredulity, and competing concepts of reality"(32). In making this claim, Dean draws on David Donaldson's "principle of charity." This principle posits as a necessary background assumption that, in order to understand another, we have to "count them right in most matters" (32). Dean argues that this principle of charity has "withered away," and for good "material-technological" reasons: so much of our communication is now mediated by machines that are "charitable in our stead," and these machines allow us to create and restrict our communication to those in like-minded communities. We increasingly communicate, often via electronic media, within geographically dispersed but narrowly conceived, like-minded communities. Fewer and fewer common assumptions are held, she contends, across these different worlds. In arguing thus, Dean helps make the case for the significance of the time-space presence of a theatrical experience such as *Nanay* and the importance of the affective intensity of witnessing across social worlds.

45. Hallward, "Staging Equality," 128, 125.

46. Dolan, *Utopia in Performance,* 19–20 (emphasis in original).
47. Burvill, "Politics Begins as Ethics," 234.
48. Berlant, "Thinking about Feeling Historical," 6, 5, 5.
49. Rancière quoted in Hallward, "Staging Equality," 115.
50. Other comments included the following: "I used to run a Home Depot with 100–300 employees being Philippino. They were a very tight community. This helps me to gain insight into their community"; "As someone who has worked in the service industry for many years, I worked with many philipinas. We always valued their hard work and ability to hold down several jobs concurrently. I remember hearing stories about working for families or hearing about caring for elderly people, but I never gained such an insider view from the stories. Many of the comments that I heard at work were somewhat fatalistic and along the lines of—'Oh, I just need to do this' and 'This is how it works.' I wish more of my co-workers could have shared their *real* feelings about how they were treated"; "I have a better understanding now of why so many Philipino boys in our high schools are so detached and have so much trouble succeeding"; "I have elderly parents requiring significant care and a sibling is pushing for an LCP caregiver. This play provided a bit more personal detail to support principled argument against my sibling, which may help convince her."
51. Geoff Meggs blog, "Nanay: Filipino word meaning 'mother,'" February 9, 2009. www.geoffmeggs.ca (accessed August 18, 2010).
52. To contextualize this statement: "While the physical space and the location of the different stories emphasize the two solitudes between the employers and the live-in caregivers, I also felt that the play was a very good opportunity for us to try to bridge those two groups. My personal experience of course has been as an advocate in the [Filipino] community. But I also grew up here in Canada. I work in different provincial governments. So a lot of the people I actually come into contact with are employers. But the play gave me more of a space to try to understand how we can bridge those two groups while appreciating the distinction between the classes, between races, between genders. I think that the talkback really emphasized for me that it's a human rights issue and it's a woman's issue. So as a mother who is a working mother, as a Filipina, it was really a good chance for me to see how those different perspectives can perhaps come together in the long term: that we have child care that is accessible for all working women here in Canada."
53. Salverson, "Taking Liberties," 247. See also Anderson and Wilkinson, "A Resurgence of Verbatim Theatre"; Martin, "Bodies of Evidence."
54. Burvill, "Politics Begins as Ethics," 233. See also Blunt et al., "My Home."
55. *Future Folk* was written and performed by the Sulong Theatre Collective at Theatre Passe Muraille in Toronto in February 2010.
56. Nestruck, "Dated Agitprop Muffles Caregivers' Battle Cry," R9.
57. Ben-Zvi, *Staging the Other Israel.*

5. Acting on Attachments

1. Massey, *For Space,* 5.
2. Young, *Inclusion and Democracy,* 222.
3. Robinson, *Globalizing Care.*
4. Engster, "Rethinking Care Theory," 62.
5. Massey, *For Space;* Weir, "The Global Universal Caregiver."
6. Tadiar, "Death by Death."
7. These comments were made at the public screening on Friday, June 4, 2010, at UBC Robson Square.
8. Featherstone, "Spatialities of Transnational Resistance to Globalisation"; Sundberg, "Reconfiguring North-South Solidarity"; Wright, "Urban Geography Plenary Lecture."
9. Popke, "Poststructuralist Ethics," 300; see also Barnett, "Who Cares?" and "Ways of Relating"; Korf, "Antinomies of Generosity"; Silk, "Caring at a Distance."
10. Butler, "Sexual Politics, Torture, and Secular Time," 21.
11. It is important in this regard to stress that, although the Canadians attempted to contact the Melo Commission once inside the Philippines, theirs was not an official government-sponsored mission, and thus it was not subject to the same kinds of constraints on interaction (nor, presumably, the same protections against state violence) as has been the case for other international observers to the Philippines, such as Philip Alston (U.N. Special Rapporteur on extrajudicial killings). (The Melo Commission was created by President Arroyo to determine the root causes of the killings and the persons or groups responsible. It conducted public hearings in which witnesses and resource persons from activist groups and the military were invited to testify. The Canadian fact-finding mission attempted to meet with the Melo Commission but were unable to arrange this. Doubting the impartiality of the commission and the safety of witnessing, the commission was boycotted by a number of leftist groups, including KARAPATAN. The Melo report was released on February 22, 2007.) KARAPATAN reported six international peace and solidarity fact-finding missions to the Philippines from 2005 to August 2006 (Hilao-Enriquez, "Philippine Government's Action on Human Rights"). Apart from Amnesty International, these included: Dutch Foundation Lawyers without Borders (July 15–20, 2006), which held interviews in Manila, Quezon City, and Tacloban City, Leyte; the Hong Kong Christian Institute (July 2006); as well as an international fact-finding mission in June 2006 described by Franco and Abinales ("Again, They're Killing"). Since this time, in response to the Stop the Killings campaign, there have been many other missions, including: the Hong Kong Mission for Human Rights and Peace in the Philippines (October 16–22, 2007); Public Services International (February 2007); the Tokyo-based Human Rights Now (April 2007); the European Union Needs Assessment Mission (June

2007); International Federation of Human Rights Leagues (August 2007). Ning identified the unusual nature of their mission: "[Other missions] mostly stayed in Manila, or they went to the urban areas in the provinces. And the victims' families came to them and explained their cases. Our mission was really different because it was fact-finding, trying to investigate cases that hadn't been documented before." The mission described by Franco and Abinales seems similar in its commitment to fact-finding in rural areas.

12. The point references Derrida's ("Force of Law") often-cited distinction between law and justice: justice is an incalculable response to the singular demand of the other, which is never assured by a rule or law.

13. Taussig, *The Nervous System*, 51.

14. This analysis is based on a long association with the Filipino Canadian organizers of the mission (through our research on Filipino migrant workers and their families in Canada), interviews with six participants of the mission, and both attendance at and participation as a panelist at a solidarity roundtable on this issue.

15. Bernstein, "Bare Life, Bearing Witness," 10, 11.

16. Nonetheless, our focus on militarization in the Philippines speaks to the implementation of state terror in other places and at other times, not least because the "Philippine model" of counterinsurgency warfare is part of the genealogy of such practices elsewhere. The "psy-war" operations and deliberate use of civilian terror in these psychological operations developed in the Philippines through the 1950s and 1960s "became standards in the repertoire of American counterinsurgency" (McClintock, *Instruments of Statecraft*, 115), and were used in Vietnam and then transported to Central America. Writing in 1992, McClintock claimed: "Most of its precepts remain intact in American counterinsurgency doctrine today" (126).

17. It is too early to say if the election of Benigno Aquino Jr. III as president in the May 2010 national and local elections will improve the situation. However, on August 9, 2011, Care2 Action sent out the following petition for electronic signature: "Demand that President Aquino take action against human rights violations committed by the military," citing the murder of seven activists and the disappearance of three others since he has come to power.

18. These are the numbers reported and accepted by the Permanent Peoples' Tribunal, Second Session on the Philippines (2007). The tribunal reported that 839 unarmed civilians were killed from the start of the Arroyo regime (in January 2001) until March 2007. During this period, another 194 were forcibly abducted and remain missing. There are a further 799 documented cases of torture. The full extent of forced migration and displacement due to fears of military reprisal is more difficult to quantify. See also Franco and Abinales ("Again, They're Killing Peasants in the Philippines") and Tolentino and Raymundo (*Kontra-Gahum*). KARAPATAN estimates that from 2007 until the end of March 2009 there were

another 180 extrajudicial killings, and 40 enforced disappearances (*Karapatan Monitor*). The number of political killings peaked in 2005–6; the disappearances peaked in 2006. KARAPATAN credits the relative decline in both in 2007 to international pressure, as well as to the fact that the Philippine government—signatory to a number of human rights covenants—underwent a Universal Periodic Review by the United Nations Human Rights Council working group in April 2008 (KARAPATAN, *2007 Year-End Report on the Human Rights Situation in the Philippines*). Abductions, disappearances, arrests, and tortures increased again in the third quarter of 2008 (*Karapatan Monitor*).

19. Raymundo, "Counterpoint," xi. As Glassman notes, after 9/11, processes of democratization and demilitarization were "kicked into reverse through a U.S. attempt to refurbish hegemony in Southeast Asia" ("Imperialism Imposed and Invited," 94). As the "second front" of the war on terror, U.S. military assistance to the Philippines jumped from 2000 to 2003, and the Philippines is now the fourth largest beneficiary of U.S. military aid (San Juan, "Neocolonial State Terrorism"). Regular military funding to the Philippines was increased threefold in November 2007, from $11 million to $30 million. The release of a further $2 million is tied to the Philippines government taking action against the extrajudicial killings, including implementing the recommendations of Philip Alston's U.N. report (Balana, "US Aid Tied to RP Action on Killings"). Critics argue that the present governmental mode is "crisis opportunism" and that the war on terror created the crisis and opportunity for a renewed war against counterinsurgents, and now leftist opponents (Tolentino and Raymundo, *Kontra-Gahum*).

20. For example, Tolentino and Raymundo, *Kontra-Gahum*; and for a longer historical view on the use of counterinsurgency tactics in the Philippines, see McClintock, *Instruments of Statecraft*. The protracted peace process and human rights agreement between the Philippine government and the National Democratic Front (representing the Community Party of the Philippines and its armed wing, the New People's Army) has broken down. As Amnesty International (*Philippines*, 7) noted: "The listing of the CPP-NPA as a foreign 'Terrorist Organisation' by the US and the EU and other allies in 2002 proved a major impediment to continued negotiations." In early 2002, the Arroyo government's renewed commitment to "crush" communist insurgency was operationalized through a new five-year anti-insurgency plan, Operation Bantay-Laya (Freedom Watch). In 2006, President Arroyo called for "all-out war" to crush the CPP-NPA within two years.

21. Agence France Presse, "Philippine Government," 2, 21. For a criticism of the 2006 Amnesty International Report coming from the Filipino left, see San Juan ("Neocolonial State Terrorism"). In San Juan's view, there is a marked discordance between Amnesty International's "realistic diagnosis of the environment" and "climate of impunity" and its "wish-fulfilling" recommendations (which relied on the Arroyo-led state to police itself).

22. Conde, "Europeans Add Credibility." Foreign Affairs Secretary Alberto Romulo reported that he sent letters on January 21, 2007, to Spain, Germany, the UK, Finland, Sweden, the Netherlands, and the European Union for technical assistance in the investigations (Reuters, "Manila Asks Europe to Help Probe Political Killings").

23. Espina-Varona, "Kin, Colleagues Brave Risk to Join U.N. Probe into Killings."

24. Alston's final report, released in August 2007, is available at http://stopthe killings.org.

25. Uy, "Alston."

26. Conde, "Europeans Add Credibility."

27. Macan-Markar, "UN Investigating Extrajudicial Killings."

28. Doty, *Imperial Encounters;* San Juan, *After Postcolonialism.*

29. Campbell, "Geopolitics and Visuality," 359.

30. For a critique of Canadians' framing of themselves as a "white knights" within international politics, see Razack, *Dark Threats and White Knights.*

31. KARAPATAN is highly visible and widely respected internationally. It made the arrangements for many of the witnesses who testified in the Alston investigation. It was one of the initiating organizations of the Permanent Peoples' Tribunal Second Session of the Philippines convened in The Hague on October 30, 2006 (see Permanent Peoples' Tribunal, 2007). In March 2007, KARAPATAN appeared before the U.S. East Asian and Pacific Affairs Subcommittee chaired by Senator Barbara Boxer (D-Calif.) on the extrajudicial political killings. On September 24, 2007, KARAPATAN Secretary General Marie Hilao-Enriquez spoke before the United Nations Human Rights Council in Geneva.

32. KARAPATAN estimates that between January 21, 2001, and September 30, 2008, thirty-four human rights workers of KARAPATAN or allied organizations were killed, another three disappeared, six survived "frustrated killing," seven were tortured, eighteen were arrested illegally, sixteen were arrested illegally and detained, and thirty were physically assaulted (KARAPATAN, *2008 Year-End Report*).

33. Mydans and Conde, "Extrajudicial Killings on the Rise."

34. Tadiar, "Death by Death," 182. KARAPATAN's analysis is that the government targeted areas for increased militarization where the influence of various people's organizations, including peasants groups, unions, and political parties, are particularly strong, whether or not they also were areas where the NPA was known to operate.

35. The following members of the fact-finding mission were interviewed by the author in Vancouver: Cecilia Diocson (chair, National Alliance of Philippine Women in Canada, interviewed May 2007); Ted Alcuitas (BC Committee for Human Rights in the Philippines, July 31, 2007); Elizabeth Grayer (Bus Rider's Union, Vancouver, August 2, 2007); Jennifer Efting (Bus Rider's Union, Vancouver,

August 4, 2007); Merryn Edwards (Grassroots Women, August 3, 2007); and Luningning Alcuitas-Imperial (Philippine Women Centre of BC, August 7, 2007).

36. The highest number of deaths is recorded in Bicol (171 as of March 31, 2009). Southern Tagalog and Central Luzon have the highest number of enforced disappearances of any region in the Philippines (29 and 66, respectively; *Karapatan Monitor*).

37. The fact-finding missions to the Cordillera region and Central Manila did not directly experience the same degree of intimidation.

38. Barnett, "Ways of Relating"; Silk, "Caring at a Distance"; see Hume, "(Young) Men with Big Guns," for a discussion of the collapse of distance for and the emotional engagement of the researcher of situations of violence.

39. Taylor, *Disappearing Acts*, 18.

40. San Juan, *After Postcolonialism*, 91.

41. Ibid., 91, 126.

42. See also Choy, "Towards Trans-Pacific Social Justice."

43. As organizers from the Kalayaan Centre have noted in reaction to a draft of this chapter, there is nothing "natural" about this political analysis. Migrant workers who have tangible experience of violence in the Philippines may not see the connection to the violence of the LCP, and so activists who went on the fact-finding mission have a responsibility to return their analysis not only to privileged Canadians but also to migrants who might not see the connections. These stories of witnessing in the Philippines are therefore openings to further politicization of migrant workers in Canada.

44. The Kalayaan Centre now houses seven organizations, addressing different aspects of Filipino Canadians' lives. The oldest organization is the BC Committee for Human Rights in the Philippines, which was founded in 1982. See www.kalayaancentre.net/content/organizations/index.htm.

45. Rafael, *White Love and Other Events in Filipino History*; San Juan, *After Postcolonialism*.

46. San Juan, "Neocolonial State Terrorism," 20, 21.

47. Grassroots Women is an organization initiated by the Philippine Women Centre of BC in 1995. For details, see http://grassrootswomen.ca/ (accessed August 20, 2010).

48. Lawson, "Geographies of Care and Responsibility"; see also Cumbers, Routledge, and Nativel, "Entangled Geographies of Global Justice Networks"; Robinson, *Globalizing Care*.

49. Massey, "Geographies of Responsibility," 182.

50. Featherstone, "Spatialities of Transnational Resistance," 405.

51. Mitchell, *Rule of Experts*.

52. For example, the Grassroots Women's campaign, "Universal Childcare Is a Woman's Right," is rooted in the belief that working-class women's lack of access

to child care has severe impacts on equality. This campaign has supported the call of Filipino migrant workers organizations to "Scrap the LCP," in recognition that the LCP not only transfers the burdens of child care from middle- or upper-class women to Third World women, but denies working-class women in Canada access to affordable child care. For Grassroots Women, genuine women's liberation will be achieved only when all working-class women, including migrant and indigenous women, have overcome the barriers to equality—in this instance, the lack of recognition of child care as a societal, rather than individual or family, responsibility.

53. Katz, "On the Grounds of Globalization."

54. Macklin ("Like Oil and Water, with a Match") notes that the mission to Sudan in which she participated was evidence that the Canadian government accepts the premise of moral (if not legal) accountability for private Canadian capitalists' unregulated conduct in Third World countries. She also suggests, however, that the mission functioned as an exercise in legitimation: after their report came out, the Canadian government said that it would take no action against Talisman Energy, the Canadian company that was the focus of their attention. After this announcement, company shares bounced from $35 to $50 per share.

55. Stavenhagen, *Report of the Special Rapporteur on the Situation of Human Rights*, 15.

56. Doel, *Poststructuralist Geographies*, 18.

57. Choy, "Towards Trans-Pacific Social Justice."

58. As Fujita-Rony ("Coalitions, Race, and Labor") points out, this calls attention to the fact that the Filipino American community is not a consolidated entity: many supported the Marcos regime.

59. Bello and Reyes, "Filipino Americans and the Marcos Overthrow"; Domingo, "Until We Have a True Democracy"; Takami, "Marcoses Found Liable."

60. Taylor, *Disappearing Acts.*

61. Hume, "(Young) Men with Big Guns."

62. Taylor, *Disappearing Acts*, 25, 261.

63. Amnesty International—as do many others—cites the refusal of witnesses to come forward as a major obstacle to efforts to investigate and collect evidence sufficient to file criminal charges (*Philippines*, 26).

64. Mario Florendo is number 115 in Bayan Muna's list of party members killed since April 2001. Bayan Muna (People First) is a legal leftist political party. It documents his death thus: on 07/30/06 in Sitio Toboy, Parista, Lupao, Nueva Ecija by elements of the 71st PA delta coy under Lt. Rubilino Cabarliz.

65. The town of Lupao in Nueva Ecija province is a deeply symbolic site: it was the site of the "Lupao massacre," where government soldiers under President Corazon Aquino killed seventeen peasants in 1987 (Bolos, "Two Presidents and the Lupao Massacre").

66. The quotations are a pastiche taken from the interviews with the two Canadian observers on this particular team: Ted Alcuitas (interviewed July 31, 2007) and Merryn Edwards (interviewed August 3, 2007).

67. Mario's wife later reported that the military's intimidation that prevented the community from mourning publicly for her husband's death was one of the hardest parts of dealing with his death.

68. Those interviewed about Mario's death also spoke of the terrorization of the entire village. All but two families had been called in for questioning (to "clear their names"), questioning that routinely involved physical violence. The military had gone house to house, counting the number of plates. If the number exceeded the number of people in the household, they were accused of supporting the NPA. These kinds of widespread tactics are clearly less about targeting specific ongoing political resistance and more about generally asserting dominance and authority and making it clear that any form of opposition to that authority would bring harsh reprisal.

69. The agreement thus came in stages: first she agreed to share her story with those who had status as church people, then with a member of the team who had the most knowledge of the protocols of taking testimony (in a legalistic human rights framework). She then indicated that she wanted Merryn to video record her testimony, after which she said that she was glad that people in Canada would know what is happening in the Philippines but requested that the video not be shown in her country.

70. In a recent critique of the way fear is rendered in the current geopolitics literature, Pain notes the disempowering consequence of ignoring the fact that some people are not afraid ("Globalized Fear?" 472). As an object lesson, Sarah Wright focuses on the ways in which MASIPAG, a network of small farmers in the Philippines, practices hope in the face of fear ("Practising Hope").

71. The quotes are a pastiche taken from interviews with the three Canadian observers on the Southern Tagalog mission: Cecilia Diocson (May 2007), Jennifer Efting (August 4, 2007), and Luningning Alcuitas-Imperial (August 7, 2007).

72. After the colonel released the KARAPATAN organizer and joined the rally, Ning left the jeepney to negotiate their passage: "I said, 'Okay, I know. I know you've already been on the phone with the Canadian embassy and this is your promise to them. You said that you're only conducting standard operating procedure. So I want to know how long it is going to take. When can we go? Because after that you promised the embassy that we can go.'"

73. The extensive use of civilian and paramilitary forces, known for their random brutality against the civilian population, marks the "Philippine model" of counterinsurgency warfare: "But the Philippine formula did not and could not overcome the basic political contradiction on which the civilian guard system was built: "Although the guards took orders from military authorities, they were the

employees of local elites, and the natural enemies not only of the guerrillas but of the bulk of the population" (McClintock, *Instruments of Statecraft,* 124).

74. The Scout Rangers are an elite special patrol force, which date from the 1950s, when many received training in the United States at Fort McKinley (McClintock, *Instruments of Statecraft*).

75. This follows the pattern of extrajudicial killings identified by Amnesty International.

76. This point has been well explored in the scholarly literature. See, for example, Olds, Sidaway, and Sparke, "White Death." At the same time, it should be noted that the international attention given to the detention of the Southern Tagalog team did allow them to project the Human Rights Violations witnessed by the other teams. See Kraemer ("Solidarity in Action") for an analysis of strategically deploying privilege.

77. In Arroyo's State of the Nation Address on July 24, 2006, Pacquiao was cited as one of the nation's modern-day heroes. After the victory against Morales, commentators were quick to draw the lessons for the nation. For example: "'What lessons can Pacquaio himself, other boxers and individuals, and the Filipino nation learn from this victory?' Answer: one needs focus, determination, preparation, and the capacity to constantly change tactics and approaches" (*Philippine Daily Inquirer,* "Sweet Victory").

78. Robinson, *Globalizing Care.*

79. Popke, "Poststructuralist Ethics," 304.

80. There is an entire world of ethical thinking to consider: Robinson *(Globalizing Care),* for instance, refuses the distinction between ethics and political economy.

81. It is important to understand as well that the international media's attentiveness to the Canadians in Southern Tagalog did not follow inevitably from their international stature; it came through KARAPATAN's labor, and its formidable organizing and extensive networks within the Philippines and beyond. It was KARAPATAN that alerted media to the experiences of the Canadians as international witnesses and used their networks with sympathetic media to orchestrate press conferences. Accounts of international solidarity and international media that miss this labor and this agency on the part of local activists both distort and reinscribe the dominance of the global North. Many journalists have themselves been killed or disappeared since 2001; as of 2006, forty-six journalists, mostly operating in provincial areas, have been killed (Arao, "Tracing the Roots of Killings of Journalists"). On the basis of this record, it has been estimated that the Philippines is the second most dangerous country in which to be a journalist, after Iraq.

82. The participants in the Canadian fact-finding mission know that they are now on a "black list" and are uncertain about whether they can regain entrance to

the Philippines. As an index of increasing limits to the Philippine government's hospitality to foreigners, three U.S. GABRIELA Network leaders, Dr. Annalisa Enrile, Ninotchka Rosca, and Judith Mirkinson, now known as the GABNet 3, were barred from boarding their planes to return to the United States after attending the 10th Biannual International Solidarity Affair of GABRIELA (a Philippines–U.S. women's solidarity mass organization) in the Philippines (July 29–August 5, 2007). In Dr. Enrile's case, her departure was delayed for a week. International solidarity activists are concerned that the Philippines' Human Security Act, passed in July 2007, further erodes the potential for international solidarity. Of particular concern is Section 58 of the act, which extends the reach of the act beyond the borders of the Philippines' territory. As a further case, in May 2009 a Filipino American woman and her two companions were abducted and tortured when they visited La Paz in Tarlac while gathering material for her writing project. Her captors called her "Maita" and asked her, "Do you think that the Canadian government can do anything for you?" She was evidently mistaken for Maita Santiago, a Vancouver activist who was Migrante International's secretary general in Manila from 2002 to 2008 but who has subsequently returned to Vancouver. This underlines both the bifurcated nature of Filipino Canadian political identities and the limits to the Philippine state's hospitality to Canadians (Pablo, "Torture Case Has Local Link").

83. Weir, "The Global Universal Caregiver."

84. Baucom, *Specters of the Atlantic,* 177.

Conclusion

1. Bosniak, *The Citizen and the Alien,* 140.

2. Ibid.

3. In Doreen Massey's words: "First there is 'home,'" then perhaps place or locality, then nation, and so on. There is a kind of accepted understanding that we care first for, and have our first responsibilities towards, those nearest in" ("Geographies of Responsibility," 9).

4. See Povinelli (*The Empire of Love*) for a fulsome critique of the work that the family does in liberal societies as a "key transfer point" for contractual economics, sociability, and liberal forms of power.

5. Mayer, "Guestworkers and Exploitation"; Weir, "The Global Universal Caregiver," 314.

6. This line of argument is suggested by Shachar's attention to the ethics of excluding children through restrictive migration policies ("Children of a Lesser State").

7. For example: Butler, *Giving an Account of Oneself;* Jenkins, "Toward a Nonviolent Ethics"; Engster, "Rethinking Care Theory"; Robinson, *Globalizing Care;* Lawson, "Geographies of Responsibility."

8. Carens, "Live-in Domestics, Seasonal Workers."

9. Oliver, *Witnessing*.

10. Ahmed, "This Other and Other Others."

11. Fraser, *Scales of Justice*.

12. San Juan, *Toward Filipino Self-Determination*, 154.

13. Ibid., 136 (emphasis added), 137.

14. Pratt, "Research Performances."

Bibliography

Abada, Teresa, Feng Hou, and Bali Ram. "Ethnic Differences in Educational Attainment among the Children of Canadian Immigrants." *Canadian Journal of Sociology* 34, no. 1 (2009): 1–29.

Abraham, Nicholas, and Maria Torok. *The Shell and the Kernel: Renewals of Psychoanalysis.* Edited and translated by Nicholas T. Rand. Chicago: University of Chicago Press, 1994.

Agamben, Giorgio. *Homo Sacer: Sovereign Power and Bare Life.* Translated by Daniel Heller-Roazen. Stanford: Stanford University Press, 1998.

Agence France Presse. "Philippine Government Rejects Amnesty's 'Blanket Accusations.'" *Manila Bulletin,* Manila Bulletin Publishing Corporation, August 16, 2006. http://mb.com.ph/node/88114 (accessed August 23, 2010).

Ahmed, Sara. "This Other and Other Others." *Economy and Society* 31, no. 4 (2002): 558–72.

———. "Affective Economies." *Social Text* 22, no. 2 (2004): 117–39.

———. *The Promise of Happiness.* Durham: Duke University Press, 2010.

Amnesty International. *Philippines: Political Killings, Human Rights, and the Peace Process.* Amnesty International, August 15, 2006. AI Index: ASA 35/006/2006.

Amoore, Louise. "'There Is No Great Refusal': The Ambivalent Politics of Resistance." In *International Political Economy and Poststructural Politics,* edited by Marieke de Goede, 255–74. London: Palgrave Macmillan, 2006.

Anderson, Ben. "Becoming and Being Hopeful." *Environment and Planning D* 24 (2006): 733–52.

———. "Affect and Biopower: Towards a Politics of Life." *Transactions of the Institute of British Geographers,* forthcoming.

Anderson, Bridget Jane. *Doing the Dirty Work? The Global Politics of Domestic Labour.* London: Zed Books, 2000.

Anderson, Kay, and Susan J. Smith. "Editorial: Emotional Geographies." *Transactions of the Institute of British Geographers* 26 (2001): 7–10.

Anderson, Michael, and Linden Wilkinson. "A Resurgence of Verbatim Theatre: Authenticity, Empathy, and Transformation." *Australasian Drama Studies* 50 (2007): 153–69.

Aranda, Elizabeth M. "Global Care Work and Gendered Constraints: The Case of Puerto Rican Transmigrants." *Gender and Society* 17, no. 4 (2003): 609–26.

Arao, Danilo Araña. "Tracing the Roots of Killings of Journalists." In *Kontra-Gahum: Academics against Political Killings,* edited by Rolando B. Tolentino and Sarah S. Raymundo, 106–26. Quezon City: IBON Books, 2006.

Asis, Maruja M. B. "From the Life Stories of Filipino Women: Personal and Family Agendas in Migration." *Asian and Pacific Migration Journal* 11, no. 1 (2002): 67–93.

Bakan, Abigail, and Daiva Stasiulis, eds. *Not One of the Family: Foreign Domestic Workers in Canada.* Toronto: University of Toronto Press, 1997.

Balana, Cynthia. "US Aid Tied to RP Action on Killings: Three Conditions Set for Additional Military Assistance." *Inquirer.net,* November 6, 2007. http:// newsinfo.inquirer.net (accessed August 23, 2010).

Balibar, Étienne. "Outlines of a Topography of Cruelty: Citizenship and Civility in the Era of Global Violence." *Constellations* 8, no. 1 (2002): 15–29.

Ball, Karyn. "Trauma and Its Institutional Destinies." *Cultural Critique* 46 (Fall 2000): 1–44.

Barnett, Clive. "Ways of Relating: Hospitality and the Acknowledgement of Otherness." *Progress in Human Geography* 29, no. 1 (2005): 5–21.

———. "Who Cares?" In *Introducing Human Geographies,* 2nd ed., edited by Paul Cloke, Philip Crang, and Mark Goodwin, 588–601. London: Hodder Arnold, 2005.

———. "Political Affects in Public Space: Normative Blind-Spots in Non-representational Ontologies." *Transactions of the Institute of British Geographers* 33 (2008): 186–200.

Barthes, Roland. *Camera Lucida: Reflections on Photography.* Translated by Richard Howard. New York: Hill and Wang, 1981.

Battistella, Graciano, and Maria Cecilia Gastardo Conaco. "The Impact of Labour Migration on the Children Left Behind: A Study of Elementary School Children in the Philippines." *Sojourn* 13, no. 2 (1998): 1–22.

Baucom, Ian. *Specters of the Atlantic: Finance Capital, Slavery, and the Philosophy of History.* Durham: Duke University Press, 2005.

Bejarano, Cynthia L. "Las Super Madres de Latino America: Transforming Motherhood by Challenging Violence in Mexico, Argentina, and El Salvador. *Frontiers: A Journal of Women Studies* 23, no. 1 (2002): 126–50.

Bell, Daniel A., and Nicola Piper. "Justice for Migrant Workers? The Case of Foreign Domestic Workers in Hong Kong and Singapore." In *Multiculturalism in Asia,* edited by Will Kymlicka and Baogang He, 196–222. Oxford: Oxford University Press, 2005.

Bello, Madge, and Vincent Reyes. "Filipino Americans and the Marcos Overthrow: The Transformation of Political Consciousness." *Amerasia Journal* 13, no. 1 (1986–87): 73–83.

Ben-Zvi, Linda. "Staging the Other Israel: The Documentary Theater of Nola Chilton." *Drama Review* 50, no. 3 (2006): 42–55.

Berlant, Lauren. *The Anatomy of National Fantasy: Hawthorne, Utopia, and Everyday Life.* Chicago: University of Chicago Press, 1991.

———. *The Queen of America Goes to Washington City: Essays on Sex and Citizenship.* Durham: Duke University Press, 1997.

———. "The Subject of True Feeling: Pain, Privacy, and Politics." In *Cultural Pluralism, Identity Politics, and the Law,* edited by Austin Sarat and Thomas R. Kearns, 49–84. Ann Arbor: University of Michigan Press, 1999.

———. "Trauma and Ineloquence." *Cultural Values* 5, no. 1 (January 2001): 41–58.

———. "Critical Inquiry, Affirmative Culture." *Critical Inquiry* 30, no. 2 (Winter 2004): 445–51.

———. "The Epistemology of State Emotion." In *Dissent in Dangerous Times,* edited by Austin Sarat, 46–78. Ann Arbor: University of Michigan Press, 2005.

———. "Slow Death (Sovereignty, Obesity, Lateral Agency)." *Critical Inquiry* 33, no. 4 (2007): 754–80.

———. "Thinking about Feeling Historical." *Emotion, Space and Society* 1, no. 1 (October 2008): 4–9.

Bernstein, J. M. "Bare Life, Bearing Witness: Auschwitz and the Pornography of Horror." *Parallax* 10, no. 1 (January 2004): 2–16.

Biddle, Jennifer, L. "Anthropology as Eulogy: On Loss, Lies, and License." In *World Memory: Personal Trajectories in Global Time,* edited by Jill Bennett and Roseanne Kennedy, 43–58. Hampshire: Palgrave Macmillan, 2003.

Blank, Jessica, and Erik Jensen. "The Uses of Empathy: Theatre and the Real World." *Theatre History Studies* 25 (2005): 15–22.

Blunt, Alison, Jayani Bonnerjee, Caron Lipman, Joanna Long, and Felicity Paynter. "My Home: Text, Space, and Performance." *Cultural Geographies* 14 (April 2007): 309–18.

Bolos, Abner. "Two Presidents and the Lupao Massacre." Gitnang Luson News Service, posted by Bulatlat. *Bulatlat,* vol. 6, no. 28, August 20–26, 2006. www.bulatlat.com (accessed August 23, 2010).

Boltanski, Luc. *Distant Suffering: Morality, Media, and Politics.* Cambridge: Cambridge University Press, 1999.

Bosco, Fernando J. "Human Rights Politics and Scaled Performances of Memory: Conflicts among the Madres de Plaza de Mayo in Argentina." *Social and Cultural Geography* 5, no. 3 (September 2004): 381–402.

———. "The Madres de Plaza de Mayo and Three Decades of Human Rights' Activism: Embeddedness, Emotions, and Social Movements." *Annals of the Association of American Geographers* 96, no. 2 (2006): 342–65.

Bosniak, Linda. "Membership, Equality, and the Difference That Alienage Makes." *New York University Law Review* 69 (1994): 1047.

———. "Universal Citizenship and the Problem of Alienage." *Northwestern University Law Review* 94, no. 3 (2000): 963–82.

———. *The Citizen and the Alien: Dilemmas of Contemporary Membership.* Princeton: Princeton University Press, 2006.

Brown, Wendy. *States of Injury: Power and Freedom in Late Modernity.* Princeton: Princeton University Press, 1995.

———. "Neoliberalism and the End of Liberal Democracy." *Theory and Event* 7, no. 1 (2003).

Brubaker, Rogers. "The Return of Assimilation? Changing Perspectives on Immigration and Its Sequels in France, Germany, and the United States." *Ethnic and Racial Studies* 24, no. 4 (2001): 531–48.

Buck-Morss, Susan. *Dreamworld and Catastrophe: The Passing of Mass Utopia in East and West.* Cambridge: MIT Press, 2000.

Burk, Adrienne L. *Speaking for a Long Time: Public Space and Social Memory in Vancouver.* Vancouver: University of British Columbia Press, 2010.

Burvill, Tom. "'Politics Begins as Ethics': Levinasian Ethics and Australian Performance Concerning Refugees." *Research in Drama Education* 13, no. 2 (June 2008): 233–43.

Butler, Judith. "Afterword: After Loss, What Then?" In *Loss: The Politics of Mourning*, edited by David L. Eng and David Kazanjian, 467–74. Berkeley: University of California Press, 2003.

———. *Precarious Life: The Powers of Mourning and Violence.* London: Verso, 2004.

———. *Giving an Account of Oneself.* New York: Fordham University Press, 2005.

———. "Sexual Politics, Torture, and Secular Time." *British Journal of Sociology* 59, no. 1 (March 2008): 1–23.

———. *Frames of War: When Is Life Grievable?* London: Verso, 2009.

Campbell, David. "Geopolitics and Visuality: Sighting the Darfur Conflict." *Political Geography* 26, no. 4 (May 2007): 357–82.

Carens, Joseph H. "Live-in Domestics, Seasonal Workers, and Others Hard to Locate on the Map of Democracy." *Journal of Political Philosophy* 16, no. 4 (2008): 419–45.

Caruth, Cathy. *Unclaimed Experience: Trauma, Narrative, and History.* Baltimore: Johns Hopkins University Press, 1996.

Castles, Stephen. "The Guest-Worker in Western Europe—An Obituary." *International Migration Review* 20, no. 4 (Winter 1986): 761–78.

Chen, Xiaobei. "The Child-Citizen." In *Recasting the Social in Citizenship*, edited by Engin F. Isin, 162–86. Toronto: University of Toronto Press, 2008.

Cheng, Anne Anlin. *The Melancholy of Race: Psychoanalysis, Assimilation, and Hidden Grief.* Oxford: Oxford University Press, 2001.

Choy, Catherine Ceniza. *Empire of Care: Nursing and Migration in Filipino American History*. Durham: Duke University Press, 2003.

―――. "Towards Trans-Pacific Social Justice: Women and Protest in Filipino American History." *Journal of Asian American Studies* 8, no. 3 (October 2005): 293–307.

CIC (Citizenship and Immigration Canada). *Facts and Figures 2006*. Ottawa: CIC, 2007.

―――. *Live-In Caregiver Program Fact Sheet*. Distributed at the National Roundtable on the Review of the Live-In Caregiver Program, Ottawa, January 13–14, 2005.

Clough, Patricia Ticineto. "Introduction." In *The Affective Turn: Theorizing the Social*, edited by Patricia Ticineto Clough with Jean Halley, 1–33. Durham: Duke University Press, 2007.

Cohen, Rina. "'Mom Is a Stranger': The Negative Impact of Immigration Policies on the Family Life of Filipina Domestic Workers." *Canadian Ethnic Studies* 32, no. 3 (2000): 76–88.

Colen, Shellee. "'Like a Mother to Them': Stratified Reproduction and West Indian Childcare Workers and Employers in New York." In *Conceiving the New World Order: The Global Politics of Reproduction*, edited by Faye D. Ginsburg and Rayna Rapp, 78–102. Berkeley: University of California Press, 1995.

Commission on Filipinos Overseas. *The Handbook for Filipinos Overseas*. Quezon City: Commission on Filipinos Overseas, 1999.

Conde, Carlos H. "Europeans Add Credibility to Investigation of Extrajudicial Killings in the Philippines." *International Herald Tribune*, February 4, 2007. www.iht.com (accessed August 23, 2010).

Connolly, William E. *Neuropolitics: Thinking, Culture, Speed*. Minneapolis: University of Minnesota Press, 2002.

―――. "The Complexity of Sovereignty." In *Sovereign Lives: Power in Global Politics*, edited by Jenny Edkins and Véronique Pin-Fat, and Michael J. Shapiro, 23–40. New York: Routledge, 2004.

―――. "The Media and Think Tank Politics." *Theory and Event* 8, no. 4 (2005).

Critical Filipina and Filipino Studies Collective. *Resisting Homeland Security: Organizing against Unjust Removals of U.S. Filipinos*. San Jose, Calif.: Critical Filipina and Filipino Studies Collective (CFFSC), December 2004. http://bayanusa .org/downloads/resisting_home_sec.pdf (accessed June 3, 2010).

Cubilié, Anne. *Women Witnessing Terror: Testimony and the Cultural Politics of Human Rights*. New York: Fordham University Press, 2005.

Cumbers, Andy, Paul Routledge, and Corinne Nativel. "The Entangled Geographies of Global Justice Networks." *Progress in Human Geography* 32, no. 2 (April 2008): 183–201.

Cvetkovich, Ann. *An Archive of Feelings: Trauma, Sexuality, and Lesbian Public Cultures*. Durham: Duke University Press, 2003.

Daenzer, Patricia. *Regulating Class Privilege: Immigrant Servants in Canada, 1940s–1990s*. Toronto: Canadian Scholars' Press, 1993.

Dean, Jodi. "Politics without Politics." *Parallax* 15, no. 3 (2009): 20–36.

DeParle, Jason. "A Good Provider Is One Who Leaves." *New York Times Magazine*, 22 April 2007, 50–57, 72, 122–23.

Depatie-Pelletier, Eugénie. "Under Legal Practices Similar to Slavery According to the U.N. Convention: Canada's 'Non White' 'Temporary' Foreign Workers in 'Low-Skilled' Occupations." Paper presented at the 10th National Metropolis Conference, Halifax, Nova Scotia, April 3, 2008.

Derrida, Jacques. "Force of Law: 'The Mystical Foundation of Authority.'" Translated by Mary Quaintance. In *Deconstruction and the Possibility of Justice*, edited by Drucilla Cornell, Michael Rosenfeld, and David Gray Carlson, 3–67. New York: Routledge, 1992.

Dodson, Lisa, and Rebekah M. Zincavage. "'It's Like a Family': Caring Labor, Exploitation, and Race in Nursing Homes." *Gender and Society* 21, no. 6 (2007): 905–28.

Doel, Marcus. *Poststructuralist Geographies: The Diabolical Arts of Spatial Science*. Edinburgh: Edinburgh University Press, 1999.

Dolan, Jill. *Utopia in Performance: Finding Hope at the Theater*. Ann Arbor: University of Michigan Press, 2005.

Domingo, Cindy. "Until We Have a True Democracy." *Amerasia Journal* 18, no. 1 (1992): 129–30.

Doty, Roxanne Lynn. *Imperial Encounters: The Politics of Representation in North-South Relations*. Minneapolis: University of Minnesota Press, 1996.

Edkins, Jenny. *Trauma and the Memory of Politics*. Cambridge: Cambridge University Press, 2003.

Edkins, Jenny, and Véronique Pin-Fat. "Introduction: Life, Power, Resistance." In *Sovereign Lives: Power in Global Politics*, edited by Jenny Edkins and Véronique Pin-Fat, and Michael J. Shapiro, 1–21. New York: Routledge, 2004.

Elden, Stuart. "The War of Races and the Constitution of the State: Foucault's 'Il faut défendre la société' and the Politics of Calculation." *Boundary 2*, no. 29 (2002): 125–51.

Eng, David L., and David Kazanjian, eds. *Loss: The Politics of Mourning*. Berkeley: University of California Press, 2003.

England, Kim, and Bernadette Stiell. "'They Think You're as Stupid as Your English Is': Constructing Foreign Domestic Workers in Toronto." *Environment and Planning A* 29, no. 2 (1997): 195–215.

Engster, Daniel. "Rethinking Care Theory: The Practice of Caring and the Obligation to Care." *Hypatia* 20, no. 3 (Summer 2005): 50–74.

Espina-Varona, Inday. "Kin, Colleagues Brave Risk to Join U.N. Probe into Killings." *Manila Times,* February 12, 2007. www.manilatimes.net (accessed November 5, 2007).

Espiritu, Yen Le. *Home Bound: Filipino American Lives across Cultures, Communities,
and Countries.* Berkeley: University of California Press, 2003.

Featherstone, David. "Spatialities of Transnational Resistance to Globalisation:
The Maps of Grievance of the Inter-Continental Caravan." *Transactions of the
Institute of British Geographers* 28, no. 4 (December 2003): 404–21.

Foucault, Michel. "The Subject and Power." *Critical Inquiry* 8, no. 4 (Summer
1982): 777–95.

———. *"Society Must Be Defended": Lectures at The Collège de France, 1975–1976,*
edited by Mauro Bertoni and Alessandro Fontana; translated by David Macey.
New York: Picador, 2003.

Franco, Jennifer C., and Patricio N. Abinales. "Again, They're Killing Peasants in
the Philippines: Lawlessness, Murder, and Impunity." *Critical Asian Studies*
39, no. 2 (June 2007): 315–28.

Fraser, Nancy. *Scales of Justice: Reimagining Political Space in a Globalizing World.*
New York: Columbia University Press, 2008.

Fresnoza-Flot, Asuncion. "Migration Status and Transnational Mothering: The
Case of Filipino Migrants in France." *Global Networks* 9, no. 2 (2009): 252–70.

Fujita-Rony, Dorothy B. "Coalitions, Race, and Labor: Rereading Philip Vera
Cruz." *Journal of Asian American Studies* 3, no. 2 (June 2000): 139–62.

———. *American Workers, Colonial Power: Philippine Seattle and the Transpacific
West, 1911–1941.* Berkeley: University of California Press, 2002.

Gilroy, Paul. *After Empire: Melancholia or Convivial Culture?* London: Routledge,
2004.

Glassman, Jim. "Imperialism Imposed and Invited." In *Violent Geographies: Fear,
Terror, and Political Violence,* edited by Derek Gregory and Allan Pred, 93–
109. New York: Routledge, 2006.

Glick Schiller, Nina. "A Global Perspective on Transnational Migration: Theorizing Migration without Methodological Nationalism." Centre on Migration,
Policy, and Society, University of Oxford. Working Paper no. 67, 2009.

Global Commission on International Migration. *Global Migration for an Intercon-
nected World: New Directions for Action.* October 2005. www.gcim.org (accessed
July 28, 2010).

Government of Canada. "Regulations Amending the Immigration and Refugee
Protections Regulations." *Canada Gazette* 143, no. 51, December 19, 2009,
3781–86. www.canadagazette.gc.ca (accessed August 9, 2010).

Gregory, Derek. *The Colonial Present.* Malden, Mass.: Blackwell, 2004.

Guevarra, Anna Romina. "Managing 'Vulnerabilities' and 'Empowering' Migrant

Filipina Workers: The Philippines' Overseas Employment Program." *Social Identities* 12, no. 5 (2006): 523–41.

———. *Marketing Dreams, Manufacturing Heroes: The Transnational Labor Brokering of Filipino Workers*. New Brunswick, N.J.: Rutgers University Press, 2010.

Gunew, Sneja. "Eur/Asian Vernacular Cosmopolitanisms: Breaching Classificatory Controls." Paper presented at Cultures of Sustainability, Sustainability of Cultures: An Asia-Pacific Workshop Series, University of British Columbia, Vancouver, July 8, 2010.

Hallward, Peter. "Staging Equality: On Rancière's Theatrocracy." *New Left Review* 37 (2006): 109–29.

Herman, Judith Lewis. *Trauma and Recovery*. New York: Basic Books, 1992.

Hilao-Enriquez, Marie. "Philippine Government's Action on Human Rights: Promotion or Infraction?" In *Stop the Killings in the Philippines*, 42–52. Quezon City: IBON Foundation, 2006.

Hindess, Barry. "The Liberal Government of Unfreedom." *Alternatives: Global, Local, Political* 26, no. 2 (April–June 2001): 93–111.

Hochschild, Arlie Russell. "Global Care Chains and Emotional Surplus Value." In *On the Edge: Living with Global Capitalism*, edited by Will Hutton and Anthony Giddens, 130–46. London: Jonathan Cape, 2000.

———. "Love and Gold." In *Global Woman: Nannies, Maids, and Sex Workers in the New Economy*, edited by Barbara Ehrenreich and Arlie Russell Hochschild, 15–30. New York: Henry Holt, 2002.

Hondagneu-Sotelo, Pierrette, and Ernestine Avila. "'I'm Here, but I'm There': The Meanings of Latina Transnational Motherhood." *Gender and Society* 11, no. 5 (1997): 548–71.

Howard, Cori. "The Steep Price of Becoming a 'Dollar Mommy.'" *Globe and Mail*, October 16, 2007, L1. www.theglobeandmail.com (accessed November 17, 2008).

Huang, Tsung-yi Michelle, and Chi-she Li. "Like a Family but Not Quite: Emotional Labor and Cinematic Politics of Intimacy." In *The Global and the Intimate: Feminism in Our Time*, edited by Geraldine Pratt and Victoria Rosner. New York: Columbia University Press, forthcoming 2012.

Hume, Mo. "'(Young) Men with Big Guns': Reflexive Encounters with Violence and Youth in El Salvador." *Bulletin of Latin American Research* 26, no. 4 (October 2007): 480–96.

Ignacio, Emily Noelle. *Building Diaspora: Filipino Cultural Community Formation on the Internet*. New Brunswick, N.J.: Rutgers University Press, 2005.

Illouz, Eva. *Cold Intimacies: The Making of Emotional Capitalism*. Cambridge: Polity Press, 2007.

Jenkins, Fiona. "Toward a Nonviolent Ethics: Response to Catherine Mills." *Differences: A Journal of Feminist Cultural Studies* 18, no. 2 (Summer 2007): 157–79.

Jestrovic, Silvija. "Performing Like an Asylum Seeker: Paradoxes of Hyper-Authenticity." *Research in Drama Education* 13, no. 2 (June 2008): 159–70.

Johnston, Caleb, and Geraldine Pratt, in collaboration with the Philippine Women Centre of BC. "Nanay [Mother]: A Testimonial Play." *Cultural Geographies* 17, no. 1 (January 2010): 123–33.

Joyce, Greg. "Caregiver Plan Indirectly Linked to Son's Death, Mom Suggests." *Globe and Mail*, February 2, 2008, S2.

KARAPATAN. *The 2007 Year-End Report on the Human Rights Situation in the Philippines.* Quezon City: KARAPATAN, January 20, 2008. www.karapatan .org (accessed February 25, 2008).

———. *2008 Year-End Report on the Human Rights Situation in the Philippines.* Quezon City: KARAPATAN, 2008. www.karapatan.org/files/2008_Karapatan _HR_Report_(updated).pdf (accessed August 15, 2009).

———. *Karapatan Monitor,* January–March 2009. www.karapatan.org/resources/ statistics/ (accessed August 23, 2010).

Katz, Cindi. "On the Grounds of Globalization: A Topography for Feminist Political Engagement." *Signs* 26, no. 4 (Summer 2001): 1213–34.

Keenan, Thomas. "Mobilizing Shame." *South Atlantic Quarterly* 103, no. 2/3 (Spring/Summer 2004): 435–49.

Kelly, Philip F. *Landscapes of Globalization: Human Geographies of Economic Change in the Philippines.* New York: Routledge, 2000.

———. "Filipinos in Canada: Economic Dimensions of Immigration and Settlement." CERIS – The Ontario Metropolis Centre, Toronto. CERIS Working Paper no. 48, September 2006.

Kelly, Philip F., Mila Astorga-Garcia, Enrico F. Esguerra, and the Community Alliance for Social Justice, Toronto. "Explaining the Deprofessionalized Filipino: Why Filipino Immigrants Get Low-Paying Jobs in Toronto." CERIS – The Ontario Metropolis Centre, Toronto. CERIS Working Paper no. 75, October 2009.

Kelly, Philip, Stella Park, Conely de Leon, and Jeff Priest. "Profile of Live-in Caregiver Immigrants to Canada, 1993–2009." TIEDI (Toronto Immigrant Employment Data Initiative), York University, Toronto. TIEDI Analytical Report 18, March 2011. http://www.yorku.ca/tiedi/doc/AnalyticalReport18.pdf (accessed August 14, 2011).

Kenney, Jason. Press conference, Toronto, Ontario, December 12, 2009. "Jason Kenney: Live-In Caregiver Program Changes, Part Two." www.youtube.com (accessed July 25, 2010).

Korf, Benedikt. "Antinomies of Generosity: Moral Geographies and Post-Tsunami Aid in Southeast Asia." *Geoforum* 38, no. 2 (March 2007): 366–78.

Kraemer, Kelly Rae. "Solidarity in Action: Exploring the Work of Allies in Social Movements." *Peace and Change* 32, no. 1 (January 2007): 20–38.

Lan, Pei-Chia. *Global Cinderellas: Migrant Domestics and Newly Rich Employers in Taiwan.* Durham: Duke University Press, 2006.

Langton, Marcia. "Even the Hard Men Know, It Must Be Said." *Sydney Morning Herald,* February 9, 2008.

Lawson, Victoria. "Geographies of Care and Responsibility." *Annals of the Association of American Geographers* 97, no. 1 (March 2007): 1–11.

Lee, Elizabeth, and Pratt, Geraldine. "Migrant Worker: Migrant Stories." In *Geographies of Mobilities: Practices, Spaces, Subjects,* edited by Tim Cresswell and Peter Merriman, 225–38. Burlington, Vt.: Ashgate, 2011.

Legg, Steven. *Spaces of Colonialism: Delhi's Urban Governmentalities.* Malden, Mass.: Blackwell, 2007.

Lemke, Thomas. "'The Birth of Biopolitics': Michel Foucault's Lecture at the Collège de France on Neo-liberal Governmentality." *Economy and Society* 30, no. 2 (2001): 190–207.

Levitt, Peggy. "Social Remittances: Migration-Driven Local-Level Forms of Cultural Diffusion." *International Migration Review* 32, no. 4 (Winter 1998): 926–48.

Ley, David. *Millionaire Migrants: Trans-Pacific Life Lines.* Malden, Mass.: Wiley-Blackwell, 2010.

Li, Tania Murray. *The Will to Improve: Governmentality, Development, and the Practice of Politics.* Durham: Duke University Press, 2007.

Liebelt, Claudia. "On Sentimental Orientalists, Christian Zionists, and Working-Class Cosmopolitans: Filipina Domestic Workers' Journeys to Israel and Beyond." *Critical Asian Studies* 40, no. 4 (2008): 567–85.

Lindsay, Colin. "The Filipino Community in Canada." Statistics Canada, Catalogue no. 89-621-XIE – no. 5. Ottawa: Minister of Industry, July 2007. www.statscan .ca (accessed September 10, 2008).

Macan-Markar, Marwann. "UN Investigating Extra-Judicial Killings in Philippines." *Pakistan Dawn,* February 13, 2007. www.dawn.com (accessed April 3, 2007).

Macklin, Audrey. "Foreign Domestic Worker: Surrogate Housewife or Mail Order Servant?" *McGill Law Journal* 37 (1992): 681–760.

———. "Like Oil and Water, with a Match: Militarized Commerce, Armed Conflict, and Human Security in Sudan." In *Sites of Violence: Gender and Conflict Zones,* edited by Wenona Giles and Jennifer Hyndman, 75–107. Berkeley: University of California Press, 2004.

Madianou, Mirca, and Daniel Miller. "Crafting Love: Letters and Cassette Tapes in Transnational Filipino Family Communication." *South East Asia Research* 19 (2010): 249–72.

———. "Mobile Phone Parenting: Reconfiguring Relationships between Filipina Migrant Mothers and Their Left-Behind Children." *New Media and Society* 13 (2011): 457–70.

Malkki, Liisa. "National Geographic: The Rooting of Peoples and the Territori-
alization of National Identity among Scholars and Refugees." *Cultural Anthro-
pology* 7, no. 1 (1992): 24–44.
Manzanilla, J. Paul. "Terror Talks: The Public Secret." In *Kontra-Gahum: Aca-
demics against Political Killings*, edited by Rolando B. Tolentino and Sarah S.
Raymundo, 96–105. Quezon City: IBON Books, 2006.
Martin, Carol. "Bodies of Evidence." *The Drama Review* 50, no. 3 (2006): 8–15.
Massey, Doreen. "Geographies of Responsibility." *Geografiska Annaler: Series B,
Human Geography* 86, no. 1 (March 2004): 5–18.
———. *For Space*. London: Sage, 2005.
Mayer, Robert. "Guestworkers and Exploitation." *Review of Politics* 67, no. 2 (2005):
311–34.
McClintock, Michael. *Instruments of Statecraft: U.S. Guerrilla Warfare, Counterin-
surgency, and Counter-terrorism, 1940–1990*. New York: Pantheon Books, 1992.
McKay, Deirdre. "'Sending Dollars Shows Feelings': Emotions and Economies in
Filipino Migration." *Mobilities* 2, no. 2 (2007): 175–94.
McKay, Deirdre, and the Philippine Women Centre. 2002. "Filipina Identities:
Geographies of Social Integration/Exclusion in the Canadian Metropolis."
Research on Immigration and Integration in the Metropolis, Metropolis British
Columbia, Vancouver. RIIM Working Paper Series no. 02-18, October 2002.
Miller, Peter, and Nikolas Rose. "Governing Economic Life." *Economy and Soci-
ety* 19, no. 1 (1990): 1–31.
Mitchell, Katharyne. "Geographies of Identity: Multiculturalism Unplugged."
Progress in Human Geography 28, no. 5 (October 2004): 641–51.
Mitchell, Timothy. *Rule of Experts: Egypt, Techno-Politics, Modernity*. Berkeley: Uni-
versity of California Press, 2002.
Miyares, Ines M., et al. "The Interrupted Circle: Truncated Transnationalism and
the Salvadoran Experience." *Journal of Latin American Geography* 2, no. 1 (2003):
74–86.
Mohanty, Chandra Talpade. "Under Western Eyes: Feminist Scholarship and Colo-
nial Discourses." *Boundary 2* 12, no. 3 (1986): 333–58.
———. "Women Workers and Capitalist Scripts: Ideologies of Domination, Common Interests, and the Politics of Solidarity." In *Feminist Genealogies, Colonial
Legacies, Democratic Futures*, edited by M. Jacqui Alexander and Chandra Talpade Mohanty, 3–29. New York: Routledge, 1997.
———. *Feminism without Borders: Decolonizing Theory, Practicing Solidarity*. Dur-
ham: Duke University Press, 2003.
Mohanty, Chandra Talpade, Ann Russo, and Lourdes Torres. *Third World Women
and the Politics of Feminism*. Bloomington: Indiana University Press, 1991.
Mydans, Seth, and Carlos H. Conde. "Extrajudicial Killings on the Rise: Stealth

Attacks Threaten Filipino Activists." *International Herald Tribune,* August 22, 2006. www.iht.com (accessed November 6, 2007).

Nestruck, J. Kelly. "Dated Agitprop Muffles Caregivers' Battle Cry." *Globe and Mail,* February 27, 2010, R9.

Ngai, Sianne. *Ugly Feelings.* Cambridge, Mass.: Harvard University Press, 2005.

Nunn, Heather. "Emotional Death: The Charity Advert and Photographs of Childhood Trauma." *Journal of Cultural Research* 8, no. 3 (July 2004): 271–92.

Olds, Kris, James D. Sidaway, and Matthew Sparke. "White Death." *Environment and Planning D* 23, no. 4 (2005): 475–79.

Oliver, Kelly. *Witnessing: Beyond Recognition.* Minneapolis: University of Minnesota Press, 2001.

Ong, Aihwa. *Buddha Is Hiding: Refugees, Citizenship, the New America.* Berkeley: University of California Press, 2003.

———. *Neoliberalism as Exception: Mutations in Citizenship and Sovereignty.* Durham: Duke University Press: 2006.

Pablo, Carlito. "Torture Case Has Local Link." *The Georgia Straight,* August 13–20, 2009, 13.

Pain, Rachel. "Globalized Fear? Towards an Emotional Geopolitics." *Progress in Human Geography* 33, no. 4 (August 2009): 466–86.

Paragas, Fernando. "Migrant Mobiles: Cellular Telephony, Transnational Spaces, and the Filipino Diaspora." In *A Sense of Place: The Global and the Local in Mobile Communication,* edited by Kristof Nyiri, 241–49. Vienna: Passagen Verlag, 2005.

Parreñas, Rhacel Salazar. "Mothering from a Distance: Emotions, Gender, and Intergenerational Relations in Filipino Transnational Families." *Feminist Studies* 27, no. 2 (2001): 361–90.

———. *Servants of Globalization: Women, Migration, and Domestic Work.* Stanford: Stanford University Press, 2001.

———. *Children of Global Migration: Transnational Families and Gendered Woes.* Stanford: Stanford University Press, 2005.

Permanent Peoples' Tribunal Second Session on the Philippines. Fondazione Lelio e Lisli Basso Issoco, Sezione Internazionale. The Hague, 2007. The verdict can be accessed at: www.internazionaleleliobasso.it/index.php (accessed August 20, 2010).

Pertierra, Raul. *Transforming Technologies: Altered Selves, Mobile Phone and Internet Use in the Philippines.* Manila: De La Salle University Press, 2006.

———. "Technologies of Transformation: The End of the Social or the Birth of the Cyber Network?" In *Living the Information Society in Asia,* edited by Erwin Alampay, 36–56. Singapore: Institute of Southeast Asian Studies Publishing, 2009.

Philippine Daily Inquirer (Manila). Editorial: "Sweet Victory." *Inquirer.net,* November 21, 2006. www.inquirer.net (accessed August 23, 2010).

"Philippines." *Internet World Stats: Usage and Population Statistics.* Bogotá, Colombia: Miniwatts Marketing Group, 2000–2010. www.internetworldstats.com/asia/ph.htm (accessed January 23, 2008).

Philippines National Statistics Office. "Number of Overseas Filipino Workers, by Place of Work and by Sex, October 2003 and 2004." From the *Survey on Overseas Filipinos,* Manila, April 15, 2005. http://222.126.95.251/data/sectordata/2005/ofo403.htm (accessed May 13, 2010).

———. "One in Three Overseas Filipino Workers (OFWs) Is a Laborer or Unskilled Worker." Press Release no: 2007-38, Manila, May 29, 2007. http://222.126.95.251/data/pressrelease/2007/ofo6tx.html (accessed May 13, 2010).

POEA (Philippines Overseas Employment Administration). *Overseas Employment Statistics, 2009.* Mandaluyong City, Philippines, 2009. www.poea.gov.ph (accessed May 13, 2010).

Popke, E. Jeffrey. "Poststructuralist Ethics: Subjectivity, Responsibility, and the Space of Community." *Progress in Human Geography* 27, no. 3 (June 2003): 298–316.

Povinelli, Elizabeth A. *The Empire of Love: Toward a Theory of Intimacy, Genealogy, and Carnality.* Durham: Duke University Press, 2006.

Pratt, Geraldine. "Stereotypes and Ambivalence: The Construction of Domestic Workers in Vancouver, British Columbia." *Gender, Place, and Culture* 4, no. 2 (July 1997): 159–78.

———. "Research Performances." *Environment and Planning D: Society and Space* 18 (2000): 639-651.

———. *Working Feminism.* Philadelphia: Temple University Press, 2004.

———. "Listening for Spaces of Ordinariness: Filipino-Canadian Youths' Transnational Lives." *Children's Geographies* 8, no. 4 (2010): 343–52.

Pratt, Geraldine, and the Philippine Women Centre of BC and Ugnayan ng Kabataang Pilipino sa Canada. "Deskilling across the Generations: Reunification among Transnational Filipino Families in Vancouver." Research on Immigration and Integration in the Metropolis, British Columbia. RIIM Working Paper Series no. 08-06, September 2008.

Pratt, Geraldine, in collaboration with the Philippine Women Centre. "From Migrant to Immigrant: Domestic Workers Settle in Vancouver, Canada." In *Companion to Feminist Geography,* edited by Lise Nelson and Joni Seager, 123–37. Malden, Mass.: Blackwell, 2005.

———. "Seeing beyond the State: Toward Transnational Feminist Organizing." In *Critical Transnational Feminist Praxis,* edited by Amanda Lock Swarr and Richa Nagar, 65–86. Albany: State University of New York Press, 2010.

Pratt, Geraldine, in collaboration with the Philippine Women Centre of BC and Ugnayan ng Kabataang Pilipino sa Canada/Filipino-Canadian Youth Alliance. "Working with Migrant Communities: Collaborating with the Kalayaan Centre in Vancouver, Canada." In *Participatory Action Research Approaches and*

Methods: Connecting People, Participation and Place, edited by Sara Kindon, Rachel Pain, and Mike Kesby, 95–103. London: Routledge, 2007.

Rafael, Vicente L. "'Your Grief Is Our Gossip': Overseas Filipinos and Other Spectral Presences." *Public Culture* 9, no. 1 (1997): 267–91.

———. *White Love and Other Events in Filipino History*. Durham: Duke University Press, 2000.

———. "The Cell Phone and the Crowd: Messianic Politics in the Contemporary Philippines." *Public Culture* 15, no. (2003): 399–425.

Rancière, Jacques. "Dix theses sur la politique." *Aux bords du politique*. 2nd ed. Paris: Éditions Osiris, 1998.

———. *Disagreement: Politics and Philosophy*. Translated by Julie Rose. Minneapolis: University of Minnesota Press, 1999.

———. *The Politics of Aesthetics: The Distribution of the Sensible*. Translated by Gabriel Rockhill. London: Continuum, 2004.

———. *The Hatred of Democracy*. Translated by Steve Corcoran. London: Verso, 2006.

Raymundo, Sarah. "Counterpoint." In *Kontra-Gahum: Academics against Political Killings*, edited by Rolando B. Tolentino and Sarah S. Raymundo, ix–xii. Quezon City: IBON Books, 2006.

Razack, Sherene H. *Dark Threats and White Knights: The Somalia Affair, Peacekeeping, and the New Imperialism*. Toronto: University of Toronto Press, 2004.

Read, Nicholas. "A Community Comes Together in Grief." *Vancouver Sun*, December 2, 2003, A1, A11.

Reinelt, Janelle G. "Toward a Poetics of Theatre and Public Events: In the Case of Stephen Lawrence." *The Drama Review* 50, no. 3 (2006): 69–87.

Reuters. "Manila Asks Europe to Help Probe Political Killings." *AlertNet*, Thomson Reuters Foundation, Manila, February 5, 2007. www.alertnet.org (accessed July 1, 2007).

Robinson, Fiona. *Globalizing Care: Ethics, Feminist Theory, and International Relations*. Boulder, Colo.: Westview Press, 1999.

Rodriguez, Robyn Magalit. "Migrant Heroes: Nationalism, Citizenship, and the Politics of Filipino Migrant Labor." *Citizenship Studies* 6, no. 3 (2002): 341–56.

———. *Migrants for Export: How the Philippine State Brokers Labor to the World*. Minneapolis: University of Minnesota Press, 2010.

Rose, Gillian. "'Everyone's Cuddled Up and It Just Looks Really Nice': An Emotional Geography of Some Mums and Their Family Photos." *Social and Cultural Geography* 5, no. 4 (December 2004): 549–64.

Rose, Nikolas. "The Death of the Social? Re-figuring the Territory of Government." *Economy and Society* 25, no. 3 (1996): 327–56.

———. *Powers of Freedom: Reframing Political Thought*. Cambridge: Cambridge University Press, 1999.

Rothberg, Michael. "Between Auschwitz and Algeria: Multidirectional Memory and the Counterpublic Witness." *Critical Inquiry* 33, no. 1 (2006): 158–84.

Ruhs, Martin, and Philip Martin. "Numbers vs. Rights: Trade-Offs and Guest Worker Programs." *International Migration Review* 42, no. 1 (2008): 249–65.

Saldanha, Arun. *Psychedelic White: Goa Trance and the Viscosity of Race.* Minneapolis: University of Minnesota Press, 2007.

Salverson, Julie. "Taking Liberties: A Theatre Class of Foolish Witnesses." *Research in Drama Education* 13, no. 2 (June 2008): 245–55.

San Juan, E., Jr. *After Postcolonialism: Remapping Philippines–United States Confrontations.* Lanham, Md.: Rowman and Littlefield, 2000.

————. "Neocolonial State Terrorism and the Crisis of Comprador/Imperialist Hegemony." In *Kontra-Gahum: Academics against Political Killings,* edited by Rolando B. Tolentino and Sarah S. Raymundo, 3–26. Quezon City: IBON Books, 2006.

————. "Toward a Decolonizing Indigenous Psychology in the Philippines: Introducing Sikolohiyang Pilipino." *Journal for Cultural Research* 10, no. 1 (January 2006): 47–67.

————. *Toward Filipino Self-Determination: Beyond Transnational Globalization.* Albany: State University of New York Press, 2009.

Sangtin Writers and Richa Nagar. *Playing with Fire: Feminist Thought and Activism through Seven Lives in India.* Minneapolis: University of Minnesota Press, 2006.

Saunders, Doug. "Why Our Thinking about Immigration Remains Borderline." *Globe and Mail,* November 3, 2007, F3.

————. "Home Alone: Millions of Romanians Have Gone West to Work, Leaving Behind Villages Filled with 'Migration Orphans.'" *Globe and Mail,* March 15, 2008, F1.

Sayad, Abdelmalek. *The Suffering of the Immigrant.* Cambridge: Polity Press, 2004.

Scalabrini Migration Center. *Hearts Apart: Migration in the Eyes of Filipino Children.* Scalabrini Migration Centre, Quezon City, 2003–4. www.smc.org.ph/ heartsapart/index.html (accessed June 10, 2008).

Schaffer, Kay, and Sidonie Smith. *Human Rights and Narrated Lives: The Ethics of Recognition.* New York: Palgrave Macmillan, 2004.

Schmalzbauer, Leah. "Searching for Wages and Mothering from Afar: The Case of Honduran Transnational Families." *Journal of Marriage and Family* 66, no. 5 (2004): 1317–31.

Seltzer, Mark. "Wound Culture: Trauma in the Pathological Public Sphere." *October* 80 (Spring 1997): 3–26.

Shachar, Ayelet. "Children of a Lesser State: Sustaining Global Inequality through Citizenship Laws." New York University School of Law, Jean Monnet Working Paper 2/03, 2003.

Sharma, Nandita. *Home Economics: Nationalism and the Making of 'Migrant Workers' in Canada.* Toronto: University of Toronto Press, 2006.

Silk, John. "Caring at a Distance: Gift Theory, Aid Chains, and Social Movements." *Social and Cultural Geography* 5, no. 2 (June 2004): 229–51.

Spivak, Gayatri Chakravorty. "Can the Subaltern Speak?" In *Marxism and the Interpretation of Culture,* edited by Cary Nelson and Lawrence Grossberg, 271–313. Urbana: University of Illinois Press, 1988.

———. "French Feminism in an International Frame." In *In Other Worlds: Essays in Cultural Politics.* New York: Routledge, 1988.

Stasiulis, Daiva K., and Abigail B. Bakan. "Negotiating the Citizenship Divide: Foreign Domestic Worker Policy and Legal Jurisprudence." In *Women's Legal Strategies in Canada: A Friendly Assessment,* edited by Radha Jhappan, 237–94. Toronto: University of Toronto Press, 2002.

———. *Negotiating Citizenship: Migrant Women in Canada and the Global System.* New York: Palgrave, 2003.

Stavenhagen, R. *Report of the Special Rapporteur on the Situation of Human Rights and Fundamental Freedoms of Indigenous People.* Catalog Number 4/3003/90/Add.3. New York: United Nations Commission on Human Rights, 59th Session, 2003.

Stewart, Kathleen. *Ordinary Affects.* Durham: Duke University Press, 2007.

Sundberg, Juanita. "Reconfiguring North-South Solidarity: Critical Reflections on Experiences of Transnational Resistance." *Antipode* 39, no. 1 (February 2007): 144–66.

Swarr, Amanda Lock, and Richa Nagar. *Critical Transnational Feminist Praxis.* Albany: State University of New York Press, 2010.

Tadiar, Neferti Xina M. "Death by Death." In *Kontra-Gahum: Academics against Political Killings,* edited by Rolando B. Tolentino and Sarah S. Raymundo, 176–86. Quezon City: IBON Books, 2006.

———. *Things Fall Away: Philippine Historical Experience and the Makings of Globalization.* Durham: Duke University Press, 2009.

Takami, David. "Marcoses Found Liable for Seattle Cannery Workers Union Murders." *Amerasia Journal* 18, no. 1 (1992): 125–28.

Taussig, Michael. *The Nervous System.* New York: Routledge, 1992.

Taylor, Diana. *Disappearing Acts: Spectacles of Gender and Nationalism in Argentina's "Dirty War."* Durham: Duke University Press, 1997.

———. *The Archive and the Repertoire: Performing Cultural Memory in the Americas.* Durham: Duke University Press, 2003.

Thrift, Nigel. "Intensities of Feeling: Towards a Spatial Politics of Affect." *Geografiska Annaler: Series B, Human Geography* 86, no. 1 (March 2004): 57–78.

———. *Non-Representational Theory: Space, Politics, Affect.* London: Routledge, 2007.

TIEDI (Toronto Immigrant Employment Data Initiative). "Immigrants Coming from the Philippines to Canada, 1980–2009." TIEDI, York University, Toronto. Factsheet 11-03, 2011. http://www.yorku.ca/tiedi/factsheets.html (accessed August 14, 2011).

Tolentino, Rolando B., and Sarah S. Raymundo, eds. *Kontra-Gahum: Academics against Political Killings.* Quezon City: IBON Books, 2006.

Tyner, James A. *The Philippines: Mobilities, Identities, Globalization.* New York: Routledge, 2009.

Uy, Veronica. "Alston: Govt Reaction to Visit 'Deeply Schizophrenic': Unoptimistic Military Will See Problem's Gravity" *Global Nation, Inquirer.net,* March 28, 2007. http://globalnation.inquirer.net/ (accessed August 23, 2010).

Valentine, Gill. "Globalizing Intimacy: The Role of Information and Communication Technologies in Maintaining and Creating Relationships." *The Global and the Intimate, WSQ,* 34, no. 1 and 2 (Spring/Summer 2006): 365–93.

Walker, R. B. J. "Conclusion: Sovereignties, Exceptions, Worlds." In *Sovereign Lives: Power in Global Politics,* edited by Jenny Edkins, Véronique Pin-Fat, and Michael J. Shapiro, 239–49. New York: Routledge, 2004.

Walzer, Michael. *Spheres of Justice: A Defense of Pluralism and Equality.* New York: Basic Books, 1983.

Weir, Allison. "The Global Universal Caregiver: Imagining Women's Liberation in the New Millennium." *Constellations* 12, no. 3 (September 2005): 308–30.

Whitlock, Gillian. "In the Second Person: Narrative Transactions in Stolen Generations Testimony." *Biography* 24, no. 1 (Winter 2001): 197–214.

———. *Soft Weapons: Autobiography in Transit.* Chicago: University of Chicago Press, 2007.

Wright, Melissa W. "Urban Geography Plenary Lecture: Femicide, Mother-Activism, and the Geography of Protest in Northern Mexico." *Urban Geography* 28, no. 5 (2007): 401–25.

Wright, Sarah. "Practising Hope: Learning from Social Movement Strategies in the Philippines." In *Fear: Critical Geopolitics and Everyday Life,* edited by Rachel Pain and Susan J. Smith, 223–33. Hampshire: Ashgate, 2008.

Young, Iris Marion. *Inclusion and Democracy.* Oxford: Oxford University Press, 2000.

———. *Intersecting Voices: Dilemmas of Gender, Political Philosophy, and Policy.* Princeton: Princeton University Press, 2003.

Zaman, Habiba. "Transnational Migration and the Commodification of Im/migrant Female Labourers in Canada." *International Journal of Canadian Studies/Revue Internationale d'Études Canadiennes* 29 (2004): 41–62.

Žižek, Slavoj. "The Lesson of Rancière." Afterword to *The Politics of Aesthetics: The Distribution of the Sensible,* by Jacques Rancière, 69–79. Translated by Gabriel Rockhill. London: Continuum, 2004.

Index

Abada, Teresa, 193n87
Abinales, Patricio N., 211n11, 212n18
Abraham, Nicholas, 205n18
abstraction, refusal of, 28
activist research, xvi, 168
advocacy groups, impact of *Nanay* on, 130
affect: affective blockage between Canada and Philippines, 78; affective force of material narrative, 76; circulating, 76, 100; complexity of emotions, in reaction to family separation, 96–97, 98, 202n49; contradictory emotions, 92, 94; and *Nanay*, 101; privileging of, over cognition, xxx; reconfigurations of affect-with-reason, xxx–xxxi; testimony and, xxvii–xxxi
affective labor, migrant domestic work as, xxix
"affective turn" in contemporary scholarship, xxix, 100
Agamben, Giorgio, 5, 28, 185n10, 186n23
Agence France Presse, 213n21
agonistic politics, between migrant organizations, xviii; testifying to trauma as form of, 70–71
Ahmed, Sara, xxxiv, 78, 165, 183n30, 183n36, 199n15, 220n10
Alcuitas, Teodoro (Ted), 148, 150, 153, 158, 214n35, 217n66

Alcuitas-Imperial, Luningning, 148, 212n11, 215n35, 217n71
alienage, troubling of liberal values by, 163–64
Alliance for Advancement of People's Rights. *See* KARAPATAN (Alliance for the Advancement of People's Rights)
Alston, Philip, 138, 149, 211n11; U.N. report, 213n19, 214n24
Amnesty International, 138, 150, 211n11, 213nn20–21, 216n63, 218n75
Anderson, Ben, xxix, 183n26
Anderson, Bridget Jane, 184n5
Anderson, Kay, 204n8
Anderson, Michael, 203n1, 207n29
Angeles, Nora, 171
anti-immigrant sentiment, provocation of, 79
apartheid, different regulatory structures for national and foreign subjects as form of, 2
Aquino, Benigno, Jr. III, 212n17
Aquino, Corazon, 10, 145, 216n65
Aranda, Elizabeth M., 196n26
Archive of Feelings (Cvetkovich), 44
Argentina, "dirty war" in, 143, 148
Armour, Norman, 203n3
Arroyo, Gloria Macapagal, 10, 145, 211n11; extrajudicial killings under, 137, 138, 157, 212n18;

Operation Bantay-Laya (Freedom Watch) under, 213n20; State of the Nation Address (July 24, 2006), 218n77
Arts Rational (radio program), 204n4
Asaki Tigers, 102
Asia, OFWs in, 12, 17, 21, 55, 58, 60, 80, 91, 93, 97, 103, 188n44, 191n77
Asian language groups: high school grade-point averages among different, 24, 174; high school graduation rates among, 175
Asis, Maruja M. B., 197n33
Association of American Geographers (AAG) meeting (2008), presentation at, 202n46
Association of Caregiver and Nanny Agents Canada, 181n7
attachment(s): displaced, 90–92; in employer scenes of Nanay, 115–16; entangled geographies of solidarity, 140–49; intensification of feelings of distance at reunification, 66–67; mothers' visits and shock of non-recognition, 55–62, 197n26; research process and long-term, 169–70
audience at Nanay. See Nanay: A Testimonial Play
August 21 Movement, 148
Aumentado, Racqel, 139
Australia, Stolen Generations' testimony in, 77, 83, 199n10, 201n45
Avila, Ernestine, 195n6

BC Committee for Human Rights in Philippines, xxv–xxvi, xxxiv, 215n44
BC Ministry of Education data on children enrolled in school, 24–27; dropout rates based on, 24, 25,

175, 192n86; information on ethnicity by language spoken at home, 24, 26, 191n82, 192n86; lack of data on immigrants coming through LCP, 26–27, 191n82; median grade point averages based on, 24, 25, 174
bahala na, controversies around translation of term, 198n2
Bakan, Abigail B., 183n24, 187n34, 194n4
Balabagan, Sara, 186n19
Balana, Cynthia, 213n19
Balibar, Étienne, 2, 184n4
Ball, Karen, 77, 199n12
Barnett, Clive, xxx, 183n31, 211n9, 215n38
Barthes, Roland, 202n47
Battistella, Graciano, 195n7
Baucom, Ian, xxv, 107–9, 161, 182n19, 183n28, 219n84; on speculative vs. melancholic realism, 108–9, 110, 111, 131; on Zong massacre, 205n17
Bayan Muna (People First), 216n64
Bejarano, Cynthia L., 199n6
Bell, Daniel A., xx, 181n7, 181n10
Bello, Madge, 216n59
Benjamin, Walter, xxvii
Ben-Zvi, Linda, 110, 131, 210n57
Berlant, Lauren, xxx, 100, 183n29, 193n94, 195n5, 197n34, 199n7, 201n31, 201nn35–37, 203n57, 204nn7–8, 210n48; on ethico-emotional performance, 76; on politics of sentimentality, 81
Berlin, production of Nanay in Hebbel Theater in, 130, 204n11, 207n28
Bernstein, J. M., 137, 212n15
Biddle, Jennifer L., 83, 90, 201n45, 203n54

sites visited by fact-finding missions in, 141

Centre for Research in Women Studies and Gender Relations at the University of British Columbia, 168

Chapel Arts (Downtown Eastside, Vancouver), 102–3; choice of location, 117–18; *Nanay* scenes set in relation to ambience and architectural form of, 102–8

charity, Donaldson's principle of, 209n44

Chen, Xiaobei, 39, 194n103

Cheng, Anne Anlin, 28, 193n95, 202n45

child care in Canada: in Canada, difficulties of finding, 113–15; in Canada, need for national, 130, 215n52

children, 16–26; age at reunification, 17–20; age at separation, 19; "decision making" concerning their parents' migration, 197n27; difficulties adjusting to life in Vancouver, 32–33; effects of LCP on, 7, 16–26; employment, determination to go beyond low-skilled, 69–70; employment, low-skilled, 35–38, 191n78; employment, to contribute to household income, 35–37; employment, to remit money to Philippines, 37–38; feelings of abandonment of, by migrant mothers vs. fathers, 46; hopes for, 15–16; invisibility of Filipino, 26, 44; morality of excluding, in temporary labor programs, 164–65, 219n6; mothers' diminished capacity to support their children at school, 33–35;

mother's sacrifice and family conflict witnessed by, 28–31; mothers' visits and shock of nonrecognition, 55–62, 197n26; of overseas migrant workers, living conditions of, 32, 194n99; reliving of mother's experiences, 7, 20–21; reunification with, difficulties of, xv–xvi, 92, 94; testimony of Filipino youths, xxvii; timing of immigration, educational attainment and, 24–26, 176–79. *See also* education of children

Children's Choice Awards for *Nanay*, 100, 101, 204n5

Choy, Catherine Ceniza, 147, 188n48, 215n42, 216n57

citizenship: boundary or threshold question of, 5, 38–39; guestworker vs. immigration programs creating divide over, 6, 187n35; irresolvable exclusion at heart of, in liberal-democratic societies, 5, 163–64, 185n10, 186n19; liberal, 5; migrant, 8–9; in Philippines, 8–9; privilege of Canadian, 160, 218n76; revaluing the politically excluded in ways other than, 97–98; rights fragmented and scattered across different nation-states, 4; separate-spheres model of, 186n33; two contradictory meanings of, 5–6, 7, 38–39

Citizenship and Immigration Canada (CIC), 27, 109

Civilian Armed Forces Geographical Units (CAFGU), 146, 157

Clough, Patricia Ticineto, xxix, 183n25

Co, Michelle, 205n15

Cohen, Rina, 187n40, 190n73, 190n75

Colen, Shellee, 46, 195n9

collaboration, research: labor of, xxxi–xxxv; reflecting on process, 168–71

collecting together, process of, xxxiv–xxxv

colonial stereotypes, 81

colonial subjugation of Philippines, history of, 8, 144, 159, 166–67, 187n39

commerce, militarized, 146–47, 159

Commission on Filipinos Overseas, 10

communicating across distance, 47–55, 70, 84–85, 86; censoring of children, 51–52; via Internet, 48–50, 196n18, 196n23; "phatic" communication, 51; struggle to embody forms of, 54–55; via telephone, 48, 50–55, 195n17, 196n21

Communist Party of the Philippines (CPP), 137, 213n20

computer, communication across distance via, 48–50, 196n18, 196n23

Conde, Carlos H., 214n22, 214n33

Connolly, William E., 183n31, 186n23

Contemplacion, Flor, 186n19

continuum of state violence, xxv–xxvii

contradictory emotions, 92, 94

corporate globalization of labor, xxiv

corruption in Philippines, 9, 134, 138, 144. *See also* state violence in Philippines, witnessing

cosmopolitan interestedness, 109, 136, 161; expansive vs. generalized, xxv

counterinsurgency warfare: American doctrine of, 212n16; "Philippine model" of, 156–57, 212n16, 213n20, 217n73

criminal system, assumptions about Filipino youth violence within, 89–90

Critical Filipina and Filipino Studies Collective, xxviii, 182n23, 194n102

Cuario, Doris, 155, 156, 157

Cubilié, Anne, 75, 81–82, 198n4, 200n28, 201n36, 201n42; ethical witnessing, notion of, 200n30

cultural relativism, xxxiv, 78

culture: of fear of military reprisal, 150–53, 212n18; of migration, 9–10; of numbness, 77; wound, 77

Cumbers, Andy, 215n48

Cvetkovich, Ann, 44, 195n10, 195n14, 197n35

cyborg mothering, 49, 70

Daenzer, Patricia, 186n34, 190n73

Dean, Jodi, 128, 209n44

debt, family conflict and, 29–30

de Leon, Conely, 184nn1–2, 184n6, 185n15, 188n53, 193n92

democracy: nonidentity of democratic sovereignty with the people, 182n22; popular democracy in Philippines, struggle for, 144, 147, 166–67; Rancière's definition of, 208n35; Rancière's notion of egalitarian and democratic politics, 207n31. *See also* liberal-democratic societies

DeParle, Jason, 201n33

Depatie-Pelletier, Eugénie, 183n1, 184nn5–6

dependence, responsibility in mutual, 133–34, 135, 165

deportation/noncriminal removals among Filipinos in U.S., xxviii, 182n23, 194n102

Derrida, Jacques, 200n30, 212n12

deskilling, 121, 200n26; implications for children's educational attainment,

elder care, 15, 200n23, 210n50
embassy representatives' attendance
at *Nanay* talkback, Philippines,
125–27, 209n41
emotions: complexity of, in reaction
to family separation, 96–97, 98,
202n49; contradictory, 92, 94. *See
also* affect
empathy, 203n49; complicit, 88,
90; dis-identification and, 132;
empathetic identification, 83, 95;
invitation to empathize, author's
photographs in Marlena's presentation as, 86–88, 202n46; potential
for, in Berlin production of *Nanay*,
207n28; sentimental appropriation
of experience,
79–81
employers: "freedom" to change,
under LCP, 184n5; as *Nanay* audience, 111, 120, 121–22, 206n23;
scenes in *Nanay*, 112–16; sensitivity of "demand," 181n7; testimony
about relationship with, 91–94, 95
Eng, David L., 195n14
England, Kim, 186n34
Engster, Daniel, 211n4, 219n7
Enrile, Annalisa, 219n82
Enriquez, Marie, 149
entrepreneurial domestic workers,
11–26, 184n1; advice to other
Filipinos, 14; children of, 16–26;
deskilling of, 15; hard work, sacrifice, and careful planning of, 11–
14, 16; multiple jobs held by, 13–
14; reasons for leaving Philippines,
11–13, 15–16; regaining professional qualifications, 14–15. *See
also* Live-In Caregiver Program
entrepreneurial migrants, 8–10
epistemic violence, xxxiii

equality: migrant labor and inequality
of nation-states, 4, 9, 144–45, 159;
in Rancière's notion of egalitarian
and democratic politics, 207nn30–
31, 208n35; systematic marginalization of Filipinos in Canada and
liberal principles of, 5; theater as
egalitarian space, 117, 127–28,
132, 207nn30–31; working-class
women's lack of access to childcare
and, 215n52
Equations (Castellanes), 57
Espina-Varona, Inday, 149, 214n23
Espiritu, Yen Le, 187n39
Estigoy, Dinah, 209n37
ethical witnessing, 81, 200n30. *See also*
witnessing
ethics: care ethics, 133–34, 135, 159;
ethical awakening to the Other,
78–83, 86–88, 201n42; of feeling
and national responsibility, ambiguity of LCP and, 78; of freedom,
2–3; materialist/phenomenologi-
cal, 160; politics and, 163–66,
219n6; politics of witnessing and,
136; relationality grounding, 116
ethnic succession, 71, 190n70
Eurocentrism, 46, 54; of feminist universalisms, xxxiv
European Union Needs Assessment
Mission, 211n11
exclusion: associated with migrant
work, targeting children, 164–65;
at heart of citizenship, irresolvable,
5, 163–64, 185n10, 186n19;
migrants' articulations of, as performative contradiction, 207n31;
nationalism feeding exclusionary
immigration policy, xxiv; temporary labor programs and enduring
social, xxvi, xxviii, 7, 28

103, 184n5; struggle between slave traders and abolitionists in late eighteenth century, 205n17; *Zong* massacre, 205n17

Smith, Sidonie, 201nn37–38

Smith, Susan J., 204n8

social death, xxvi

social hierarchy, self-affirming empathy stabilizing existing, 80–81

social science, speculative realism as language of, 108, 109

solidarity, international, 136, 218nn81–82; entangled geographies of, 140–49; as generative, 146

South Africa, Truth and Reconciliation Commission hearings in, 77, 199n10

South Asian Youth Alliance, 95

Southern Tagalog, mission to, 139–40, 160, 217nn71–72; international attention given, 218n76, 218n81; key sites visited by fact-finding missions in, 141; theatrics of intimidation in, 153–58, 215n36

sovereign power, 5, 185n10, 186n23; categorical distinction founding, 28; Live-In Caregiver Program as instance of, 3; testimony to trauma challenging, 70–71; violence of, 38; vulnerability of Filipino domestic workers to arbitrary exercise of, 4, 6; "wild zone" of, xxvii

Sparke, Matthew, 218n76

spatiotemporalities structuring temporary migration, xxiii

Special Civilian Armed Auxiliaries (SCAAs), 146

speculative and melancholic realism, distinction between, 108–11

sponsoring family members, 86; children too old to be sponsored as dependents, 20–21; fees and show money required, 190n67; government information on numbers of sponsored persons, 27; LCP and, 4, 6–7, 64; regulations, 122; rupture of attachment to caregiver in Philippines and, 64–66, 67; saving for, 13–14

Stasiulis, Daiva K., 183n24, 187n34, 194n4

state power, demonstrated by Philippines embassy representatives at *Nanay* talkback, 125–27

state racism, 3, 185n9

state violence, 5, 44; continuum of, xxv–xxvii; contradiction between popular sovereignty and, 182n22; in liberal democratic countries, 70, 135–36; made visible by testimony to trauma, 70–71

state violence in Philippines, witnessing, 133–61; appeals to international community and, 137–40; Canadian fact-finding mission, 134–37, 149–60, 211n11, 215n36, 215n43, 217nn71–72, 218n76, 218n81–82; community terror in Central Luzon, 149–53, 158–59, 215n36; entangled geographies of solidarity, 140–49; making connections between LCP and violence in Philippines, xxvi, 158–61, 215n43; protection of international observers against, 147; "theatricality" of state terror, 148–49; theatrics of intimidation in Southern Tagalog, 153–58, 215n36

statistical information: disjuncture between statistical analyses, 8; efficacy of numbers, 26–28

Stavenhagen, R., 216n55

difficult contract created by, 87–
88; power and paradox of, 81–82;
response-ability of those who
testify, 82–83; of terror in Central Luzon, 140–42, 149–53; translations of, 82; to trauma as form
of agonistic politics, 70–71; witnessing between fragments, 90–
95; witnessing complicity and
implications to loss and suffering
in, 88, 90
text messaging, communication by,
51, 195n17, 196n21
theater: as egalitarian space, 117, 127–
28, 132, 207nn30–31; impact of
performance outside, 128–31;
political potential of, xxix, 117, 128
Theatre Passe Muraille (Toronto),
210n55
theatrical performance. See *Nanay: A
Testimonial Play*
"Third World women," epistemic violence within Western scholarship
on, xxxii
Thrift, Nigel, xxix, 183n26, 183n31
time-space presence of theatrical experience, significance of, 209n44
Tolentino, Rolando B., 212n18,
213nn19–20
Torok, Maria, 205n18
Torres, Lourdes, 183n34
translation: intercultural, 111, 132; of
testimonials, 82
transnational mothering. See mothers
and mothering; mothers' stories,
listening to
"transnational" research through attachment rather than physical mobility,
182n12. See also Philippine
Women Centre of BC, collaborating with; research into action

trauma of separation, xxvii, 45–46, 70;
family dislocation and, 62–66;
mothers' visits and, 59–62; parallel
between photographic wound and
experience of, 87, 88; tendency to
"gentrify" trauma, 71; testifying to,
as form of agonistic politics and
means to build political community,
70–71. See also family separation
trust, long-term attachments in
research process and, 170
Truth and Reconciliation Commission hearings in South Africa, 77,
199n10
TVI Pacific, Canatuan Gold Project
of, 146–47
Tyner, James A., 187n44, 188n46,
189n64

Ugnayan BC. See Filipino-Canadian
Youth Alliance (FCYA)
unfaithfulness as destabilizing potential, 63–64
Union of Democratic Filipinos, 148
United Nations Human Rights Council, 214n31; Universal Periodic
Review of Philippine government
(2008), 213n18
United Nations Supplementary Conventions on the Abolition of Slavery,
the Slave Trade, and Institutions
and Practices Similar to Slavery, 2,
184n6
United States: colonial subjugation of
Philippines, 166–67, 187n39;
demographics of OFWs in,
188n44; Filipino male guest work
in, history of, 187n39; military
assistance to Philippines after
9/11, 213n19; "noncriminal
removals" among Filipinos in,